DOUBLE LIVES

DOUBLE LIVES

Writing and Motherhood

Edited by Shannon Cowan, Fiona
Tinwei Lam, Cathy Stonehouse

McGill-Queen's University Press
Montreal & Kingston | London | Ithaca

Legal deposit first quarter 2008
Bibliothèque nationale du Québec

Printed in Canada on acid-free paper that is 100% ancient forest free
(100% post-consumer recycled), processed chlorine free

McGill-Queen's University Press acknowledges the support of the Canada Council for
the Arts for our publishing program. We also acknowledge the financial support of the
Government of Canada through the Book Publishing Industry Development Program
(BPIDP) for our publishing activities.

LIBRARY AND ARCHIVES CANADA CATALOGUING IN PUBLICATION

Double lives : writing and motherhood / edited by Shannon Cowan, Fiona Tinwei
Lam, Cathy Stonehouse.

Includes bibliographical references.
ISBN 978-0-7735-3377-6

1. Women authors, Canadian (English) – 20th century – Family relationships.
2. Women authors, Canadian (English) – 20th century – Biography.   3. Motherhood
and the arts – Canada.   4. Children of authors – Canada.   5. Motherhood – Canada.
I. Cowan, Shannon, 1973–   II. Lam, Fiona Tinwei, 1964–   IIII. Stonehouse, Cathy

PS8237.M64D69 2008   C810.8'0355   C2007-907402-2

Set in 10.5/14 Garamond with Filosofia and Filosofia Unicase
Book design & typesetting by Garet Markvoort, zijn digital

For Robbie, Zaira, and Freya,
with love & gratitude

contents

BECOMING A WRITER

MOTHERING FIRST

THE MUSE

words of advice

Preface

marni jackson

I was just sitting down to write this, having procrastinated for a full six hours of housework, including mopping the basement floor, something I do perhaps once a millennium. I wrote the word Preface. I boldfaced it. Then the phone rang.

It was my son, calling from Montreal, where he is finishing his university degree and playing music on the side (or vice versa). He is twenty-three. He hasn't lived at home since he was seventeen. I told him I was working on my last piece about motherhood, and we had a good laugh about that. Then he filled me in on his week – not so great. He was offhand about it, but I found myself still faintly gripped by that old, deep mother-ache: I want him to be happy. As a matter of fact, I would carve out my heart and liver and Fed-ex them to Montreal if that would do the trick.

I have a friend, a psychotherapist, who admitted to me she can't sleep until her live-in, responsible, twenty-two-year-old son comes home at night. If he comes home at two a.m., she's still awake at two a.m. "I know it's crazy, but I can't help it." This may be sobering news to those of you embarking on new motherhood and hoping to "get back to normal" in four months or so. No: the new normal is this passionately divided, more amplified you.

Now and then our son comes home to visit, where he occupies his old room, the one we are reclaiming for an office. When he goes to bed, he still leaves his jeans shucked on the floor, standing in two crumpled leg-towers. He sometimes stays out late, as twenty-three-year-olds do. My husband sleeps on, just as he did when his son was three weeks old and breastfeeding 118 times a day. But come two a.m., my eyes pop open. I can sense his empty room down the hall. I know by the slant of the light that his bedroom door is still open: he's still out there, my son, in the perilous world.

I get up, go down to the kitchen, make some tea, and reflect on my ridiculous position. I'm like an old soldier with post-traumatic syndrome; certain situations can still flood my nervous system with inappropriate anxiety. I flip through a magazine, feeling the same alert core of focus that I felt during those early, anxious nights of motherhood: nights of fever, whooping cough, and asthma. The time he was so sick I slept under the coffee table, as he slumped in the armchair with the remote, hacking and coughing, ordering a set of Miracle Blades from the infomercial on T V.

Four a.m. Cold tea. Is he staying over with friends? He's probably biking home right now with one rear light, in his dark clothes. Do I have the phone number of his friend, Reese? What sort of mother am I, not to know the last names of her son's friends, and their phone numbers, even if they are twenty-three? I idly study the photographs of him stuck in various corners of the kitchen. On the walls are the prints and paintings he's done over the years. So much of him, still animating the house.

But I'm tired of being a mother, I have to write tomorrow, and I feel silly losing sleep. I go upstairs to bed, gently rotating my husband onto his side to pre-empt any snoring. I am determined to forget that I have a son. I am just letting go, sinking into a dream, when I hear the sound I was waiting to hear – the ringing, metallic *chunk* of the wrought-iron fence as he wheels his bike through the gate.

Now I can sleep.

❧ I was thirty-seven when I had my first and only child, after supporting myself as a freelance writer since college. I had almost finished a novel, and I was collaborating with three other women on a theatre project. My husband was a musician and a freelance writer, too. We rented two floors in a house on Brunswick Avenue in Toronto and bought our first couch ever when I was pregnant. We weren't married, we had no money, and I wasn't at all sure this whole family-and-motherhood thing was going to pan out.

Somehow, the play got finished (my collaborators also babysat). When my son was about two, I tried to revise the dormant novel, but I couldn't get back inside the story. The wildly adventurous person who had written it seemed to have fled. I limped to the end of a draft, but then I put it away. I think I was depressed. My son was going through a sequence of illnesses, I was trying to support my "creative" writing by doing scraps of freelance journalism, and my husband was often away on assignments. I was too ground down to do the sort of deep, sustained, solitary work that a novel requires.

So instead, I began to write about what was keeping me from writing. I would go through those intense, soul-fraying mornings that every new mother goes through, race to my desk when he finally slept, and try to give them some sort of shape and weight and meaning by writing them down. I felt I had simultaneously found myself and been erased. I grew huge inside, a zeppelin of contradictory emotions, while apparently becoming invisible to the world on the outside. I was also desperately afraid of losing my self, so I wrote away, in delight and fear and consternation.

Oddly, nothing seems to have changed in the fifteen years since *The Mother Zone* appeared. The writers in this collection feel, just as passionately as I did, that motherhood is still not properly seen, valued, supported, understood, acknowledged. None of the love-and-work dilemmas that I despaired about back then seem to have been resolved, despite the current wave of "mother-lit." I think this new generation of mothers are more determined than ever not to let motherhood change their lives – and therein lies a new problem, because, of course, having children transforms you. It keeps on transforming you. And the hardest thing to prepare for is this constant change.

Although motherhood is now more accepted as a topic of discussion and a subject for books, the conflict between career and family has, I think, become more pressing for young women. The surrender to the mother-years seems to come at a higher emotional price for women who have forged independent lives and careers. The stakes seem to have gone up, on both sides.

One sign of progress has been the deeper involvement of many fathers in childrearing. (They have wasted no time in writing books about that, too!) And same-sex couples are quietly reinventing and often improving on the old nuclear family. Still, in hetero households at least, the limp vegetables in the crisper generally fall to the women – and that goes for the sleepless nights as well.

You can occasionally detect the exhaustion and the faint hysteria of the new mother in some of the essays that follow – and this is a good thing.

The writing gets stripped down to the essentials; there isn't time to waste words when you have the space of a two-hour nap to get something decent down. Perhaps this is what made Grace Paley such a deliciously elliptical short-story writer and why the career of Carol Shields, the mother of four, began with a slim but eagle-eyed novel about domestic life, called *Small Ceremonies*.

The reason we don't have more books that reflect the richness of motherhood as a drama and an intellectual challenge is simple: mothers in the thick of it are too tired and strapped for time to write them. And when time finally opens up, maternal amnesia sets in. The children grow up, and the texture of those early, intimate days is lost. But motherhood sets the bar high, very high, for empathy, self-questioning, and joy: all helpful for the writing life. In *The Mother Zone* I wrote about the curious commute a writer-mother must undertake between the rather seductive surrender of self demanded by new motherhood and the confidence, ego, and sustained focus that writing demands. It is a bumpy commute.

Perhaps this is why Jane Austen and Virginia Woolf could pour themselves so passionately into their work; no one else demanded that much of them. Writing is a kind of ongoing conversation or quarrel with one's self. When children come into the picture, the voices multiply, overlap, and become confused. What I discovered in my own new motherhood, and in the process of writing a book about it, was that the self is not a watertight vessel that sails you through the rough seas of family life. It is and has to be more permeable. Many novelists describe the surrender of their creative will to the apparently autonomous whims of character that can emerge in the process of writing fiction. Their characters sometimes seem to dictate what will happen next in a novel – like a wilful two-year-old. In *The Mother Zone* I argue that motherhood is a fruitful dialogue between Self and Other that mimics – even as it interrupts – the imaginative journey of writing. British paediatrician D.W. Winnicott[1] talks about the "good-enough mother" whose gradual "failure to adapt" to the omnivorous demands of their baby in fact fosters separation. This shuttle between oneness and twoness, and a sense of never quite living up to the demands of one's subject is also typical of the writing life.

As Rachel Rose writes in her contribution here, "Letters to a Young Mother Who Writes": "If you find yourself in the situation of recently having created life, it won't hurt to recognize the spiritual doors that have opened to you. And why should such an opening be free of pain? Even following the barn owl for a day makes the back ache and the knees stammer. The other name for such good work is joy."

This is what the writers in this collection are onto: just get it down on paper, either your magnificent idea or the details of your day, while and whenever you can. One thing motherhood cultivates – although never enough! – is patience. And although children grow up and leave home, your words, written on the fly or in exhaustion, will still be there, awaiting the patient work of transformation.

NOTES

1 Winnicott, "Transitional Objects and Transitional Phenomena."

Introduction

SHANNON COWAN, FIONA TINWEI LAM,
AND CATHY STONEHOUSE

Double Lives explores the intersection of two consuming passions: the passion to write and the passion to mother. At the core of each is the yearning – and struggle – to create. Of course, these passions can coexist, even nourish and foster each other. Our title implies this parallel existence; it also suggests a certain duplicity. The two passions can be in direct conflict when there is too little in the well – be it time, space, energy, or inspiration. Each may demand all – or even more than – one has to give and begrudge even a moment's neglect. Imagine a child's cry from another room in the midst of a writer's long-awaited, hard-earned moment of quiet or at the start of a crucial but fleeting epiphany. And when one is not an established writer, and perhaps even if one is, making regular, uninterrupted time and space for writing seems self-indulgent, selfish, unjustified. Giving to one passion may truly feel at the time like a betrayal of the other. The choice may either be an uneasy, sometimes fraught compromise, or a sacrifice. And how is that choice experienced as opposed to perceived – selfless and noble, or selfish and ruthless? Is conflict inevitable, unavoidable, untenable – or is it momentary, resolvable, survivable, without ultimate loss?

Even with the beacons of Tillie Olsen, Adrienne Rich, Carol Shields, Alice Munro, and Margaret Laurence, among others, to guide them, writer-mothers still face very real obstacles. Hemmed in by interminable feedings and diaper changes, a writer new to mothering might ask herself if she will ever write again. Similarly, a mother who is new to writing may struggle to integrate yet another unpaid, home-based responsibility – this time not to others, but to herself. Both may seek answers in the real experiences of others; yet although there is a wealth of Canadian fiction and poetry on mothering and even mothering and writing, there has been a dearth of memoir or personal narrative published in Canada on the subject, with the notable exception of Marni Jackson's *The Mother Zone*, first published in 1992. Although there has been a groundswell of theoretical analyses of the historical and sociopolitical construction of motherhood as an institution or practice, there is a need for frontline, real-life stories by writer-mothers, whether active or "on hold."[1]

Writing is intellectual work and mothering all too often seen as its antithesis. Writers are assumed to need quiet, solitary space, thinking time, reading time – all things mothers rarely get. Writing is seen as "scribbling," a hobby for women – unlike ballet, filmmaking, or metal sculpture, "you can do it while he naps." Even today, writers who become mothers are more or less exiled from literary community by default, unless they hide or suppress their parenting life. Many famous mother writers avoid talking about their mothering in public. Despite the reading public's fascination with the writing process, the endless books of interviews with writers, revelations about the writing life, books about how to write or become a writer, almost nothing gets said about the effect of raising children on writing and how writer-mothers have coped.

Double Lives seeks to redress this gap by providing well-written original personal essays of literary quality that explore the experience of writing while mothering. Its focus is restricted to personal narrative rather than academic analysis, not because such analysis isn't required but because the firsthand experiences of mothering writers have never been collected in this way before. Providing access to writers' personal lives and stories can offer a kind of long-distance mentoring. We hope to reach out not only to writers who are mothers at various stages in their writing careers or in their mothering, but also to writers considering motherhood, mothers who wish to write but who cannot for whatever reason, and any mother who is presently engaged in a dire struggle to write. As mothers and thinkers we feel the need to rescue mothering from the separate, nuclear familial realm into which it has been exiled; we feel the need to bring the work of parenting back into dialogue with the work of culture. Literature needs this, as does society.

Inevitably, all anthologies are incomplete. We have included as wide a range of contributors as possible, with essays by those who are just starting out, as well as those in mid-career or further along. We have also deliberately avoided courting only big-name writers and instead have included the voices of less well-known writers, some of whom have chosen to postpone writing and put mothering – or economic survival – first. Their voices have often been marginalized or dismissed, even though they represent the majority of women who aspire to write but cannot because of the social and economic constraints related to raising children.

We initially considered including male writers, but in the end focused on women, as it is women who still bear the brunt of child-rearing responsibilities, especially in the early years. It is mothers who are the focus of campaigns to take care of children in the home, mothers who more often end up with children after relationship breakdown, female writers who have the challenge of breaking down stereotypes about who gets to write, how and when. Even though some men have written about fathering and child-rearing, this experience rarely seems to impact a male writer's career, perhaps because it's easier to find a woman partner who will take on the family while the man gets down to writing. Men do not usually have to choose between art and family: they can have one or the other or both fully, and keep the family at arm's length, or even abandon the family with impunity. Biologically and culturally, women are tethered – and when they loosen those tethers, they are more likely to be riddled with guilt, loss, or regret, and/or criticized and condemned.

Nevertheless, our mother-writers are a diverse group. The essays in *Double Lives* have been penned by single or divorced mothers; biological and adoptive mothers; mothers with special-needs children; straight and lesbian mothers; mothers who have been on welfare and those who are financially secure. The authors also range in age and generation, including grandmothers who reflect upon the past from a distance and new mothers who reflect upon the intensity of their transition into parenthood. Also included are voices from different parts of Canada and from a variety of cultural backgrounds. The essays also vary widely in style: some authors have taken a broader, more philosophical stance; others describe the minutiae of an immediate experience. All of them, however, vividly depict not only the synergies but also the compromises and surrenders their authors have made in weaving together their writing and mothering lives. Taken as a whole, these essays represent a rich spectrum of experience, whether they explore the immediacy of a moment by moment struggle or provide the wisdom gained from time and retrospection.

Yet there are still voices missing, notably those women whose literary aspirations have never had a chance to emerge owing to the exigencies of their lives: women living on the street or in extreme poverty, criminalized or institutionalized, or just getting by. To have the time and language to reflect on such lives, let alone commit thoughts to paper, is a privilege. We are also aware of the absence of women who have chosen to avoid motherhood in order to focus on their art. One author in the collection does discuss the excruciating decision of giving up custody of her children in order to write. Other authors talk about sacrificing writing in order to parent. The common theme among the writers in *Double Lives* is that none regret having had their children – despite enormous frustrations and the realization that much has been sacrificed. Although some women may regret choosing motherhood, this book's focus is on those who negotiate and desire both social identities, mother and writer. To this end, we offer this collection as a spark, a thorn in the side, an inspiration. The exploration has just begun.

As editors, we have grouped our authors' essays into five categories, although inevitably some themes recur, being common to the experience of almost all mother-writers. The contributors in Room to Write demonstrate in different ways how having or not having a "room of one's own," whether in the form of a separate office or of uninterrupted mental and emotional space, influences their writing. Jane Silcott attempts to start a new piece while her child is at home sick. Susan Musgrave struggles – ironically enough – to write about *Motherhood and Other Possibilities* through mothering a newborn and then a demanding teen. Denise Roig moves her desk all around the house and eventually out of the house. Cori Howard faces constant interruptions during telephone interviews. And Robyn Sarah struggles to write, revise, and mail out poems through endless domestic chores and sleep deprivation.

In Becoming a Writer, seasoned authors Di Brandt and Luanne Armstrong look back to their rural roots. Métis writer Sharron Proulx-Turner describes her journey through childhood abuse into motherhood and writing. Catherine Owen details her journey as a teenage mother and how she managed – at great personal cost – to put writing first. Like Brandt and

Proulx-Turner, Fiona Tinwei Lam reveals the significance of culture and family history upon her writing.

The authors in Mothering First discuss their choice to put their writing ambitions or career on the back burner. Catherine Kirkness and Theresa Shea illuminate the primacy they have given to rearing their school-aged children above all else. Elizabeth Greene finds insight and inspiration in her dream-life, while raising a son diagnosed with autism, eventually coming back to writing when her son attends university. In contrast, Deirdre Maultsaid describes a trip to Gibraltar with her sons, where constantly tending to their needs drains the potential for inspiration, despite the glowing and historic setting. Stephanie Bolster offers the perspective of a writer who has had an established writing career prior to becoming a mother.

A number of essays focus on how mothering has spurred creativity in The Muse. Poet Anne Simpson provides a lyrical treatise on the similarities and synergies between mothering and writing. Recalling the early days of raising her child while working as a housecleaner, Noreen Shanahan ponders whether her now teenage son has been her muse. Sally Ito's dreams during pregnancy inspire and shape a novel. Having written prize-winning essays about her experience raising an adopted daughter from China, Susan Olding confronts opposition and judgement from senior writers and colleagues at a famous writers' colony just as her writing career appears to be gaining momentum. Linda Spalding unfolds memories of time spent as a child with her grandmother and how this ultimately influenced her to become a writer.

Finally, the authors in Words of Advice reflect back on what shaped, inspired, and moved them as mothers who write in order to pass on to readers what they have learnt. Janice Kulyk Keefer describes how her children's ways of thinking and seeing the world have informed her own vision and writing. Joanne Arnott discusses what books and people influenced her through a sometimes fraught, sometimes joyous journey as a mother of six children. Renee Rodin depicts her creative liberation as a writer during the heyday of the feminist movement while she was a young single mother on welfare. Rachel Rose closes the book with a luminous, Rilke-inspired essay, "Advice to a Young Mother Who Writes."

Mothering small children provides challenges for editors, too. During the creation of this book we have rarely met in person, although we live relatively close by (two of us in the same city). Instead we have conducted editorial meetings via email or late-night conference call after the kids were in bed. During the time this anthology has been gestated, our kids have grown from infants and a toddler to small children, while another baby has come along.

As these life changes have occurred, our perspectives have shifted, yet one question remains: has much changed since Tillie Olsen wrote her ground-breaking work *Silences*? Here was an author who put off writing while supporting and raising four children and who eventually wrote of her atrophied abilities, of her desperation, and of the many woman authors whose talents were horribly blunted by their obligations and society's expectations.

Virginia Woolf was right when she said that, in order to write, an author needs a room of her own, physically, emotionally, and mentally. Without one, her passion is subsumed; her creative energy is channelled elsewhere – to help and support others.

For the most part, the writers in the collection champion motherhood, perhaps in defense against the image of the childless (usually male) writer, but also perhaps because they have taken on that challenge, that identity. As editors we are aware that motherhood is complex, and mothers' motivations particularly so. For this reason, we have chosen to focus on breaking one particular silence, and to let women do so in their own words, however surprising. Some things may have changed since we began gathering essays for this anthology, but its relevance to our lives remains clear. In the words of Adrienne Rich, whose pioneering work on mothering remains an inspiration, "I knew I was fighting for my life through, against, and with the lives of my children ..."[2] So here it is: a collection of personal, literary nonfiction on the experience of writing and mothering by Canadian women writers. Proof that despite real challenges, mother-writers have voices as rich and varied as these contributions suggest.

NOTES

1 For more information, please refer to York University's Association of Research on Mothering, ARM: www.yorku.ca/arm.
2 Rich, *Of Woman Born*: *Motherhood as Experience and Institution*, 29.

room to write

Drafts 1–12 (Not Including 11)

Jane SILCOTT

I've been writing this essay for months. I think of "essay" as an idea stretched out and held up to the light – examined from different angles, pulled so thin there are holes. Patched with opposing arguments? Seeing what fits. I've started and restarted it many times, hoping for one long stream that I could keep to, one concentrated moment. Of course, that was a fool's idea, a dream. I offer you this instead. Stops and starts, which may be the only point I have to make after all.

Draft #1

It's interesting right now that I'm writing an essay on motherhood and writing – or more accurately – I'm not writing. I'm thinking about how I'm not writing, and why I'm not writing, and while I'm doing all that not-writing I'm imagining smarter, more confident mother/writer superwomen all pattering away at their laptops producing brilliant cogent thoughts while their happy, perfect children chortle and suck and goo somewhere close – but not too close – by.

Meanwhile here I am flat on the couch drinking wine and thinking of an old boyfriend. I have one foot propped on a hot-water bottle and a cat purring at my shoulder. My children are downstairs with my husband. They're watching hockey. I don't approve of this activity, but they've done this so I can write. How can I complain? During dinner, my daughter came and curled onto my lap. I wrapped my arms around her and held her close, sniffing her hair. I was thinking of my father who was hardly ever around – like most 1950s dads, he worked a lot – and how he'd do exactly this sort of thing, snuggle close and say excessively affectionate things: "light of my life" or "darlings, this is all I need." I resisted saying something similar, aware of how embarrassing I used to find it. The old boyfriend skitters through my brain, offering a life so dramatic and eventful I don't have time to have children. I'm too skinny and well rested, and my hair looks fabulous.

Did I say that?

I take another sip of wine. I love my children. Really I do. Ask any mother, and she'll tell you the same. Mother engineers, mother lawyers, mother gas station attendants – they're so glad to go out to work in the morning. But they love their children. I know because I love mine, too, and without them – well-rested and skinny or not – my life would be sad and thin with a paucity of love. Yes. A paucity. I have another sip of wine, pet the cat, and remember how the old boyfriend looked at me when I said I was tired of rock stars and airplanes.

DraFT #2

When I started this essay some months ago I thought of the yin/yang symbol, black on one side of a sensuously curving line, white on the other, with a black and white dot on each opposite to indicate complexity and cross-pollination. The mother/writer sides of myself, I decided: two peacefully coexisting halves, all together making a whole.

I tell this to a friend, and she laughs and laughs. Mother/writer together! You've got to be kidding. I walk away feeling depressed, thinking of all the times I've tried to write with children in the room or nearby or even when they were in school. She's right. There can be no coexistence: just two hard-edged selves glaring across a great divide. I will have to give up the essay altogether – too dark a vision – what if my children read it some day?

Then I remember another symbol from when I was younger and studying aikido, a martial art. The dojo adopted for its logo an image of two cranes facing each other, their heads curved in opposite directions. It looked like an embrace, the outer edge of the outstretched wings forming a circle, the dark shape between them a sinuous path. Aikido teaches people to guide an aggressor's negative energy in a spiralling motion back into the ground, like a screw. The Sensei wore a flowing black skirt called a *hakama* that swirled around him when he moved. I fell in love with the beautiful gracing arc of it. So, I reason, when I'm still oddly reasonable, that's what being a mother is: taking the interruptions, the needs, the assaults on the delicate psychic state required for writing and swirling with them, moving aside slightly, taking them by the wrist, firmly, so as not to lose contact, and moving from the hara (or hips, or belly – the centre of all things – yes, since childbirth, even more so, more centre, more oomph) and whipping those little suckers around so their force is subverted and comes with me into my force. Give me white, I'll meld you into my black – or the other way around. All done with love, of course. *Ai* means love or harmony in Japanese; *Ki* is energy; *Do* is the way. So "the way of harmonizing energy."

Beautiful. Perfect. So whole. Just like bread.

DГaFT #3

The essay is due. I have a day. Fine. Six hours. I can do it. Focus. Concentrate. Oodles of time. My son wakes up with the flu. Can't go to school. My husband, deftly ignoring my seething disharmonious state, prances off to work. He's fine, he says. He'll watch TV. You can work.

Sperm donor walks down the stairs to the car, unaware of wifely daggers sticking out of his back, blood dripping onto our red painted stairs (lucky, so the neighbours won't notice the gore and I won't have to waste time cleaning them). Sweet-faced poor ailing son curls onto the chesterfield upstairs with the TV remote. I put a blanket on him.

I'm fine, Mum, he says. Gorgeous, oh, achingly gorgeous child. (It's the sheer translucence of them, not just their skin, but their hearts and their needs and their minds, all of it shining through those soft, still unformed faces.)

Do you want some water? I ask.

Sure, he says, and I think he's agreeing because he knows I feel guilty about having to work. He always knows. He can read me like no one else can. My too-wise boy. My first born. The melting point of my life.

Okay. I steel myself against this vision and come downstairs with the laptop. Shut it out. Mother self, go away. There's nothing more I can do anyway. He isn't throwing up yet. I will squeeze in a few minutes of writing before it hits. I know when it does that all thought of words will disappear, no matter how far in them I am. As I stare at the blank face of my computer screen, I imagine how the puke will spill out onto the carpet and hit the door and the walls. I see myself gathering him into the bathroom and helping him clean up and find fresh pyjamas. I know I'll feel all choked with love and concern and that writing will just seem like one stupid distraction when life, biology, my higher purpose is just this: being a mother. At this point in the fantasy, the white side of the yin/yang symbol sloshes heavily over into the black, and I feel a little dizzy with my sense of goodness. I'm positively radiant with it, in fact, a veritable Earth mother goddess, queen of vomit and bleach. Isn't that what most religions teach – to find yourself you have to give yourself? Surely after almost twelve years of broken sleep, I should be a Buddha by now. The computer screen is still blank, an irritating hum emits from the machine; upstairs the soothing murmur of the TV and the pull of my son's face. Wouldn't it be easier to give this up and just be his mother?

DraFT #4

I go to the library to look for books about writing and motherhood. All of them are out, so I bring home *Silences* by Tillie Olsen. It's about a whole panoply of reasons that writers go quiet – not just children, but publishing difficulties, bad public reaction, and other humiliations. Some of these reasons are so dire she prefaces one section with a warning: writers, don't read this.

I don't. I scan for words that might speak to me. In the opening chapter Olsen talks about the "receptive waiting" that writers must do to create works of art, and I feel slightly calmed. So, it's true, writing is different. I'm not crazy when I insist on needing time to gather my thoughts. "An undistracted center of being" is required, Olsen says, quoting Paul Valery, "and when the work comes, the response must be immediate, otherwise: all may vanish as a dream ..."[1] This is worrying again. I have a hard time completing and implementing a thought about dinner. What hope is there for all the half-baked ideas I've got for poems and stories, let alone this essay? Still,

I read on: "... only the removal and development of the material frees the forces for further work."

What does this mean? The unfinished novel, this essay, the scraps of poems are all blocking me from doing other writing?

This is too depressing.

I go for a walk.

Some time later I hear Margaret Atwood speak at the Vancouver Writers' and Readers' Festival. I'm sitting comfortably until I hear her say "block" and "unfinished work." "You have to send these things out," she says, "or you can't move on to the next thing."[2]

I feel my dark little writer side judder a little; the surface looks mottled with something like rust, and there are odd, lumpy bits pressing against the edges. Is my unfinished work developing malignancies?

I go back to Olsen for a "misery loves company" session. This time I find her invoking Franz Kafka. Kafka worked for an insurance agency and wrote when he could, but the frustration of not being able to develop his ideas strained him. Listen: "I finish nothing, because I have no time, and it presses so within me ... Yesterday for the first time in months, an indisputable ability to do good work. And yet wrote only the first page. Again I realize that everything written down bit by bit rather than all at once in the course of the larger part is inferior, and that the circumstances of my life condemn me to inferiority."[3]

Kafka died of tuberculosis at the age of forty-one. Olsen intimates it was the continual strain of stopping and starting his creative work that killed him. Listen again: "Outwardly I fulfill my office duties satisfactorily, not my inner duties however, and every unfulfilled inner duty becomes a misfortune that never leaves ..."

Not that I'm comparing myself to Kafka, of course, but next time a child interrupts me while I'm writing, may I say it's going to be the death of me?

Of course, there's another solution. More than once on the playground, talking with other mothers – architect mothers, nurse mothers, teacher mothers – I hear dark jokes and intimations, and I think of Annie Dillard, a writer I love, who says that, in order to write, "You must go at your life with a broadax."[4]

Ah. I had no idea this was going to be such a violent essay. Sorry. I think again of the old boyfriend. At least with him I could have died of something simple, like falling out of an airplane. I wouldn't end up alone (my children forsaking me for airing such thoughts) or in a small and hopeless room dying of a brain-wasting disease from too many stopped-up ideas.

DraFT #5

Toward the end of her life my mother's mind turned into a kind of jelly jam. She lost her ability to speak: *word salad*, the caregivers described it. As she disappeared behind the wall of her disease, I held more tightly to the things I knew of her. A nightgown, her handwriting on an old letter, a photo. One time the home she lived in hired a greeting service, so I received a "call" from her on Mother's Day. The syrupy male voice told me she was thinking of me on that day. I phoned the home and railed at them for doing that – the horribly surreal effect of some corporate entity claiming to know what was in my mother's mind infuriated me. I don't know why I've put that in here. I miss her, that's all. She wasn't a standard sort of mother. She went golfing any day she could and, while she made us family dinners, quite often she spent half the time on the phone with one of her golfing friends while we ate. Did she resent us? I don't think so. I think she loved us well enough, but maybe we weren't everything to her. She had her own life separate from us, that's all. Is she a good model for me? Do I really have any choice but to follow her lead?

My mother (sigh) my self.

DraFT #6

Online I google "mothers who write" and come upon an essay titled "Babies and Books" in the magazine *Literary Mama*. In it Jane Lazarre, author of *The Mother Knot*, speaks of "the need to learn to insistently be an artist in the midst of family," and, "The only thing that seems eternal and natural in motherhood is ambivalence ..."[5] Ambivalence: ambi (both) valence (relative power to react or interact).

I read on. US academic Toril Moi in her introduction to philosopher Julia Kristeva's *Stabat Mater* (subtitled *The Paradox: Mother or Primary Narcissism*), says that we need a "'post virginal' discourse on maternity ... to provide both women and men with a new ethics ..."[6] My mind, blurring the academic language and sweeping right past the ethics, reads "post-virginal Virgin Mary" and imagines Mary taking off her blue robe and handing it, along with Jesus, to a wet nurse. Mary waves goodbye as she walks into another room to write her side of the story.

Recently a friend said to me and some others about to hike a mountain, "I'm going to climb this as a virgin goddess."

"Fine," we all said, wondering what we were getting ourselves into.

"The original meaning of 'virgin' is to be whole unto oneself," she explained.

"Ah," we answered, "Can we be virgin goddesses, too?"

DraFT #7

I'm thinking about dualities again, the splitting of cells, my body. My son coming out of me with the help of a surgeon's knife, my daughter, smaller, knowing the way on her own. Again I know why I'm here feeding and loving them: they are pieces of me walking around out there in the world. In my mind, they are the white part. (And this part is getting stretched thin as they take more and more of me out there with them – wait, I want to call, what about me? Can't I come with you?) I clutch at them, but it's no good. Of course I have to let them go. Does this make sense? Complaining, then clinging. Of course it does. It's all there.

Ambivalence.

DraFT #8

Most days I write in a space under the roof with a skylight and window looking out to the mountains. Air passes through. The table is piled with books, the wastebasket with papers. Under the table are boxes of files and magazines and a sewing basket. Shelves tucked between the framing of the walls are painted pink. The carpet and the chair are green.

I rise early to peck at this keyboard. If I didn't do this, peck and search and sift through language and memory and idea, would I know my own thoughts? My daughter's door clatters open, and I hear her footsteps. In a moment she is in the room. Her body is long and bony, but it still curls like a comma in my lap. I feel her skin against mine, her warmth, her soft bad morning breath in my face. She is beautiful and perfect, and this moment could be no better. How can writing compete?

Stop.

After a while, my daughter says, I'm going to go have cereal, and I say, no, don't leave me, and we both smile. This is a game we play, don't grow up, don't go away. I need you here. But under it, I am ready for her to leave, to pull the computer back onto my lap and to work.

Sometime after my mother died I realized she wasn't gone at all. Her hands, her way of exhaling air when she was frustrated, the fierce stare over the tops of her glasses, all of these are mine now. She's not gone. She's moved in. My children have pieces of her, too: my son's posture playing sports, my daughter's quick, bright eyes. This is my parturition. My mother divided into me, me into them.

Continuum. Whole. Rounding the circle.

DraFT #9

For a whole week I leave the family entirely and go to Banff for a poetry workshop. Do I need to say it's heaven with mountains? A bathroom all to myself, not to mention a bed big enough for three families, but mine to spread out on all alone. There are a lot of mothers here. We mention our children in passing the first few days, commenting on the blissful state of solitary bathing and sleeping, but these are glancing asides, the main point is poetry, line by line, word by exquisitely considered word. Toward the end, tired by the intensity of the workshop, we exchange more information: names, ages. Home is beginning to pull at us, or are we preparing ourselves for the shift across the line?

While I'm still there a new friend says, "Maybe you're not good for them right now." What is he seeing? Poem lust? A word-addled brain with no room for children? I come home and stare at the people I love. I feel separate from them – divided – no black in the white or white in the black, just two sides bifurcating and me tumbling into the chasm between. Is this the place where cells split? Is it the source, like a well? I feel myself falling through anger, resentment, fear, pain, the deep chronic ache of my own inadequately mothered self (she loved me the best she could, was it her fault it could never be enough?).

At the bottom of it, am I doing this to my children?

DraFT #10

As I sit and stare at the mess of words on this screen – the jumble of ideas, the conflicting images, the false starts and asides, the coy remarks – the dark side of my writer self settles in.

I get up and pace, staring at the papers on the table, the pens, the coffee cup. Upstairs is silent, but the house is filled with my awareness of him. If my son weren't home sick, I would still come to this place of confusion and despair – it always hit somewhere through the writing process – and I would put on my shoes and go out for a walk.

I tear the pages, throw an empty plastic cup across the room and watch it bounce. That doesn't help, so I put the words all spilled and ruined on the pile of ashes, which could be more words or just wood, I don't remember. How many tantrums make a novel? How many an essay? I touch the flame to the pages and sit on the couch to watch them burn.

DraFT #11

(Burned.)

DraFT #12

Teacher strike. Five children upstairs. I'm on the couch again, not thinking about old boyfriends or alternate lives, but just this life. How to survive it? If I think too much about it, I can't. Yesterday, after teaching for the morning, I came home and took over from a friend. The children played happily upstairs, and I sat outside on our sunny porch. A man I knew slightly, an odd-looking man on a bicycle, rode past the house. I sat on the porch, drinking tea, hearing my children and their friends playing safely – at a happy remove – and wrote a poem.

That was a good day. Today not so good. It comes and goes, like anything. Yin/yang? I don't know. Aikido? Maybe. Or a dark and swirling chasm – the one side where I feel stuffed into a mould that doesn't always fit, the other side where I feel free. I'd like to hold to the aikido model if I can: remember to step gracefully aside and keep my centre firm while I hold those little suckers close and make the most of them as we spin slowly, slowly toward the firm and reassuring ground.

notes

1 Olsen, *Silences*, *14*.

2 Atwood, "Five Visits to the Word Hoard," Bill Duthie Memorial Lecture, Vancouver Writers and Readers Festival, October 2005.

3 Olsen, *Silences*, 15.

4 Dillard, "Holy the Firm," *The Annie Dillard Reader*, 429.

5 Lazarre, *The Mother Knot*, quoted in Malin, "Babies and Books: Motherhood and Writing," *Literary Mama*, www.literarymama.com/litcrit/archives/000105.html.

6 Moi, ed., *The Kristeva Reader*, quoted in Malin, "Babies and Books: Motherhood and Writing," *Literary Mama*, www.literarymama.com/litcrit/archives/000105.html.

The Crib and the Desk

DENISE ROIG

There I am. Break page of *The Gazette* Books section – big colour pic – newly adopted baby girl in my arms, smiling for all I'm worth. Georgia's three-month-old, still-bald head shines from the flash. I'm tilting her bottle at the just-right angle. Her hand is in mine. After home studies and social workers, after being fingerprinted by the RCMP and trekking halfway around the world, here we are. A family. In the background is my desk and in the foreground is Georgia's crib. Beneath the photo is a review of my first book of short stories.

I wonder now why our baby is in that photo. Do women writers usually pose with their children when a book of fiction gets reviewed? (Do men?) But in winter 1996 – fresh from strenuous travels to the former Soviet Republic of Georgia to adopt the baby who would become *our* Georgia – I didn't give the picture much thought. I was happy with the review. I was happy with my baby.

Then I received word that another writer, a woman with older children, had told my publisher, "I can't believe Denise has put her baby's crib in her office. Doesn't she know that'll never work?"

I still smart when I remember that remark. As if I hadn't read Virginia Woolf. As if I was unaware of what adding a baby into my writing life would do. As if I was some kind of newcomer to this juggle. (I almost wrote jungle.) I was forty-eight with an eighteen-year-old daughter I'd mostly single-parented since the age of three, and I knew a thing or two about the collision of making meals and making stories. Not to mention making money.

We *can* do it all – write a poem and do math homework and approach agents and do Girl Guides and book tours and Christmas cookies for the teachers and final edits and try to make a living from teaching writing and negotiate sleepovers and sit at the computer waiting for things to come.

We can and we do. Most of the women writers I know are doing all that. And more. My particular writing heroine is the late Grace Paley, short-story writer, poet, essayist, mother, and political activist. She would have written more, she explained late in her life, except there was the rest of the world to worry about.

But now, at nearly sixty, with a thirty-year-old about to get married and have babies of her own, with an amazing, smart eleven-year-old who has cerebral palsy and a hearing impairment, with a book of nonfiction that seems to be coming out in centimetres not pages, with short stories stewing on back pots, with ongoing teaching and freelancing to pay my way, with various social justice projects to help me feel I *am* paying my way, it occurs to me that I've been mothering nearly as long as I've been seriously writing, and that I am, in a word, tired. This particular meeting of desires and needs – to mother, to write – feels supremely demanding. Rich and fraught, it requires more than I have some days. And don't even *use* the word balance.

Still, I keep returning to that photo of Georgia and me. We're so young, so untouched. I search my face for shadows to come, Georgia's small, cradled body for hints of physical and emotional difficulties. I look, too, at the way I'd arranged the furniture: crib in the foreground, desk in the background, chair for mom and babe in the centre.

I recently read *About Alice*, Calvin Trillin's book about his late wife. He attributes the success of their marriage – like mine, of two writers – to realizing early on that there are two kinds of families: "your children are either the center of your life or they're not, and the rest is commentary."[1] He didn't need to say what kind of family they'd had together.

I was moved by this, especially coming from a man, and from a writer more known than I will ever be. Are my daughters more important than my writing? If Georgia is running a fever at school, do I tell the nurse, "Sorry, I'm in the middle of a really crucial scene right now?" The choices, of course, are usually not this dramatic. They're much more subtle. Do I volunteer to work at Georgia's class bake sale when I've marked WRITE! for that day on my agenda? Do I take on yet another helpful activity with her – vision therapy, hyperbaric oxygen therapy, Kumon reading classes – when we're so stretched already?

At sixty I don't have the sheer physical energy I had at even fifty. Nor the patience. How do I make the most of what I've got now? How do I accommodate the needs of the people I love most in the world and my own (not inconsiderable) need for time, space, and quiet to write?

Desk here, crib there, crib down the hall, desk down the street – thirty years of making adjustments and making room. Family, it seems, is only about movement. Writing, too, now that I think about it.

FEBRUARY 1996 – BACK OFFICE

I've just dropped Georgia off at the sitter's and come dashing home to the computer. Beauch, my husband, is in his office at the other end of the house, working on the book we're writing about adopting our daughter. We already have a title for it: *Bringing Georgia Home*. He writes one chapter, I write one chapter. We're hoping the alternating voices work.

I looked at my watch: 10:10 a.m. We mounted a half-flight of stairs. Dodo rang the doorbell, over which was taped a hand-printed sign in Russian. "Knock if no electricity," Dodo translated. This door was in even worse shape than the one outside.

When no one answered right away, Dodo knocked. A tall, gray-haired woman opened the door. "Gamarjóba!" she greeted us and led us through a narrow entryway, into a large, dim room. "Olga!" she said, pointing to herself.

We heard her before we saw her: Natia Merabovna Lomsianidze bellowing her five-week-old lungs out.

I stood there wanting to move toward her, took steps that must have looked tentative. Daly, Dodo and the woman were conferring excitedly in Georgian.

"She is hungry," Dodo said.

Olga led us to the couch. The baby – red-faced and gray-eyed with little tufts of dark hair – lay on her back, tiny legs kicking the air, arms raised to heaven. Olga knelt and scooped and there she was, Georgia Natia Beauchemin, in my arms, looking into my eyes.

"Ahhhhh," breathed the women.

*Olga handed me a small plastic bottle, took off the orange shawl she'd been
wearing around her shoulders and wrapped it around the baby. She led me to a
wood chair; gently, firmly, pushed me down into it. I slipped the nipple into the
waiting mouth, held my breath. We watched each other. Beauch put his arm
around the back of the chair to include us both. I could feel his body shaking.*[2]

Of course this can work! When Georgia's at the sitter, I reclaim my office
space. I don't even *see* the crib. I want to tell that doubting woman writer,
the one who knows so much: *Check this out!*

APRIL 1996 – BACK OFFICE II

"Yes, there's a problem," Georgia's pediatrician, an expert in international
adoption, confirms.

I've sensed for a while that things are unfolding slowly, have come to hate
those child development books. Georgia has trouble lifting her head. When
you hold her, even at six months, she's a sweet, heavy, unsupported lump.
She didn't smile until she was nearly three months old. (But then, what a
smile. It lights up my worried heart.)

As we climb the stairs of our flat after the doctor's appointment – stunned
into a rare lack of words – the phone rings. It's Ariel, oldest daughter, calling from Amsterdam. Nearly two years ago she ran off from the post-high
school, Italian foreign-exchange program we'd sent her on and has been
roaming the globe with her twice-older boyfriend doing hair wraps on the
beach in Eilat, picking olives on Crete, cooking in a tapas bar in Tel Aviv.

They've had the uncanny knack of landing in the most troubled corners
of the world – standing outside the Tel Aviv arena the night Itzak Rabin
was assassinated, missing a suicide bombing in Dizingoff Centre by ten
minutes, arriving at Gatwick the week of IRA bombings, hitching through
Bosnia as a shortcut to Greece. I've been holding my breath for months.

"I'm coming home Saturday," she says.

"I have two daughters with developmental delays," I tell my mother on
the phone.

Many months later, my mother says, "I'd never, ever heard you sound
bitter about being a mother before."

My father, a visual artist, had every right to feel bitter about putting his
art on hold while he supported our family of six. He laboured for years at
a civil-service job he only occasionally liked, heading up an environmental

controls office for the US Air Force, an artist among generals. He painted at night, sculpted on weekends, and earned two more master's degrees in his (spare!) time. He also was the parent of a disabled child, my next youngest brother who suffered an inflammation of the cerebellum at thirteen months and has required therapy of all kinds ever since. At fifty-one, my brother still calls my parents every day.

My father has never said, "Christ, this is tough." He is the gentlest and most gentlemanly of men. But at some of the most critical moments in my life, he has also been frontally honest.

"Remember – you wanted this," he said a few years later when we were visiting. We were in his studio on the hill above their house in LA, just the two of us, his muscular, sensual sculpture all around. I must have been complaining about the load I was carrying – child with a disability, intense husband, students with no respect, no time to write. "You wanted *all* of this," he reminded me.

Yes, and I want my wandering older daughter back. But I'm scared, too. Who is Ariel now? And, more practically, where will she sleep? Where will I write? Now that Georgia sleeps through the night, she's down the hall in the tiny room at the front of the flat, and Beauch has moved his office into the large dining room where we never eat anyway. My office at the back of the house has been divested of its crib and restored to its usual writer's mess. I light scented candles on my desk.

FEBruary 1998 – DINING room

The Russian woman who arranged our adoption has just told me the most wonky, wonderful stories of her recent return visit to Moscow, and I have to get them down NOW, while the lattes are still working. I whip off my coat, turn on the computer. Am I going to tell these stories in the first person or third?

"Take them, take them!" Vicky waved at me in the café. (Doesn't she know how dangerous it is to tell a writer anything?)

I wasn't happy at first about writing in the dining room, which now also includes Beauch's ugly little computer desk, our dining room table and chairs, china cabinet, book cases and Georgia's doll house.

I didn't really want to share an office again. But here I am in a big, bright room with my own window, and I don't know why but the words are coming and coming. The Russian stories bring the count to five. I've never worked on five short stories simultaneously. I go a little way with one, get stuck, go to another. It's like having five little babies who nap and eat at (conveniently) different times.

My real babies are thriving in their ways.

Ariel, big girl, is in her own apartment and in art school at Concordia, finding her feet (hands, eyes, talent) at last.

Georgia is in a daycare that integrates a special-needs child into each class. She's getting physiotherapy, occupational therapy, speech therapy. I drive around a lot from one cheery, encouraging therapist to another.

At two-and-a-half, Georgia is finally walking and starting to talk (first word: *ma*; second: *danger*), thanks to the saintly, unflagging efforts of all those therapists and her own nonstop will. We're trying not to break that will, but it has a dark side. Georgia has terrible tantrums, uncontrollable meltdowns many times a day. Even the behavioural psychologist I drag us to weekly is impressed.

He doesn't actually treat Georgia; instead he coaches me in his methods. It's pure reward and punishment. For twelve minutes every day, Georgia and I sit at the kitchen table. "Hands on the table," I command. She puts her hands on the table. I pop a kernel of popcorn, or a chocolate chip, in her mouth.

But when she runs amok, it's in-the-corner time. Give in now, and you will be giving in for the rest of your lives, the psychologist has warned us. In the corner of our hallway, Georgia arches her back. She thrashes. She screams so loudly I worry the police will come. Whole evenings are obliterated. Tears, promises, exhaustion follow. If she throws a tantrum on the way to daycare, it takes an hour of tea and chores before I can settle down to write.

January 1999 – rented space

It's almost too quiet in here, this studio on the third floor of an apartment building near the Vendôme metro station. I want and need silence, but this feels too anonymous.

We've switched places with Ariel, who after two years of living on her own in this building, told us, "I need to be with family." We didn't argue as we borrowed a trailer, unplugged and replugged the computers again, moved Ariel into the back bedroom, my old office. Truth is, I love having her home again. It feeds me, watching the art she is making.

Georgia's tiny front room is now a little girl's room. The crib is gone. She's on a futon, easier for both of us to negotiate than a crib. She careens around the house, a tall girl with a magic smile who loves cats and her big sister. That was her third word, a hard word, "Ariel."

I should love the studio's absolute, resounding silence, the girls out of sight, the phone barely ringing. But I feel out of touch with myself here. Partly it's the hours: nine to five, too much like a regular job. We drop Georgia off at daycare, then drive to "the office." It's good for discipline, but if something comes to me at five a.m. I can't get up and natter at the keyboard in my pajamas. I do work here, but it's mostly the other work: writing for money, prepping for teaching writing to kids who think they're already writers. One of my university students this year is writing sci-fi porn, really bad outer space sex. It would be funny if I didn't have to take it seriously. My own writing sits like a garden in winter. I write that line in a short story about a teacher with a demanding, blackmailing, bipolar student.

The best thing is the single, huge window near my desk and the sense of being perched in the tree outside. I watch the seasons colour the tree.

MARCH 2000 – DINING ROOM II

Ariel's painting the little front bedroom a dreamy shade of aqua. She hangs gauzy silk-screened fabric she's printed in school. In the interest of economics, we've moved the office home again. Georgia's taking over the bigger back bedroom – all those toys and books and dolls – while our office has been moved back to the centre of things, the dining room.

After a year of near-deafening quiet, how am I going to write in here? A rice-paper screen separates our two work areas, apt since we've abandoned our joint writing project about Georgia. It was wonderful fun until we had to edit the thing. Between our disagreements over each other's tone, structure, and stylistic ticks, plus rejection letters from publishers, the project finally foundered. We are each other's best editors, we agree, just not when it's on the same book. We'll print the whole ungainly, uneven thing out for Georgia when she's older. It is her history, after all.

I'm dubious about our new-old space, but in Dining Room Central, Beauch is rewriting his second novel. I'm finishing off some of my half-done stories. One is about a priest who gets married and who wants to write and tries to be a husband. One is about the parents of an autistic boy who are losing it themselves. I begin to dare to imagine another book.

Bed, desk, sink, closet, a statue of the Virgin Mary on the lawn. That's it. This is my safe house, a monastery forty minutes, but light years, from home. I come with a poet friend to hole up and write from Friday afternoon to Sunday afternoon.

I'm usually nervous when I arrive, but a happy nervous. Will I be able to write this time? I have no excuses here: no pediatrician's appointments or clothes to fold or homework to supervise. I open the door to my very own room and am carried off. It's story time. Sometimes I look up and six hours have gone by. I edit a second book of stories here.

We write, we eat, we sleep. Several times a day we attend the offices chanted by the monks. We're not supposed to talk – it's a silent space – but when my friend and I meet we whisper, "How's it going?" There's only one it here.

The first time I came here for a writing retreat, Georgia was still a baby. I woke several times during the night that weekend, thinking I heard her crying down the hall. Now I only call home once a day, after supper.

"I love you. I miss you," Georgia says, but I can hear she's also anxious to get back to the endless board games she plays with her father in my absence. Beauch has taught her poker, too. "Are you writing a lot, Mom?" she asks.

january 2007 – river

If I sit up really straight I can see the Saint Lawrence River from my desk. This is our first house; small, but the view is big. Beauch is in the finished basement, typing away. It's dark down there, but he claims to like it. My office is painted the same dreamy aqua as Ariel's bedroom in our old flat.

She lived here for six months when we first moved in and left her trademark blue. But Ariel won't be coming back now: she and her fiancé (a son at last) have just bought a condo across town. Kids are born – then blink! – they move out. My father has warned me about this. "Don't forget who you are," he told me last year. "You are a writer."

I'm working on some new short stories and a nonfiction book about my recent year in a Montreal pastry school. It's slow, but it's coming.

Georgia's bedroom, with its brass day bed, packed bookshelves and flat-screen computer, is next to my office.

"I'm going to be right next door. I have to do some stuff on the computer," I tell Georgia every night. Bedtimes have often been battle zones, with me still having to lie down with her to get her settled. It's as if she can't bear to release the incredible control she must keep on her body all day.

But lately she's begun to say, "Okay, Mom, good night."

She brought a math test home this week (on data management, no less) with *90%* written on it and a sticker from the teacher that said: "You're a star!"

"Brainiac," I say. She grins.

Georgia swims and rides horses, especially proud of a first-place ribbon she just won for jumping. Her disabilities are, in her words, "No big deal." She still has the occasional meltdown. After a bad one, Beauch and I talk, not too enthusiastically, about seeing a shrink again. At some point, we know we'll probably have to. There's a lot coming up. Adolescence, for starters.

And, for me, the beginning of my seventh decade. I no longer feel I have all the time in the world to write, to travel, to do everything I wanted to do. But then that's life for all of us, isn't it? Why shouldn't I be feeling the press of time?

Old photos do that to you. I'm still studying the one that ran with the first review. I was nearly fifty, but I look so fresh, sitting with such certainty in my little world of crib and desk. Maybe that woman writer was right: I was naïve. I didn't know how the two would collide this time around.

They also met in a most surprising way. At that same desk, in late 1995, two months before the review, working late one evening, the phone rang.

"There's a baby," Vicky told me. "She was born October 19. She's yours if you want her."

October 19: why did that date sound so familiar? And then I realized this was the date I had launched my book just a few weeks before. On that night I had stood in front of a crowd of family and friends at a bar on St. Laurent and read a story and signed books and been incredibly happy.

Later still, I remembered what story I'd read. It was called "Tiny Dancer," and it was about a couple with a sick child who has to wear a helmet because he can't keep his balance. He dances in an empty bedroom at the end as the parents watch from the doorway: "When Berry finally lost his balance, Ned bent to lift him. And as he straightened up, he looked at Fran and she looked at him and something not unlike joy passed between them."[3]

Halfway around the world, Georgia was born the same day my book was born.

notes

1   Trillin, *About Alice*.
2   Denise Roig and Raymond Beauchemin, *Bringing Georgia Home* (unpublished ms.).
3   Roig, "Tiny Dancer," *A Quiet Night and a Perfect End*.

Motherhood and Other Possibilities

susan musGrave

wInTer, 1988–89

One factor that sets women writers apart, Marilyn Yalom says in *Maternity, Morality and the Literature of Madness*, is their tendency to see writing books as conflicting with, or as a substitute for, having babies. According to Yalom, who studied writers such as Sylvia Plath, Anne Sexton, and Virginia Woolf, all of whom endured a psychosis, the conflicting pressures of art and maternity can add overpowering stress to any fissure that already exists in the psychic structure. Another example she cites is the French writer Emma Santos, who had a stillborn child. Santos perceived this as a kind of punishment for the book she was working on, the price of words.

My husband and I are attending our first prenatal class because we plan on having a natural childbirth. My husband isn't going to fall asleep during my contractions; I am going to do my bit by staying calm, imagining the wings of a butterfly and floating my way through transition.

Our instructor, whose nametag identifies her as Cherry, is busily distributing pamphlets on the care and prevention of hemorrhoids. When all the couples have arrived and arranged themselves on feather pillows and designer mats, she asks each of the "moms" to share something about herself. "For instance," I think I hear her ask me, "what do you do?"

"I'm a writer," I say, trying to sound convinced. Throughout my pregnancy, I've been determined to hang on to this image of myself, though lately, instead of writing, I've been pricing crib monitors and, instead of reading Dostoyevsky, speed-reading *Diaper Dialogue*.

"A writer, that's super!" says Cherry, "but I asked when you were *due*."

My baby is due on Christmas Day. But even a more daunting prospect, my new book, *Motherhood and Other Possibilities*, a collection of personal essays, is due nine months later.

Up until now I have mostly written poetry. How difficult it is for women to be poets, sympathizes Robert Graves, in *The White Goddess*. There's a temptation, he says, for us to commit suicide in domesticity. "No poet can hope to understand the nature of poetry unless he [*sic*] has had a vision of the Naked King crucified to the lopped oak and watched the dancers, red-eyed from the smoke of the sacrificial fires, chanting, 'Kill! Kill! Kill!' and 'Blood! Blood! Blood!'"

"It's normal for expectant moms to have strong feelings," Cherry is saying, as she dims the lights and begins a slide show. I try to focus my thoughts on the primitive, respiration-like movements on the screen, where the baby has reached thirty-two weeks and is becoming, Cherry tells us, aware of other voices outside Mom's body. "Eavesdropping begins in utero," my husband whispers. From living with me he has learned that a writer's job is to eavesdrop on the world.

If it's a boy you are carrying, Cherry says, right about now his testicles will be descending into the scrotum. With that we break for a snack of apple juice and sugarless cookies, then get down on the floor again to practice our deep breathing. No husband can hope to understand the nature of motherhood unless he has had a vision of his wife spread out on a hard oak floor panting *Puh! Puh! Puh!*

We wind up with some muscle relaxation exercises. I can feel the stress building in the fissures that, since the day I was conceived, have existed in my psychic structure. A few more classes like this one, and I'll be tossing aside my good intentions of having a natural birth and be chanting "Drugs! Drugs! Give me drugs!"

One young mother-to-be approaches me as I'm rolling up my foamy. She wonders if the urge to write is the same as the urge to have a baby. She's always wanted to write a book, but every time she sits down to do it she finds herself pregnant.

Driving home from our class I wonder if I've been naive. I hadn't counted on parenthood involving any major adjustments in my work habits. Despite what other women writers have told me about the difficulties of pursuing a career after becoming mothers, I am certain that having a baby is going to be no more difficult that giving birth to a poem.

On Christmas Eve I call my editor to say I am taking a few days off. My current book is on schedule and can be put on the back burner. I am prepared to give birth and then, after a week's maternity leave, I'll be ready to go back to work. The house is ready, too; I've had it decorated for Christmas since the day after Halloween. Every cookie tin is filled. I've made soup and booties; the freezer and the baby's chest of drawers overflow. "What are you going to do next?" my husband asks. "Make curtains for the car?"

He is helping me pack my suitcase for the hospital. I give him the agenda: a quiet Christmas Eve rehearsing my breathing patterns. Christmas morning we'll exchange gifts, before lunch I will have dashed off a dozen thank-you notes for the baby's gifts I've received, and, after eating turkey dinner for two, I'll go into labour at a civilized hour. I'll take Boxing Week off to bond and be reunited with my Mac by January first.

Christmas Day comes, but no contractions. On Boxing Day well-meaning friends begin calling to suggest everything from bumpy car rides to gin fizzes in hot bathtubs and greasy duck dinners to help things along. My mother brings over a bottle of cod-liver oil, saying let nature take her course.

On New Year's Eve we undecorate the house. My husband unpacks my suitcase and says I might as well get some use out of the new nightie he'd bought me to wear in the hospital. Knowing we are going to forfeit a tax break, and that our child will have to wait an extra year before starting grade 1, we go to bed sober.

On New Year's Day a friend calls to suggest I consider a Caesarean section. I say I don't want my baby robbed of the excruciating pleasure he will feel during his journey down the birth canal, and I hang up the phone. Another friend calls to propose medical intervention. After consulting one of my pregnancy guidebooks, which links inductions to sadomasochistic behaviour later in life, I take the phone off the hook and let nature take her course.

Two weeks behind schedule, in the middle of the night and the middle of a blizzard, we arrive at emergency. My husband holds my hand as I lie shell-shocked in the labour and delivery room until dawn, panting for drugs. My doctor believes in letting nature take her course, too, and I end up having a natural childbirth by default.

My husband is a trooper. He doesn't yawn once, and afterward he doesn't ask if I still think having a baby is anything like giving birth to a poem.

Three days later I pack, strap the baby in her car seat and leave the hospital. A true Renaissance woman, I am itching to get back to my computer.

The first day home I put our daughter to bed in the corner of my office that we've converted into a nursery. As I sit down to begin a new chapter I think how lucky I am, I have an advantage over other women with careers. I can be home with my baby and still continue to work.

Writing, for me, has always been instinctive. What I hadn't counted on was a baby having instincts, too. The moment I boot up my computer, her instinct tells her it is time to have her Huggies changed. Instinct tells her to wake up when I lie down, to eat when I am hungry, to spit up when my editor calls to ask how is the new baby ... and the current book.

Overcome by the conflicting pressures of staying up all night and trying to write for a living during the day, I go back to bed one morning and stay there. I've been home for two weeks and haven't completed a sentence. My unfinished book would have to be put on the back burner, literally. One blank page at a time.

My husband tries to console me. He says I owe it to myself to take a couple of months off work. If other women have to go through what I had gone through in childbirth, he adds, he sees little hope of the human race continuing. He offers to take our daughter while he washes a week's dishes and prepares our evening meal so I can be alone in my office. He'll bring me a cup of tea.

He's right. Even if I am not writing much these days, I have research to do.

♣ "Art cannot be achieved by those for whom anything else matters more," writes Carolyn Heilbrun, author of *Reinventing Womanhood*. "Art, like passion, is not a part-time occupation."

I reread this sentence and realize in my twenties I would have bought that romantic notion, but I no longer believe it to be true. Back then I believed that domesticity and the creative process were incompatible, that in order to be a real artist you needed a remote cabin, paper, food, and a part-time lover. It's hard to admit, but having a baby has changed the way I feel.

I read the next sentence out loud, following my husband into the kitchen as he struggles to get the dote into her corduroy Snugli. "The real artist is engaged in a full-time struggle, which is harder for women, among other reasons, because they do not have wives."

He secures the Snugli to his chest so she can watch him do the dishes and prepare his specialité – Ketchup with Meat. "Who hasn't got enough wives?"

"'Most of the great women writers,'" I keep reading, "'have been unmarried. Those who have written in the state of wedlock have done so in peaceful kingdoms guarded by devoted husbands. Few have children.'"

My husband adjusts the heat under the saucepan of hot water in which he is heating the baby's bottle. "I thought you were going to work."

In the peaceful kingdom of my office, I curl up with my books. Heilbrun cites Virginia Woolf as one of the lucky ones who found a nurturing man; Woolf knew that women with diapers to change and meals to arrange could not be artists, as well. To be truly an artist, she said, is to retain control of one's destiny, and women struggling their way to a sense of identity through the encircling meshes of domesticity were not artists, but victims.

For the women who did manage to write, the options were limited. Death and marriage were the only two possible ends for women in novels and were, frequently, the same end, Heilbrun writes. So full of anxiety were women before the current women's movement that, when imagining other possibilities of female destinies, they went to great pains to conceal their authorial identities. (George Sand, for instance, became a male impersonator.) It's hard now to conceive of certain subjects being considered "unwomanly," but it wasn't so long ago that Charlotte Brontë's closest friends were describing her novels as coarse and unbecoming in their presentation of passion.

These days, women can write openly about intimacy; when Anna Quindlen, columnist for the *New York Times*, says, "another year has gone by and still the Nobel Prize has not been awarded to the inventors of the Snugli baby carrier," it's because she sees her life as interacting with her art. So does Sharon Olds make poetry out of her son's first birthday party, or the right way to insert a diaphragm.

Neither Quindlen nor Olds gave up writing when they became mothers. A passion for writing never decreases, just as when your second child is born and you don't love your first any less.

"When I was twenty-five," Quindlen writes, "I always felt as if a bus were coming around the corner with my name on its front bumper, and that I'd damn well better have spent the day working on a good opening sentence for my obit. Now it seems as if there are so many years ahead ... and if I get the forty additional years statisticians say are likely coming to me, I could fit in one, maybe two new lifetimes. Sad that only one of those lifetimes can include being the mother of young children."

Today's writers – men *and* women – know that art can be achieved by those for whom other things, like family, matter more. When Ken Kesey, author of *One Flew over the Cuckoo's Nest*, was asked why he hadn't published a book in many years, he replied, "I felt like you can write forever, but you have a short time to raise a family."

He was right. And if I could not finish my book because something else mattered to me just as much, if not more, then the book would have to wait. Raising a child, like passion, would not be my part-time occupation.

I had left home when I was sixteen; I assumed my daughter would do the same. I could write forever, but, for the next sixteen years at least, my daughter would be my full-time job.

sixteen years later

Bearing in mind the slogan, "If you love something, let it go free," I have put my sixteen-year-old daughter on a plane to spend a month in Australia with my goddaughter. I'd found a seat-sale ticket, got her a valid passport. I'd set her up with a bank card; every weekend I would transfer $50 into her account so she would have spending money. What *was* I thinking?

Her phone card alone cost $50 a day. On day three, my daughter, weeping over the long distance, says she'd been locked out of her lodgings by accident and is camping in a strip mall on Downer Street. The pay phone has a ring of lip gloss around it because she's been talking to her friends on Vancouver Island all day. There is nothing else to do in Australia; she'd maxed out her VISA on designer sunglasses in the airport gift shop (I'd given her a credit card with a $500 limit – "for emergencies"), but it hasn't stopped raining since she arrived. She's seen no wildlife except for some gross birds that tried to steal her last cigarette. She has only seen one hot boy, and he was underage. All the kids she's met are into crystal meth, and they want her to try it, too; would I buy her a ticket home instead?

I set aside *Motherhood and Other Possibilities* (I'd planned on using my daughter's vacation as a chance to pick up where I'd left off, so many lifetimes ago) and tried not to panic. What else was a mother to do? I'd loved her, let her go, and now she wanted to boomerang back. I went on the Internet, googling "Things to do in Adelaide when you are 16." What I found wasn't hopeful:

unless u wanna go to a museum or church there is hardly nething fun to do. me and my friend had an idea so ill share it wit u. it mite keep u amused for a day, or 5. depending on how good u can read bus timetables! what u do is just catch random busses around so u get totally lost. wen u get somewhere good pretend ur tourists, and hook up wit guys youll never c again! at the end of the exciting day ... try to get home!

I emailed my friends: do they have any ideas as to what might keep my daughter occupied in a less random way? "It would be great if my daughter could see more than the inside of a pay-phone booth, though that in itself could be a rich experience," I wrote, trying to stay positive.

"Remember that song by Shel Silverstein, 'Hello mudda, hello fadda' about being at camp?" my friend, Lorna replied, in response to my desperate email. "The chorus is 'Take me home, oh mudda, fadda, take me home/ I hate Granada/ Don't leave me/out in the forest where/ I might get eaten by a bear.' Then a couple of stanzas, later, 'Waita minute/It's stopped raining/guys are swimming/guys are sailing/playing baseball/gee, that's better/ mudda, fadda kindly disregard this letta.'" I remembered the song alright, but my recollection of summer camp was that it had *never* stopped raining and we were forced to stay indoors and participate in drug-induced Satanic rituals and underage orgies (of which I remember little since we were hypnotized first).

Another friend, Marilyn, wrote, "Just about everybody I know who has sent a kid 'abroad' has a similar story. The only one that didn't work out was the one who helped her son come home early – a mistake I think." A third, Katherine, said that she had sent her daughter to Calgary for a respite when she was seventeen. "She spent most of her first days on the phone ... fearing she was missing all that was happening in bad old Sidney." The consensus seems to be that my daughter will fend for herself, find out something about the world, and, after a week or so, want me to disregard her initial homesickness.

My friends were right. She befriended a boy who collected trolleys in the supermarket parking lot and got to see the inside of an Australian parking lot as well as the phone booth at the mall. She photographed wildlife in a zoo. She witnessed a purse-snatching (by some crystal-meth-addicted youths) and helped police retrieve the victim's purse. She partied with new friends who drove her to the airport to catch her plane back to Canada on her last day ... which is when I get the final, most heart-rending phone call of all.

"Hello? Mumma? My passport's been stolen. They won't let me on the plane. Help me, mumma. I just want to come home!"

♣ I never gave up writing, but parenting, over the years, involved a major adjustment in my work habits. As my daughter grew from an infant into a child then a teen, I wrote plenty of other books – children's stories, novels, volumes of poetry – but my definitive work on the art of motherhood seemed destined never to end. I had the title and a beginning, and a fair chunk of the middle was complete, but the end, every writer's favourite two words – THE END – eluded me.

I suspect it's because there is never an end to it, being a mother of children who need you there to rescue them, as long as you survive. There never were, as it turned out, other possibilities.

Opposing Forces

cori howard

My first clue that motherhood and writing are opposing forces came when my first child was four months old. I had perfected the position – phone cradled on my shoulder, hands typing on the computer, feet propped up on desk, tiny baby sleeping face up on thighs. This was no easy feat, but my baby seemed to like it and rarely woke up as I clattered away on the keys. My light bulb moment came when I was working on a story about Canada's most eligible bachelors for *Elle* magazine. I can't remember now whom I was interviewing, and it's not because I had mommy brain – although I did have it and still do. It's because I want to forget that interview. Halfway through, my baby woke up and projectile vomited all over my lap, the computer, the phone, my hand, himself.

It was disgusting and really shocking. But what's interesting about this story is that – get this – I didn't stop. I didn't say, "Hang on a second," or "Can I ask you a favour and call you back in five minutes?" I just kept typing through the vomit, wiping as much of it on my shirt as I could and breastfeeding to prevent him from crying and disrupting the interview.

What was really happening in this moment was a refusal to admit that I couldn't do it all. I had been raised on the abominable myth that women can have it all, do it all – career, family, everything. What kind of feminist would raise their daughter believing that kind of crap? Anyway, I was still new to motherhood and in the throes of a pretty major identity crisis, so I was still grasping onto my life as a freelance writer.

I finished that interview, but I was obviously not as focused as I could have been on my subject, and my story inevitably reflected that. I was laid off shortly after that incident. My editors at the magazine insisted it had nothing to do with the quality of my work. They said it was the budget. But they always say that. So, full of self-doubt that had been building since the baby was born and reeling with hormones, I cried on the phone. I begged them not to do this to me. I was emotional and out of control. I wouldn't have wanted to be my editor.

"Please," I sobbed. "You can't do this. Could you just give me another month?"

"No, I don't think so," replied the editor, tersely. "But you could write a few freelance articles for us, and we can pay you for that."

"Oh," I continued, hiccupping with hysteria. "And what about after that? You said we were going to sign the contract just two weeks ago."

"Cori, we just don't have the money right now to pay someone on a regular basis."

Of course, I soldiered on with my writing career. I had to. I needed money. I had just been laid off from a staff job as a reporter for *The National Post* a few months earlier. *Elle* had agreed to hire me as a part-time editor, and I was using the rest of the time to bond with my child and figure out another way to make a living as a writer. But who has time to figure anything out when you're becoming a new mom? When you're trying to make organic apple purée, find the best cloth diapers, and walk and walk and walk until the baby finally takes a nap? And here's the key thing: Who has the mental energy to write after a day of breastfeeding and lolling on the floor goo-ing and gaga-ing at your delicious baby?

Mental freedom is a precious commodity in my life right now. Five years after the vomit incident, I have two kids. The first one is now four, and I have, as I write this, a one-year-old baby girl. And what I've learned over the last few years is that, in order to write, I need time to think. I need free brain space, time to let thoughts come and go, and that doesn't come easily or often. Predictably, I do a lot of writing in my head while I'm lying in bed breastfeeding baby number two to sleep. Some of it I do in the swimming pool on the rare occasion that I get to go out and do some exercise. Sometimes, I will get inspired and ignore my kids while they play and I stare into space, chasing ideas around my head. But then, I can rarely follow up those moments with the free time to sit down and get all the stuff out of my head and onto paper. I could get up after the kids fall asleep to write some stuff down, but I'm usually way too tired. I could come home after swimming and write some stuff down, but there are usually two eager kids waiting to see me and an even more eager husband/mother/father waiting for the hand-off. And I definitely can't do it after ignoring my kids because I've already ignored them and they're crying now: someone got hurt or needs some apple juice or wants some attention. When I think about this stuff, though, I don't feel frustrated or mad. I just can't believe how unprepared I was for this life of motherhood and writing. And I write nonfiction. I feel very sorry for my friends who are mothers and fiction writers. That's even harder. At least I can rely on other people's stories. I only have to imagine how I'll write the story. They have to imagine the story and then how to write it. My imagination these days is all spent trying to keep up with my four-year-old's demands to tell him another story. "Can this one be Scooby-Doo meets Superman meets The Incredibles?" This is a daily question in my house. Maybe I should be writing books for Disney.

Beyond the limits of my imagination and the shortage of mental space, there is the tender issue of how to actually conduct a phone interview at home with children around. I have a two-storey home and figured this wouldn't be an issue. If I'm on the phone, they can be either upstairs or downstairs for the half-hour it usually takes. But nothing is simple in a world with small children.

Just the other day I was writing a story for *Maclean's* about online pedophiles and criminal prosecution. I was interviewing a potential pedophile on the phone. I had dialled his number on the off-chance he'd be home. I told my husband what I was doing. Prepared him for what might happen if I actually got through. So when I did actually get him on the line, I shoved our baby into my husband's hands, whispered to him to take the four-year-old upstairs, at the same time explaining to the guy on the phone who I was and what I wanted. The first twenty minutes went well. I was getting some great information when I heard the padding of feet on the stairs. Then I see my son come into the kitchen where I'm at the computer. I whisper to him frantically to go back upstairs and try to ignore him. But he's ignoring me and soon he's singing a quiet song to himself and lying on the kitchen carpet. Again, I whisper to him to stop. Again, he ignores me.

This time, I am not going to keep going. I am no supermom. I have surrendered to the reality of motherhood and writing. I am a mother. I am a writer. Mostly, they overlap, and, when they do, it will be a crisis and each crisis will require a new and creative solution. In this case, I ended up putting the potential pedophile on hold.

"Ty, go up and see your Dad. I'm almost finished," I whisper, covering the receiver.

"No. I don't want to. He's being mean," he says and then starts singing again.

"Ty. Stop singing and go upstairs right this second."

"Mom, please. I don't want to. I'll be quiet."

"TY. GET UPSTAIRS THIS INSTANT." I'm screaming now and not happy that my parenting skills have devolved to this.

I give up and manage the finish the interview with my son lying like a dog by my feet. As soon as I hang up the phone, I race upstairs to scream at my husband.

"Why did you let him come downstairs?"

Dirty look. "I couldn't help it," he says between clenched teeth. "I have two kids here. It's not easy."

"But all I needed was twenty more minutes. This is serious stuff. This is my career. You can't just let them come down in the middle of an interview. Now I won't be able to write a good story."

Another dirty look.

"Okay," I say, still fuming. "Maybe this just isn't working. I can't work at home. That's great. What the hell are we going to do if I can't write? All I needed was a few minutes on the phone. I don't think that's too much to ask. You cannot let the kids come near me when I'm working. Why is that such a hard thing to ask?"

Stony silence. I want to punch my fists into the wall. I can't believe something so simple is so unattainable. I can't believe I'm going to have to write like this for the rest of my life. I'm miserable for the rest of the day.

Mostly, I'm miserable because I screamed at my son and at my husband. The story will get done. It just does. I feel sick that I screamed at my son to stop singing. I want him to sing. Just not when I'm working. Sadly, I'm sure I'll yell at him again. My husband knows I'll yell at him again and pretty soon, I'll be yelling at my daughter. So when my kids grow up, they'll think of writers as intense, spacey types who spend a lot of time staring at computer screens and yelling. Good. I don't want my kids to be writers. It's no way to make a living.

Despite all the yelling though, there is proof that I'm evolving. My family is evolving. I have totally surrendered to the reality that the old way of doing things is gone forever. Now, I schedule interviews around the availability of my husband, mother, father, television shows. I drag my sorry butt out of bed at 9 PM, after the kids are sleeping, to write. My husband does the best he can to keep the kids away from me when I'm on the phone. As for my kids, well, they sing better than they vomit.

A Double Life

ROBYN SARAH

One October morning in 1974, a young woman sat in a rented cabin on Vancouver Island looking out on the Strait of Juan de Fuca and recorded in her journal a landmark quietly passed:

> My twenty-fifth has been and gone; and having received my birthday cards early, I didn't even notice. Remembered when I awoke this morning ... Just as well – if I'd remembered yesterday, I should have brooded: Twenty-five – and no book – and no child.

> I've got to just say to myself: If it's writing that you want to do – if you really want to do it – then you will do it no matter what – child or no child. So there is no need to make an issue out of having a child – "whether" and "when." Just "yes" and "whenever."[1]

Seventeen months and three journal volumes later, only the scenery had changed. In a third-floor walk-up over a storefront on Rue Villeneuve, in Montreal's Mile End district, the same woman wrote:

> ... this morning I suddenly understood something I have known all along. It is this: The book is waiting for the child. But the child is waiting for the book. You go first. No, you. No, after you. After YOU.

My obstructed offspring. Too polite, both of them. The book, the child, both inside me and yet not inside me. Each waiting for the other to decide to come forth ...

Looking back from the vantage point of my mid-fifties, it's clear that, from very early on, the creative and procreative were associated in the mind of that young woman I was. The book and the baby exerted separate but equal claims on me; even in the abstract I felt them to be, if not in actual conflict, somehow dancing around each other. They were in some way equivalent. My yearning for motherhood, once it fully kicked in, was the only thing I'd ever felt as fiercely as the calling to write that had been with me since childhood. The first, I understood to be my destiny as a woman; the second, my personal destiny. If they seemed sometimes to be jockeying, still it was unthinkable that I should have to sacrifice either one for the sake of the other.

In April 1977 – a year after that second journal entry – I received a letter accepting my first poetry manuscript for publication. I was by then pregnant with my first child. All was in order. The real jockeying had yet to begin.

♣ I grew up accepting without question my mother's mantra that a woman's deepest fulfillment in life was to have children, that a childless woman was to be pitied: even if she was rich in achievement and enjoyed a full life in other respects, *as a woman* she was incomplete. Alongside this notion (and even as feminists were trumpeting a woman's right to pursue aspirations of her own outside of the home) I absorbed dire warnings from the literary set to which I was early drawn:

Once you have a baby, you'll stop writing, you won't need to write any more.

Write while you can. Once you have kids, you'll never have the time.

Look at the women writers of genius, the ones who produced literary masterpieces – none of them had children.

It was hard to disregard the warnings. The disheartening litany was there for anyone to recite to herself: the Brontë sisters; Jane Austen; George Eliot;

Emily Dickinson; Willa Cather; Katherine Mansfield; Virginia Woolf; Katherine Anne Porter; Dorothy Parker; Eudora Welty; Carson McCullers; Flannery O'Connor; Marianne Moore; Elizabeth Bishop ... Childless, all. The rare exception seemed only to prove the rule. Maybe it was indeed possible to combine motherhood with a career as doctor, academic, lawyer, executive – but it did rather seem as if the calling of a writer required vows. Nothing so extreme as retiring to a nunnery, perhaps – not in an age of birth control – but it looked as if one might have to renounce "womanly fulfillment."

In my early twenties, at the age when we are all invincible and know we can have everything, I was made uneasy by these mantras – the one about womanly fulfillment, the one about women writers. On a gut level I was afraid that both were true. But this meant that ultimately I would have to betray myself – if not as a woman, then as a writer. I would have to choose, and the choice would soon be upon me. Procrastination seemed my best defense.

Plea-bargaining came next. I decided it would be okay for me to have a child as long as I published a book first. That way, I would already be a writer when I became a mother, so could presumably continue in both identities. But did I have the discipline, the self-confidence, the sheer persistence to complete a book in my early twenties – let alone get it published? I was flighty in my enthusiasms and attentions, divided in my energies; I suffered from dry spells and depressions, and despite my best intentions I wrote sporadically if I wrote at all. I could not even settle on a genre – wavering between poetry and fiction. So it was that at twenty-five (that stock-taking birthday), finding myself still bookless and childless, I changed my tune. How long could I delay starting a family in the hope that a book would materialize first? I had a lifetime in which to write books, but the biological clock was ticking. I had to trust the writer in me to survive motherhood and throw my scruples to the winds.

To my surprise (one of a long series of surprises) pregnancy didn't happen the minute I announced myself open to it. In fact, it didn't happen for nearly two years. Cycles of hope and disappointment, and a secret terror that I might remain childless despite my intrepid declaration of willingness, became the new drama in my life. Against it – as I embarked on what was to be a twenty-year day job as a college English teacher – I continued to struggle with my writing. Desperation probably did not help either cause.

In June 1977 I gave birth to a son, and in February 1978 my first poetry collection was published. The baby, so long and anxiously awaited, very much upstaged the book: for the moment, I was more than happy just being a mother. To be able to stay home on maternity leave, not to have to teach for a semester, was heaven. My muse, never very constant, visited fitfully at best; even journal entries tapered off to an average of one a month. And soon enough, not entirely by design, I was pregnant again – pregnant and back at work (a half-time course load), because we could not afford for me to extend my full maternity leave. But the half-time salary wasn't enough to pay for child care or help in the house. We were two parents spread pretty thin, our work schedules dovetailed so we could alternate the home shifts. We were also trying to run a small press, Villeneuve Publications, at home on a moonlight basis – with no manpower but ourselves, and no outside funding. (Were we crazy? Probably.)

On 11 March 1979, I wrote: "Trying desperately to finish some poems for my reading next week – the pressure is good, writing is being done – but I am overexhausting myself. The new babe tickles my insides and is beginning to seem more real. Teaching (my poetry course) goes well, but I come home so tired I have heart palpitations ..." And beneath that entry (the last I was to make until August) in a different colour of ink, undated, the note: "During this period wrote 'Maintenance,' 'An Early Start in Midwinter,' 'At Dawn,' and completed 'In Winter Rooms' from notes begun a year ago ..."

Our daughter was born in July 1979. Our son had just turned two. My total output as a writer over a period of five years – from the beginning of my first pregnancy until my second child turned two – was thirteen poems, which we published in 1981 as a chapbook, *The Space Between Sleep and Waking*. I don't mean that thirteen poems were all that I thought good enough to publish: I mean they were all that I wrote. Yet there is no question in my mind that it was during this period I found my voice as a poet. Taking my place in the chain of generation – the physical, emotional, and spiritual voyage of becoming a parent – was what liberated the writer in me and grounded my poems, giving them a gravitas that had been lacking before. My serious writing began in tandem with motherhood, which was paradoxically at once its spur and the greatest challenge to its happening at all.

In a modest way the new work was immediately recognized – by reviewers, by editors, and by the local poetry scene in which I was suddenly in demand as a reader. "Maintenance," the long poem that opens the chap-book, was anthologized seven times in the next eight years and translated into French and Spanish. It is not and has never been a favourite of mine; in fact, at first I worried that it was not a poem at all. I can only attribute its staying power to the sheer energy of the strongly felt – and, perhaps, to a universal human sentiment the poem speaks to, a longing to rise above the daily grind, voiced in its opening words: "Sometimes the best I can do / is homemade soup, or a patch on the knee / of the baby's overalls. / Things you couldn't call poems ..."

The poem goes on to catalogue the over-and-over-again nature of house-hold tasks, "the eaten / replaced by the soon-to-be-eaten, the raw / by the cooked, the spilled-on / by the washed and dried, the ripped / by the mended," taking time out for a comic digression about neglected corners "where the dust lies furry and / full of itself ... The dust! / what I could tell you about / the dust ..." It takes issue with the idea that there is any poetry to be found in the Sisyphean labours of maintenance, or that there are "compensations":

> ... It doesn't work that way.
> The planes are separate. Even if there are
> moments each day that take you by the heart
> and shake the dance back into it, that you lost
> the beat of, somewhere years behind – even if
> in the clear eye of such a moment you catch
> a glimpse of the only thing worth looking for –
> to call this compensation, is to demean ...

The poem's subject is not those moments of grace, but the deadening hours no one talks about:

> I mean the day-to-day,
> that bogs the mind, voice, hands
> with things you couldn't call poems.
> I mean the thread that breaks.
> The dust between
> typewriter keys.

"Maintenance" was the *cri de coeur* of a would-be writer turned mother, and it was the poem that would follow me around for the next decade, upstaging poems I thought were much better. For a long time I wished I'd never written it.

❧ The oldest of five children myself, I was spared the shell-shock some young mothers experience with their first child: I knew what a baby was. But nothing could have prepared me for the second. It was the difference between a baby and "kids." If one child was a more or less portable append-age to adult life and freedom, "kids" by comparison were a ball and chain. If one child was company, two were a crowd. If before there had been three relationships to juggle in the household – mom and dad, mom and child, dad and child – the addition of one little person added not one but three new relationships to the pot, doubling the number to make six (all in con-stant flux) – an eye-opening lesson in domestic politics. If before, I had begun to feel pulled between the baby and the typewriter, now I felt pulled between baby and toddler, between husband and kids, and soon enough – within eighteen months – between job and home. The typewriter didn't even figure. The typewriter was barely on the screen. (And it was a type-writer in those days – not a screen.)

I look around me today and see young women embarking simultaneously on family life and literary careers with a professionalism that is intimidat-ing – seemingly without angst, taking it for their right, gracefully manag-ing (or seeming to manage) what for me was a season of crashing around in the woods, stumbling and bumbling through days without any shape to them, as I wrestled with various demons: guilt, frustration, distraction, fragmentation, drivenness, fatigue, my own nature, and the fact that there was never enough money to free me from teaching (at least a half-time load) or from the burden of housework and child care. It is true that brute economics accounted for some of my woes: had we not needed a second income just to get by, my output as a young writer-mother might have been enhanced (and my life made significantly less stressful). But when I com-pare the literary climate then and now, so much more seems to be going on. So very much has changed.

Today's young women writers take for granted the coming into its own (thanks largely to the women's movement) of women's writing. They take for granted the presence of women writers in the public eye – women who both write and have families – serving as role models. They benefit from a well-established "creative writing culture" in which young writers can easily avail themselves of mentorship from established writers – and into which they themselves can hope eventually to be received as paid mentors. Generous publishing advances, grants and book awards, contests with generous purses, international book fairs and authors' festivals, a dizzying array of literary journals, the advent of websites, ezines, and internet technology in general – all add up to a very different writing and publishing world from the one in which I made my early forays. Yet I can't help wondering what the publicity machine is *not* telling me about how it is now for young writer-mothers. Those Books Page feature photos of young women on tour with their prize-winning novels; those urban-cool, glamorous back-cover author photos with bios that casually mention children ... has it all really become so easy? Or have the stresses simply changed their form as the ante has been upped?

❧ It is hard for me, even now, to read my journals from the years of early motherhood. "The planes are separate," I wrote in "Maintenance," and the journal swiftly became the place where I cried out against the one that threatened to silence me. Where other mothers kept baby books, recording the day-to-day joys of watching their infants grow, my journal became a howl of frustration – the record of a monumental struggle to find the time, the peace, and the *will* to keep up some kind of writing life amid the domestic hurly-burly. It became the place in which I tried to figure out how this thing was to be done – and debated, often with anguish, whether I could do it without short-changing my children, whether I had the *right* to do it.

The other plane, the joyous one (those "moments each day that take you by the heart") did sneak into its pages here and there, but only in glimpses. I have to dig for those moments elsewhere, now, in musty storage: the yearly calendars in whose day-squares I jotted the milestones of first steps, new words spoken, new accomplishments; the shoeboxes full of snapshots; the piles of lovingly kept drawings and paintings pocked with thumbtack holes from when they adorned the kitchen wall; the children's own early scribblings; their baby voices on an old audio cassette or two; the odd tiny garment too adorable to pass on. A friend of mine once remarked that living with young children was like living with autumn trees – they dropped such a wealth of lovely ephemera, things you wished you could save – things that didn't keep for very long, but that gave so much passing pleasure. I wish I had recorded more of the lovely ephemera. So much of the dance has survived in memory only.

My journals record a different story, a hard reckoning. Silence from March until August 1979, after my daughter was born ... and then this:

(end of August 1979) I don't know the date ... Am I beginning this journal again? I even phrase this as a question. I have been reading Tillie Olsen's *Silences*. Perhaps it is already too late for me to redeem myself as a writer. I am twenty-nine; I have produced almost nothing – one small-press book of poems and a handful of others I deem worthy of keeping; stories I could count on my fingers. And just when I had begun to want to make the commitment to an unproved talent, I started a family. My years are flying. The book [*Silences*] depressed me but at the same time it furnishes the necessary challenge, it forces me to face the truth of where I am, and what I (the writing me) am up against. It has been like cold water in the face. The rude, necessary shock – the waking.

I vow, then – (how many vows have I made before?) I vow what I know I can keep. I shall at least keep the journal again – daily if possible. I shall write letters again, to people who will maintain a correspondence. I shall send my work-at-hand out to publishers. I shall make notes for new work.

♣ It was a vow I kept from then on, to the best of my ability and with some ferocity; and I kept it in the conviction (rightly or wrongly, I'll never know) that otherwise I stood in real danger of losing my hold on writing for good and all. From then on, even if I managed only a few lines, I wrote in the journal regularly – if not daily, at least not lapsing longer than a week or two, except for times of serious illness in the family. I established a *habit* of putting pen to paper, a way of reminding myself that the writer still existed. But entries from the next couple of years record the nature of the struggle:

(31 August 1979) Afternoon, sun on my desk, lukewarm tea and both kids asleep: this equals paralysis ... What shall I do? Finish cleaning

the house? Sit down with tea and a new book? Write a letter? Take a nap? Make a journal entry? Often by the time I have committed myself to one or another, one of the children has waked. And I have cleaned part of the kitchen, read part of a chapter, written a paragraph of a letter I will not finish, let alone post – and had a 15-minute sleep, the kind of sleep that (unless you can do it every couple of hours) is worse than no sleep at all ...

(20 September) I can't do anything with these isolated hour-long blocks – nothing but journal *&* letters and it's hard enough doing those. One problem is being afraid to type for fear of waking the kids – and this is why I still have not made the submissions I intended to ...

(1 October 1979) I do not know what form to attempt to work in ... The journal is helping me, though. Slowly it is becoming habit to grab a pen the minute the kids are asleep. And "talking to myself" in this way gives me the lovely, inviolable sense of privacy that I need in order to feel like a writer again.

(4 October 1979) Right at this moment I am thinking: they will wake up soon, they are due to wake up, so there's no use starting anything. and I glance out at the garden and think I'll go pull some beets *&* carrots for supper ... and it is exactly this that I need to overcome. The *fear* of interruption. For it is a waster of my best time, my only time.

(8 October 1979) I need a daily block of time I can count on not being interrupted. Even two hours would do. But the only time I get two hours is after 10:30 at night, and by then I am too tired to do good work ...

(23 October 1979) ... these moments of holding my breath, trying to write something before the baby wakes up ... And last night she woke twice – at 4 a.m. and at 6 a.m. – and I had gone to bed at 1:00. This DOES ME IN. Every time the carriage squeaks, I think it's over. She's stirring. THE END. It's a farce – pure and simple ... And at night – they're NEVER both asleep before 10.

(24 October 1979) ... Last night I finally moved my typewriter to the back room and typed clean copies of most of my newer work. Now to send them out ... Evenings, after all, are the only working time that makes any sense – even if I can't begin till 10:30. That still gives me two good hours – three if I'm willing to sacrifice sleep time. It's worth it.

But this period of determination and slow forward movement soon began to founder as sleep deprivation, life complications, and the always-changing needs of growing children asserted their claims. Sometimes the fight seemed *not* worth it:

(15 December 1979) To find these moments ... why does it become harder and harder? No peace, the house a mess, an endless list of things to be done ... Groceries to buy, things to fix, clothes to mend ... L needs boots, N needs bumper pads for her crib, I need a winter coat – and if errands are done, there are all the other things – unexpected visitors, social obligations, doctor and dentist appointments for all of us, kids getting sick, kids teething ...

(17 January 1980) ... I haven't written anything. But tonight, for some reason, I feel a rebirth of patience *&* hope, a confidence that I can rebuild and reorganize a life that gives me ways to work. For the moment, thinking of the kids, putting them first, *not fighting it*, is freeing something in me.

(28 January 1980) ... It's so depressing, these afternoons when the children sleep, to want more than anything just to crawl into bed myself, when I could be writing. But my mental horizon is empty – no ideas, none. Or none that I can see clearly enough to know what to do with. Just a faint blob or two that may or may not turn out to be ships ... Am I going to give up and take a nap? I'm afraid I am.

(23 February 1980) ... for now, a kind of resignation has overtaken me. Winter, illnesses, the demands of two babies ... I am theirs, my life is theirs, there is nothing left over. If occasionally I read, or visit friends alone, it's enough. Night after night I have sat up staring at blank paper, too tired to think, let alone write – my head filled up

with trivia and mundane anxieties – heating bills, head-lice, tomorrow's supper, playgroup meetings ... I have decided there's no point flagellating myself. It certainly has not made me write anything. For a while I shall not try. I shall use those two hours for other things, sleep not least among them, and see if it makes any difference ...

❦ I had begun to realize it wasn't just my time that was being taken over by things domestic; it was my mental space. I might arrange, briefly, to free myself of *physical* responsibility for the children, but it was very hard to banish them from my head:

(10 October 1980) ... When F offers an hour here or there, I am completely distracted by the sound of the kids' voices and cannot get work done ... I scarcely know what my work is anymore, I fret to be doing it but have utterly lost the habit, the drive, the momentum ... Even if they go out, I cannot get my mind off the kids *&* the current difficulties ...

Beyond the logistics of child rearing which seemed to occupy more and more of my mental files (medical decisions, daycare and schooling decisions, researching of options, appointments to be made, schedules to juggle), there was the prosaic texture of household routine, the stultifying sameness of it – an external life not conducive to inspiration:

(19 November 1980) I need a new sort of journal, I need to get away from this dismal whining ... if this is to degenerate into mere diary, at least let it be interesting ... (Interesting! she cries, in a house smelling strongly of baked beans cooked for tomorrow's playgroup lunch.) It is midnight; I'm writing in bed ... I am going to write for a few moments every night, I will try to think of what stood out about each day ... Ha! All I can remember of today is the rubbery texture and pasty taste of a failed baking attempt this afternoon (to try to salvage the stewed figs my dear children refused to eat). I spent the whole afternoon in the kitchen ... *This* I'm supposed to write about?

Return to teaching in January 1981 brought welcome stimulation, but it also brought dreaded new claims on my time and mental energy. Now, in addition to domestic demands, I faced the psychological effect of seeing job work (papers to mark, course preparation) spread out on my desk if I sat down to write. Once again I moved my typewriter to the little back room off the kitchen, where I could at least turn my back on the drying rack with its load of diapers and the inevitable scattering of toys on the floor and not feel guilty about piles of unread essays at my elbow.

But ultimately even my escape to the back room could not furnish the kind of space I needed. The mere fact of being at home seemed to keep me mired in maintenance; it didn't even matter if the kids weren't there:

(15 June 1981) ... Monday, spinning my tires ... Somehow between breakfast and F's departure [taking the kids outside to play] I lose my will to sit down and work. It has already been sapped by the chaos of house & children. They leave, finally; I lie down setting the alarm to ring in 20 minutes – a kind of meditation before going to my desk. But in 10 minutes the phone rings ... I set the clock again to ring in 20 minutes. In another 10, F comes back in, with N demanding a cookie. I hold my breath and wait for them to leave; they leave; I get up, put on water for more tea, take the clothes out of the wash-ing machine. I notice that the garbage stinks. I take it downstairs. I notice that the can stinks. Pour bleach into it, water, swish it out, pour it down the toilet. Am drying it out with wads of toilet paper when the phone rings ... it's M [a woman friend] just wanting (needing) to talk ... [after several more interruptions] By now it is after eleven and I feel hopelessly dissipated, useless, uninspired, and already wondering what to make for supper ...

Continuing to believe in myself as a writer became a challenge – became, perhaps, *the* challenge – as I struggled to carve out a little time to work, only to find myself misusing it, failing again and again to rise to the occasion:

(22 July 1981) Another morning slept away ... I despair of writing. It has been a year. Perhaps I am a casualty. I have been effectively silenced, finally, by motherhood ... A year is too long, never before has it been a whole year ... I keep setting time aside to write, F takes N out while L is at playgroup, but it is all to no avail ... By the time they are out the door (always late, usually after bickering) the will

& desire to make something of the time has fizzled and died in me, leaving an avenue open for the poisonous guilt that whispers: "How dare you put Art first? You who have not proved it in yourself."

❧ Does it need reiterating, at this point, that my children were wanted children? Does it need saying that I loved them, delighted in them? At no point did it cross my mind, even for a second, to regret my choice to have children. Wanting and loving my children, yet feeling sometimes half crazed with frustration because it was so hard to get to my desk: for many years, these two things coexisted in me, neither cancelling the other out. At first the frustration was in trying to find time at all; later, when the children started school, it seemed to be in finding *enough* time, *sustained* time, *dependable* time. But really, it was a question of learning how to *use* the time.

Very soon after that last journal entry, mysteriously, I began writing poems again. I found a writing routine that worked for me, and it has remained my modus operandi to this day – that is, when I am writing. Over the years I've learned that long fallow periods are part of my rhythm as a writer (as they were even before I had children) and that this is something I must simply accept and work around.

I had not been silenced by motherhood. Having a family slowed me down, no doubt, and I can't deny it had an impact on the amount and kind of writing I produced. For a few years it restricted me to poetry, because poems were all I could hope to finish in the snatched evening hours I finally learned to claim for myself – but poetry is the most stringent of written forms and proved to be not a bad training. Motherhood forced me to be endlessly inventive, ever seeking new ways to nurture an inner solitude and buttress it against the clamour of family needs; it also taught me to cherish that hard-won ground. As household routines changed, I switched back and forth between evening and morning hours, moved my desk from one room to another, for a time even rented a studio away from home. I learned to schedule all my teaching on two consecutive days, preferably late in the week, in order to give my writing week maximum continuity and a running start. I learned that what mattered most was not the *amount* of time I could set aside for writing, it was the regularity and (for want of a better word) *sanctity* of it: if I had only an hour, the point was to *give myself* that hour and keep on giving it to myself, even if much of the time I had nothing to show for it afterward. If I used the hour simply to stare at a sheet of blank paper, that was *okay*: the point was that I was *not allowed to use it for anything else*. I learned that to court a muse, one needs musing time; and that for a mother, this does not necessarily mean *thinking*, so much as it means emptying the head (of trivia and daily concerns.) Motherhood kept me on my toes, constantly having to reassess and fine-tune the balance of my chosen double life – but it did not silence me. Ultimately, it may even have saved me from publishing work that was immature, lacking in urgency, or otherwise less than my best.

What kind of writer would I have become, had I not had children? Where would my life have taken me, what material would it have yielded? Would I have been more prolific? Would I have had different things to say? These are moot questions. I had children, and sometimes the best I could do was homemade soup. I had children, and often as not, dust jammed the typewriter keys. But in flashes there was that other plane. I had children, and they brought me back in touch with all my past selves: that is what children do. I had children, and for them – with them – I recreated a lost realm, the embrace of a primary home. In becoming a mother I felt myself viscerally linked to all humanity and all of human history. These are no small things. Caught in the powerful undertow that is generation, I felt the elemental currents and cross-currents of time, the layering of natural and human cycles; and those currents, as I regained voice, became my chief delight as a writer.

Time, once the tyrant, became my subject.

notes

1 Author's private journals.

becoming a writer

My Breasts Had Become Eyes

DI BranDT

I grew up in a traditionalist Mennonite farming village in southern Manitoba, surrounded by other villages, filled with dozens and dozens of boisterous, cheerful, eccentric aunts and uncles, cousins, second-cousins, third-cousins, cousin-aunts, cousin-uncles, great-aunts, great-uncles, great-cousin-aunts, great-cousin-uncles, grandmothers, grandfathers, great-grandmothers, great-grandfathers, and dozens and dozens of babies and young children. "Playing house" was a challenging game in our villages, including much complex pretend labour, planting and harvesting vegetables, canning, cooking, baking and serving meals, measuring people's bodies and designing and sewing clothes for them, all the while minding numerous children of varying sizes. We liked to play house outside, under the ash and elm trees, with pebbles and twigs and seeds. Sometimes we served real fruits and vegetables newly picked from our mothers' orchards and gardens: raspberries, apricots, currants, carrots, peas. We had large families of dolls and imaginary friends. But often we used real babies in our play, lugging them around happily in their blankets and toddlers' shoes, feeding them tidbits and dressing them up with ribbons and leaves, making up elaborate dialogues and scenarios involving them as central characters, ready to give them back to their mothers at a moment's notice when they turned cranky. It never occurred to me that I wouldn't have nearly a dozen children myself, as each of my grandmothers did. I was very good at looking after babies and children, better than at some of the other physically demanding tasks of running a farm household. I looked forward to the time I'd be reigning over a grand extended family, supervising numerous children and grandchildren engaged in large complex garden, sewing and other design projects, as they did.

And then everything changed. Public school education became widely available in the Mennonite villages, families became smaller, farming practices became mechanized. I wasn't physically robust and found the tasks of running a farm household daunting and challenging. But I loved school, I loved reading and writing, I loved poetry, I loved English and German literature. By the time I finished high school, in the late 1960s, I had acquired a different dream: I wanted to attend university and study English literature and maybe, maybe – an extremely forbidden thought in the villages, which were fiercely committed to orality and traditionalist separatism – even write books. Could I still have children and a garden and bake pies and have dinner parties and design clothes? It never once occurred to me that I would be asked to make a choice between these things. I got married very young, by today's standards, though it was a normal age in the villages, nineteen years. I was halfway through an undergraduate arts degree at the University of Manitoba. My husband was twenty-two years old, and also a student, completing a degree in Fine Arts. We were going to be artists together, like John Lennon and Yoko Ono.

I was completely unprepared for the way people treated me after I got married: are you still planning to finish your degree, they would ask. Suddenly I seemed to be a second-class citizen, expected to vanish behind my husband as a kind of submissive unpaid servant. There were numerous discussions in cities everywhere in those days on the question: should women work? Or, even, could women work? Would women want to work? Could women be artists and writers? Could women earn university degrees and hold positions of public influence and responsibility? These questions astonished and perplexed me, having been surrounded by complex, highly skilled, much valued and prominently featured women's work and creative expression all my life. Women were in so many ways the keepers of Mennonite culture; they ruled in the home, the nursery and the garden and the kitchen, and in the village and family gatherings, filled with singing and poetry and the display of the children in their holiday clothes and newly memorized recitations and musical performances, even though they deferred to their husbands in matters of money and church policy. Men's lives were considerably more isolated than women's; they worked alone or in small groups in the fields and were very relieved to return home to the women's much richer and more culturally sophisticated social realm every evening. What on Earth should women do if they weren't allowed to, or considered capable of, "work"? And why indeed would we be considered incapable of it?

My parents were solidly against my acquiring a university education and becoming a writer, but not because it represented "work" or cultural creativity, only because it seemed to be taking me so far away from their traditionalist peasant ways, far enough to represent a serious threat to the continuation of Mennonite culture in my generation. They were right – university education does disrupt traditional knowledges in serious and perhaps irreversible ways, a terrible cultural loss and one I am deeply regretful for now, though I could hardly wait to get away then and try out the many new adventures of urban life in the early 1970s, heavily inflected by hippie counterculture, the mass media, and feminism. I eagerly threw away my mother tongue, Plautdietsch, and the rich ancient folk ways of my people, without much of a pang. Could I be a poet, a writer, and a mother at the same time? Having grown up in a family where my mother and grandmother recited poetry regularly and loved to read books, even though they were very hard to come by in our village, and where family gatherings prominently featured poetry recitations and performances by all the children, from age two to adult, poetry and mothering seemed inextricably linked, and, indeed, my own creative writing career began to take off after my children were born, in the mid 1970s. It was when my professional confidence began to blossom, when I began to find my way from my private scribblings into the public world. How I loved sitting on the floor with my children and their friends, making up poems while they played with their dolls and crayons and kittens and blocks and puzzles and paper and scissors. Early childhood was a perpetual state of intense creative chaos, an environment in which I and my poetic instincts thrived. I was blissful, I felt tuned to the cosmic wellspring of creativity and expressiveness. But it was also a very fraught time, given its many cultural pulls and stresses in so many aspects and directions.

My university professors in those days seemed more supportive of my professional aspirations than my family did, though I don't recall receiving any professional mentoring from them in terms of career advice of the sort my male student friends regularly received. There were very few creative writing courses or local publishing venues then, most of the literature we read was by dead white British males. I kept on writing poetry, and stories, as I had done from the time I learned how to read and write, but I did it mostly in secret, while hanging out with the children, working on other things in my adult life. Occasionally I showed my poetry to my artist husband, who never wavered in his belief in my writing talent from the time we met until I was finally published, many years later. My most important support group during those years was other young women my age, all involved, as I was, in feminist "consciousness-raising" and reclaiming our lost cultural territories as women, as culture-keepers, as literal and symbolic mothers. Though it was not all smooth sailing. I was fascinated and shocked to discover how anti-maternal much of feminist discourse and activism was; motherhood was a much more divisive topic in feminist academic circles than, say, lesbianism. Motherhood, it seemed, had acquired many negative associations in contemporary culture that I had not anticipated and didn't really understand, such as "weakness" and "exploitation" and "sentimentality" and "softness" and "passivity." To me, mothering seemed directly the opposite of these associations in every way, requiring great strength, cunning, fierceness, political vision, and the ability to multitask on a daily, hourly basis.

The act of juggling professional academic and writing careers and mothering in the 1970s and 80s, as I experienced it, was no easy feat. It was physically and emotionally and spiritually exhausting – though more so because of the oppositional attitudes and venues inherent in their different spheres than in the activities themselves. Professors and publishers expected much more demonstrated achievement from young mothers than from other students and emerging professionals, in spite of, indeed, because of, their domestic interests and commitments, even though we had considerably less time and resources to devote to our studies and writing projects while our children were young. The presence and noise of young children was frowned upon in restaurants, libraries, galleries, theatres, and other public places, making us feel like second-class citizens with our children in tow. (My friend Jackie Dumas, the novelist, and I once spent a hilarious dinner party imagining the kinds of huge impressive paraphernalia for our maternal labour that men seem to favour for theirs – huge strollers with air-conditioned cabs and CB radios and flashing lights to give absolute priority to domestic traffic with young children; removable roofs on our kitchens and helicopter deliveries through the ceiling of freshly picked salad directly from Mexico lowered in a servable net; large choruses singing the Hallelujah chorus every time we breastfed. Why indeed should we be always trying to take up as little public space as possible with our domestic labour and our children, when men seemed to be trying to take up as much public space in every endeavour as possible? It was the year the City of Edmonton was repaving Whyte Avenue in front of Jackie's bookstore; she was mightily fed up with watching the workmen in front of her house interrupt her bookstore business with great noise and smell and long coffee breaks. It was the year my youngest daughter left home; I was nostalgically bereft and relieved to have my own life back, all at once.)

Our husbands and boyfriends did not always appreciate the implications of our feminist negotiations in those early years of feminism, even if they were for us in principle. They did not have the same skill levels in childrearing as we did. They did not have access to the same transformative rhetoric as we did. In the 1960s and 70s, the predominant liberatory rhetoric for young men in North America was "going on the road," an anti-domestic narrative that did not in fact mesh well with the aspirations of feminism or increased domesticity and emotional sensitivity for men. It was hard for them to give up some of the patriarchal privileges they had taken for granted, such as priority of place in public positions, self-sacrificial support from their wives and girlfriends, and control over household finances. As women, we had to learn how to support each other professionally and domestically at the same time, from the ground up, so to speak, since most of us had been taught to see these things as mutually exclusive in some way and to relate to each other as rivals and domestic friends rather than professional and personal colleagues. I found it hard to have to choose between a life of numerous children and an academic career. Though I only had two children of my own, I often looked after their friends, and sometimes think I raised a whole neighbourhood, in spite of my other equally absorbing and stimulating career as an academic and a writer. It was a busy noisy boisterous time! There were so many children, so many boots and hats and scarves to look after, so many cats and dogs and lizards and gerbils to feed, so many meals to cook, so many beautiful child paintings on the walls, so many delightful childish entertainments to enjoy. And, sometimes, so much exhaustion, so much anxiety, trying to figure out how to find enough hours in the day, enough dollars in the household budget, especially after my marriage ended and I was left a single parent with sole custody on a graduate student and later freelance poet's income.

As we now know, changing cultural scripts is a very deep serious matter and cannot be done in a single generation or by an act of will by an individual or a handful of people. The feminist revolution is by no means complete, though it is amazing to think about how many deep changes we have made in the way women and men relate to each other in the domestic and public spheres in the past few decades. The world is now a completely different place than it was in the 1950s and 60s; women regularly hold public positions of power and influence, and no one thinks you have to choose between a career and children any more. Men, too, are beginning to understand in large numbers that emotional intelligence and domestic sensitivity are good traits to have and that giving up patriarchal privilege may come with great benefits, such as greater involvement in family life and greater intimacy skills and satisfaction, and less disjuncture between public and private aspirations and ideals. We should not forget how many of these changes came about through the strength and influence of women from cultures other than the dominant mainstream. Paula Gunn Allen insightfully pointed out in her influential 1982 essay, "The Red Roots of White Feminism" that all of the liberatory movements of modernity, including the French Revolution, the American Revolution, feminism, 1960s counterculture, and even the invention of modern democracy, were inspired by the cultural legacy and ideals of traditional First Nations gynocracies and the ritual of the "vision quest," which makes possible grand political visionary gestures and mobilizes the psychic and social energies needed to make them true. This is as true for Martin Luther King's "I have a dream" as for the feminist belief that "the personal is the political," and the prophetic ecopoetics of Dorothy Livesay's "believe in the trees."

Recently I had a visionary maternal experience myself. I was grieving, yet again, the great relationship rift between me and my mother, who was often overwhelmed by the task of mothering her children and didn't ever really bond with me, neither in childhood, nor later in my adult life, though she did seem ever so much happier and more capable of a warm nurturing relationship with my daughters, her grandchildren, in her later years. This is a topic that has preoccupied me greatly over the years; three of my book titles have the word "mother" in them (*questions I asked my mother; mother, not mother;* and *Wild Mother Dancing: Maternal Narrative in Canadian Litera-*

ture); all of my writing has been in some way centered around the recuperation and restoration of maternal energies, in me, in my relationships with other people, in my intellectual work. I have been much preoccupied also with learning to understand what Paula Gunn Allen meant when she wrote that, in indigenous cultures, the womb is a second brain and that women are mothers not only as childbearers but as the dreamers who give birth to the world. This recuperative work has taken me in many interesting unforeseen directions. I found many wise strong loving adoptive and symbolic mothers – teachers, professors, older writers, therapists, friends – who gave me the love and advice and advocacy and support that my own mother would have liked to give me if she'd been able. I have given, in my turn, similar adoptive and symbolic maternal love to many younger women, and also men – my daughters and their friends, the children of my friends, students, and younger writers. I greatly mourned the end of my reproductive years, but now that I've entered the age of grandmotherhood (and eagerly waiting for grandchildren!) I am happy to discover how the territory of the maternal expands, in middle age, to include many young people, many people, many living beings, the world, the Earth itself. I begin to see myself as a keeper and passer on of maternal wisdom, and knowledge, and skills, a mentor to the next generations. Mothering, at this age, is not so much about looking after people, feeding, cleaning, caring for, as it is about becoming a guardian, an elder, a woman of strength and insight who can help advise the world in its intricate decision-making as we lurch into the unknown but not unanticipated future.

I was mourning the great emotional distance between me and my mother. And then suddenly, in a flash! I saw, I knew, that she too had trauma experiences in her childhood and youth that she was not allowed to tell anyone or seek help or consolation for. And I realized that her emotional rejection of me was not about me, but was the effect of her enforced splitting off from deep experiences at a tender age. I saw that all the recuperative work I'd done in trying to restore the mothering I needed to get, and the mothering I wanted to give to the world, was gathering together to release that great wound and set us both free to enjoy the rest of our lives unfettered by that black hole of unnamed grief between us. After that I had an extraordinary dream. I dreamed that my breasts had acquired the most beautiful turquoise blue shaded eyelids, with lovely eyelashes that fit snugly and perfectly over my nipples. When I awoke, I understood that my breasts had become eyes, beaming beautiful white light both inward and outward. My friend and mentor Walter Isaac, a Buddhist contemplative, tells me this is the image of Tara, the Buddhist avatar of compassion and maternal love, who has eyes in her breasts and in her hands and in her feet. I have also sometimes felt eyes in my hands, beaming white light into whatever they touch. (Not everyone likes being touched by white light: it is a challenging energy that rouses the spirit and requires an active response. It's good to have those beautiful shaded eyelids and hands that can close.) This is how mothering and creativity and writing have come to mean the very much the same thing for me, how they are intricately woven together in my life, now.

Other Is the Longest Part of Mothering: Writing and Parenting on the Edge

catherine owen

Being a writer and being a mother have one thing in common for me: I didn't choose to do either of them. As early in my life as I can recall, I was in love with language. At the breakfast table, I read cereal boxes and fruit tins. On the road, I recited signs. Before bed, I sounded out Dickinson and Whitman from my *Child's Treasury of Verse*. By the time I wrote my first facile ditty, beneath a tree outside of my French Immersion Preschool, putting pen to paper felt like a smooth and luminous transition, a logical extension of my obsessive mouthing of words. I never felt that writing was an ambition, a dream or a hope. It just was.

In parallel fashion, children were always a part of my life. As the oldest of five, and later as a babysitter, I was surrounded by small bodies crawling and crying around my feet with all their complex and simple needs to be fed, clothed, and sung to. I often felt an affinity with infants in their direct and sensory connection to the planet, their easy tears and laughter, their existence outside of labels. Children just were. I never longed for them, never imagined a future of marriage and babies. If I had, it would have been at an appropriate age with money in the bank, a job, my education behind me.

Yet when I became pregnant at sixteen, there was no question that I would not keep the child. My parents are Catholic. I would (they had no doubt) give birth after spending several months in a home for unwed mothers, and I would later marry the hapless, incompatible father. Of course, I did just that. At the time of Damian's conception, I was drinking more than I was writing anyway. Yes, I'd graduated from tales of bananas and aliens to hard-core fiction about punks and Jack Daniels, heavy-metal tunes entitled "Hell Hole" and "Love at Knifepoint," but I wasn't doing anything serious. I was mainly trying to gather "experience," à la Bukowski or Kerouac. Only they, as I'd failed to account for, weren't young women.

The pregnancy thus came as both a surprise and a relief for me. I was catapulted into caring for myself, and with the multivitamins and energy shakes, strangely, came poetry, or, at least, a renewed commitment to it as a determined pursuit. Though I toyed with fiction at first, by the time my son was six months old, I had realized that it was really rhythms and forms that woke me up at night along with his incessant breastfeeding.

I began to write every moment I could. Though I had dropped out of high school, I returned, taking Distance Education courses in English Literature and Creative Writing, under the pretext of graduating, but mainly so I could validate time spent away from my son, sending him to his grandparents four mornings a week. Within nine months, I had both a diploma and a dozen boxes spilling with drafts.

Of course, it wasn't that simple. I was always trying to fit poetry in. I remember stirring soup with Damian on my hip and Plath's *Selected* in my hand, or drafting a poem about an old boyfriend while building a Duplo tower, over and over again, my son's plump fist knocking it down as I felled my former flame with the "might" of my pen. And the father hounding me: "Can't you just not? For once?" Any artist who mothers is a mansion with many rooms, upon which doors are opening and shutting simultaneously, some in the smallest gust, others slamming with typhoon brutality.

(22 November 1993) When Rachael cries, in some part of me I ignore it. When Damey becomes furious, I shrug it aside. All to return to the shelter of my writing.[1]

Watching the birth-video[2]

sixth birthday and you see yourself
purple, pressing out of my opening,
and want to hold your pale limbs,

exotic cry,
close.

i watch my sixteen year old body
as helpless as yours, legs supported,
lips thick and wet, but there is nothing
about my cry I want to
carry.

In 1991, I was barely coping. Finally in college, I had gotten up the nerve to perform my first reading at the Burnaby Art Gallery. I selected three trembling poems, recited them in dry-mouthed terror and dashed back to my seat, nauseous with failure. No one knew I had a child, once again dropped off guiltily with a grandparent, so I could pretend to be the young, unfettered poet everyone thought I was. Worse, I found out I was pregnant again, just after I had won the Emerging Poets Prize from the Burnaby Writers Society and was beginning to truly acknowledge my poetic aims. The father and I were dwindling away from each other and yet the phone call I made for an abortion was cancelled at the last moment. In a feminist literary course I was taking, we were reading *A Room of One's Own* and Woolf's description of Judith Shakespeare's dilemma: "who shall measure the heat and violence of the poet's heart when caught and tangled in a woman's body?"[3] bit into me with its hard truth. Anger swelled up as colostrum tightened my ducts and my womb rose achingly beneath my ribs. I was trapped. I decided to endure the pregnancy in denial, continuing to attend classes until the April before my daughter's May birth. In April, I also performed my second poetry reading, with Evelyn Lau, to a capacity crowd. I wore a billowy flowered shirt, and no one knew I was eight months gone. Afterward, people swarmed up to me, crowing, "So young and so talented! Imagine what the future will hold!" I knew what it promised: two energy-sapping infants and the hell of a marriage that was never right enough to go wrong. Following Rachael's birth, though she was a placid, silken child, I was deeply depressed. My typewriter congealed in the corner; I had dropped out of college following too many embarrassing incidents with my breast milk "letting down" in the middle of geography lectures; I spent my days slumped in various parts of the house, head dizzy with senselessness, kids latched onto nameless pieces of my body or playing aimlessly around my feet. I needed out.

Then, in November 1993, I signed up for a four-day workshop with Patrick Lane in Sechelt. This was it. On the ferry over, the dark burden lifted. I read, took walks, listened to a performance by John Pass and Theresa Kishkan, and received critique on all the stumbling, gutsy poems I was writing at the time. I knew myself again, and myself was a poet. A few months after I returned home, I left the father of my children and set the three of us up in our own apartment, joined by another poet, Chad Norman, who later became my husband. We slept in the living room so I could have the bedroom as a studio. Though the depression receded, the anxiety assumed a new face. Now that I was firmly and assuredly a poet, at twenty-two, I had a lot of work to do to catch up to Sexton, Levertov, Tsvetaeva, and others in my recently discovered pantheon of female poets. This meant time, space, and financial support, little of which I had. Since leaving the children's father, I had gone on welfare. While he hadn't put up a fight for custody, neither did he pay a cent toward child support. Every other weekend, he would pick them up for a trip to Subway or to watch an inappropriate movie, but the stress I experienced waiting hours for him to appear left me wishing less for this child-free time than for the emotional release that would follow his complete disappearance from their lives.

Fortunately, I did possess a persistent in-house editor in Chad; many nights after the kids were asleep, following countless readings of Frog and Toad and relentless humming, I sat with him over the pieces for my first, self published book, *And the Silence, Stones*, quibbling over diction and line breaks. I was so impatient, burning with language and a youthful sense of the immortality of my quest. Yet with so many interruptions, how would I ever achieve the intensity of the Aeneid, the concentrated grace of Ovid's *Metamorphoses* or even the jaunty savoir-faire of cummings or Birney? I sat on the toilet quite regularly, gripping my writing book and scrawling maniacally while one or both children clawed at the door as I gnashed out: "Just a minute. Just a minute!" desperate to recall a rhythm before it faded into domesticity.

(29 October 1997) Infuriated and distressed. The computer crashed just after I had finished all my revisions. I swore and banged my fist on it. Then the kids began to cry and argue.

Three things saved me during those years: Chad, my parents, and school. Chad introduced me to (and took me boating with!) unforgettable poets like Al Purdy, Joe Rosenblatt, and Phyllis Webb, thereby deepening my lived comprehension of Canadian poetry. During this time, my parents cared for the children on a regular basis so that Chad and I could scoot around the islands, performing readings as part of the Stray Dog Poetry Project. From 1997 to 1999, they also opened their home to my children and me, when I decided to cut the welfare ties after several years and began to pursue my degrees in earnest. Though inhabiting a dark and narrow basement with two boisterous offspring and a husband on night shift was stressful, in doing so I avoided a student loan that would later have impeded my freedom to create art. In the process, my struggles toward degrees at Douglas College and SFU presented me with continual goals and regular successes. All produced poetry. Though I still battled with melancholic feelings of guilt, the "doors" were beginning to shut a lot more gently now, or perhaps I had become so used to interruptions that I scarcely sensed the chaos anymore.

(7 November 1997) Too weary for new poems today and anyway I have revisions to do of the week's two pieces, but the kids have four days off now, alack!

Forgiveness, for my daughter[4]

When all I could offer
you
were the bones
of my being
you
carved them into a cradle
and slept.

Mother's Day, 2005. I have been giving poetry readings for fourteen years. But never before on Mother's Day. Even though my children have not lived with me for six years, it was still a difficult decision. Perhaps it was harder because they don't live with me. Every occasion I have the opportunity to spend with them and don't, a sharp jab of "bad mother!" pierces me. In

1999, when I was starting my Masters degree, I was slapped with a double revelation: no one would rent a two-bedroom apartment to a family with two children of the opposite sex, and renting a three bedroom was financially inconceivable. Further, my son was facing continual conflict with his stepfather. My ex stepped forward to announce that he could offer the stability the children required; he had a full-time job and the three of them could move in with *his* parents, allowing them to remain in the same neighbourhood and with the apparent security of another extended family. With terrible reluctance, I let them move in with him, hoping that his erratic outbursts would not scar them as they had me. Chad and I then relocated to Commercial Drive, where over the course of two years, my degree was completed as my marriage unravelled. I wrote an excessive amount in the children's absence. I also cried. And drank. Though parenting as a writer had always been complex, seeing them solely on weekend visitations was insufficient, hollow. All the justifications were meaningless. Yet, once I had made the decision, no reversion was possible. Their father gripped the power the renewed possession of his children had filled him with. Now if I was ten minutes late to pick them up, he would phone the police, deny me access based on a rigid court order. At times, all my books, all my readings seemed merely acts of cruelty, neglect. If I hadn't been an artist, I would never have made such a choice, I would have found a way to earn more money, to parent more closely. And yet none of these rationalizations were sufficient to stop me from writing; it was as necessary as my breath.

Today they whined when they heard I would be halfway across Canada reading with Joe Rosenblatt at Pteros Gallery on Mother's Day, less, I felt, because they'd miss me and more because they know how effective such guilt-cries have been in the past. Yet, despite the ache in my conscience, a much-too familiar pang, I had to go. Before the event, as people were starting to trickle into the exhibit, I phoned them, Rachael at her father's and Damian at my parents, where he has lived for the past eighteen months, since one of his father's hard rages led him to renounce his filial bonds. My son could scarcely tear himself away from the ball game to bounce out a greeting before he was gone, while my daughter's answers of "Meh" to all my questions, concluding with a painfully disembowelled "So Happy Thingy Day, yeah, so love ya'" CLICK, were scarcely reassuring. Had I snapped yet another fragile filament of our intimacy by choosing my art over them? Or was their lacklustre response a sign that I had made the right decision? The reaction to my reading was nurturing at any rate and those few moments of ecstatic warmth carried me through the recurrent cold doubt at the heart of all these years of choices.

(27 November 1997) Amazingly, I wrote three new pieces today, one based on images I collected yesterday while putting Rachael to sleep.

Awakening on a Dry Morning[5]

I have just opened my eyes
but am already a mother.

There are small clothes around me
and brightly coloured strangers.

I cannot wake to them gradually; they need to eat;
my breasts and arms are theirs.

Their voices are like seeds inside me,
always bursting their green call.

Now that I have teenagers, with their iPods and Dippity-Do, I actually feel pricklings of nostalgia, as foolish humans will, for their childhood. As one forgets the agony of giving birth, so one, over time, develops amnesia for the extensive periods of conflict and turmoil, recalling mostly those moments of epiphany and inspiration, those instances when writing and parenting seem kin. I remember the peacefulness that flowed over me in the early years of mothering when I would sit before the typewriter with a child in a sling. It slept beneath my breasts while I tapped away like a heartbeat, the rhythms of its breath and my work complementing each other. Then, as they became toddlers and school-age children, it was their level of attention, awe, and even ire I found inspiring, along with their imaginative and linguistic-based innovations.

My daughter loved anything small and would spend hours crouched over an ant hill, fierce in her rapture for these odd specks of darkness as they darted in and out of their pyramid. For my son, any destruction of nature was tantamount to a crime. One day, he tore into the house, angrily weeping and stabbing his finger out at the road. When I asked him what was wrong – "Murderer!" – he sputtered hotly, his shoulders shaking, raging that a neighbour boy had let his soccer ball roll over an unsuspecting beetle. My daughter tickled spiders' bellies, turned salt and pepper shakers into stocky bridal parties and every night, when she was three, regaled us with her "chicken dances" and songs about a "lost dog named Rosie," one of the tunes featuring a tricky rhyme between "home" and "known." My son had his own world, Dameyland, founded on a scientific principle he called "the speed of darkness." With this universe, he had developed his own original lexicon. Aliens were "uniques," to move was "to duffle," and the mystery of life was mysteriously dubbed "QUAIMUTU." How could this not be an inspiration for a writer!

When they were in elementary school, any time I tried to recite one of my poems, I was met with shrieks, plugged ears, or absence, as the offended child dashed from the room. Now, though my daughter still expresses resistance, as she does to anything that smacks of "being good for her," my son has become a helpful critic. Formerly displaying a mathematical bent, in recent years, he has become involved in the world of acting and filmmaking, his newfound appreciations enabling him to both listen to and read what I have written. While sometimes his remarks run to the personal – "Oooh, you bitch, Mom!" over a catty description – more often they are lucid comments on content or form. The other day, he burst out with, "Mom, you're just such a feminist diva!"

Yet I must confess to feeling increasing relief as they get older. Not only is our relationship becoming more artistically empathetic (at the best of times), but my guilt over being relentlessly divided between my care and love for them and my nurturance of my art is diminishing. When I'm with them, I try to live wholly in the instant of their brief youths. When I'm alone and writing, I strive to resist the sour alleyways of regret in my psyche. At thirty-three years old, I have two teenagers, several degrees, seven books, and a band. Somehow, it's all been possible. The doors are open; the doors are swaying in the slightest breeze; there are, sometimes, no doors.

> I could leave you, you my lover
> I mean, could find myself in another

country, a fish slid free of the fissure
       between ocean *&* boat.

Of course it would hurt, would
       for a while, hone the axe

between my thighs
       and I would want for you at night

with the tree's desire for amnesia.
       But you, you my children, I could not

cast from me, could not abandon your lives
       to time's cold contract, though

it would have been easier
       not to have loved you,

to have had only these ghosts
       with their quick *&* stinging bodies

and not the languorous, treacherous, endless
       ache that is you both

and our bond that is.[6]

notes

1 Author's own journals.
2 Owen, *Her*.
3 Woolf, *A Room of One's Own*.
4 Owen, *And the Silence, Stones*.
5 Owen, *Her*.
6 Excerpt from Owen, *Fyre* (2005, unpublished ms.).

A Mother, Writing

LUANNE ARMSTRONG

On my nineteenth birthday, I gave birth to twin daughters. Immediately after they were born, a starched-looking nurse whisked them away to the nursery. I lay in the narrow white hospital bed, curled up on my side, under the bright fluorescent lights, on scratchy white sheets, my brain a puddle of incoherence. After finally falling asleep, I dreamed that I was running away, carrying my new twin daughters in my arms under a grey sky, on grey sand, beside a grey ocean. When I began to sink into the sand, I realized I had run into quicksand. I held the babies up as high as possible, and then, as the sand began to cover my face, I threw my children, hard, at the people who had been following me, from whom I had been so frantically running away – my mother and my husband. Then I sank into the sand and died. I woke up almost immediately, gasping for air, panic-stricken.

At some point, when I was a teenager, I decided to never have children. At six, I had decided to be a writer; I knew I wanted to write from the first moment I read a whole book. It seemed obvious to me that having children would not go with that ambition. Besides, I knew nothing about children. Growing up, I followed my father around on our small farm and dreamed of being a cowgirl. My mother, stuck in the house, seemed trapped by work and poverty and caring for four children. I was determined not to replicate her life.

I became pregnant at eighteen while living with my first boyfriend. Because I was both shy and ignorant, I had let him take responsibility for birth control. I was trying to finish my first year of university. As my belly grew, I sat in our small apartment in Vancouver, staring out at the rain, reading French existentialist philosophy. I didn't read any books about children or mothering. I couldn't stand to think about it.

The man and I married, and he tried to prepare us to be parents. A couple of days after the birth, we brought our daughters home. I wrapped them up the way the nurses had showed me and then I stared at them in their cribs. I was afraid of them. They were mysterious with their gasping gaping mouths, their random hands, blindly seeking, and their eyes that looked everywhere and nowhere.

"Alright," I said. "You can have me, all of me." I meant it.

The next day I returned to university while a kindly neighbour woman babysat. A few days later, my mother and my grandmother came to visit. They seemed bewildered by my desire to keep going to school.

"Your life is over now," my grandmother said sternly. "You must live for your children."

But instead I went on being a student and a mother, and, I hoped, eventually a writer. Most of the time these roles seemed to be irreconcilable, but it wasn't possible to give either of them up. Persistence, however difficult, seemed the only option. But such persistence made my life tense, frustrated, and fraught with tension. Despite my vow, I was often an inattentive and exasperated mother. I snapped at them when they interrupted my reading. I left them with too many different babysitters so I could go to school. But I loved them. And they, to my astonishment, loved me back.

I practiced writing in the bits and pieces and cracks and fractures of my life, and I learned to live there as well. I read constantly; books piled beside the bathtub, and beside my bed as my husband slept beside me. I took courses in English, history, and philosophy and discovered Canadian poetry and Canadian novels. Leonard Cohen had just started publishing, and I fell in love with his work. I began writing poetry in secret.

♣ A long while later, I was sitting in the dark in a small white house in a hot and ugly city in the Southern US. I had a different husband now, and two more children, two sons, one a year old and the other only two. After a loud and terrible fight with my drunken husband, I had slammed the door behind him and all the glass had fallen out in pieces on the floor. We had no money. The fight had been about him getting fired for being drunk. But my parents had sent me a little bit of money, and I had hidden it. I began planning my escape, back to the farm, back to safety and a place to try to understand what had gone so terribly wrong. I left with my four children late one night, taking a taxi to the bus station. I left everything behind, including journals full of poems and stories.

I walked into the welfare office of my small hometown. When I came into her office, the social worker looked at me with suspicion.

"What did you do with your husband?" she asked, as if he were a piece of luggage I had misplaced.

I tried to bite down the various flippant answers that rose came to mind. Because I hadn't eaten or slept much for weeks, I looked like a refugee from a camp somewhere, dressed in clothes that I had worn to rags over the last couple of weeks. But I was proud of the cheque she finally, begrudgingly handed over. For the first time, I felt that I owned my life. I was twenty-four.

I bought a twenty-eight-foot trailer from a neighbour with money I borrowed from my parents; the neighbour brought it down on a flat bed truck and placed it across the yard and around a bend in the driveway from the huge green farmhouse where I had grown up. The first night after the kids and I moved into the trailer, I sat alone in the dark. I'd bought groceries and clothes and shoes for the kids with the welfare cheque. They were all asleep in their bunks. I put on some music I'd borrowed from my mother, Tchaikovsky's *Winter Nights*. I curled up alone in the close and holy music-washed dark. I had been away from home for six years. Now two husbands and four kids later, I was back, utterly bewildered and shamed by how different my life was from what I had planned.

I talked endlessly with several other single women in the community about how to get off welfare and get real lives. Maybe we could go back to school, we thought, but what could we study that would guarantee us a real job and a good living? How could we ever manage school with our kids when all the schools were far away at the coast?

Becoming a writer seemed impossible. The social worker who drove out from town once a year just sighed when she saw the trailer and the chaos we lived in. She also turned a blind eye to the few hundred dollars I made in the summer from the garden. What would happen when the kids were all in school? I'd have to get a job then, she said. I agreed with her. I wanted to give my kids someone, something, to live up to.

Time passed. Every spring I ordered a box of seeds and started baby plants under grow lights in my parent's basement. By the end of February, I'd start pruning the apple and peach trees, and by March it would be time to start the tomato and pepper seedlings for the garden. By the middle of April, it would be time to start planting the garden itself. I usually finished planting by the end of May. Then there were the usual summer chores of picking fruit and getting in the hay. I bought a food drier and a freezer, plus my mother and I canned fruit together. In my spare moments, I swam and lay on the beach reading books on women's issues, or hung out with my other single-parent welfare-women friends, talking, talking, talking.

Winters were difficult. I chopped wood and tried to keep the house warm and clean and the kids clean and fed and onto the yellow school bus every morning at 8 a.m. I began to attend peace and environmental meetings. My youngest son, now four, headed off for his grandmother's every morning after the other kids caught the bus, and I had an hour alone.

I tried to start writing a novel. But I had no idea how to write one, despite writing for years in fifteen-minute segments in the local bakery while my laundry went round and round in the dryers next door.

The time was coming when I would have to make some decisions about the rest of my life, but I kept shoving it away. One spring morning in early May, I put on some loud symphony music and opened the doors and windows. I shook out the rugs and took the ashes out of the stove and set the houseplants outside and rinsed off the dust. And then, dancing and singing, I vacuumed the whole house. Daffodils and tulips were blooming at the front of the trailer; the alder and birch were haloed in electric green mist. It was enough to be alive as the trees and flowers were alive, demanding nothing, simply radiating joy. The universe unfolded around me, a huge white flower. After a while I came back to myself sitting on a rock in the sun, with ants crawling up my ankles. I went back in and finished the vacuuming.

The next morning, when I picked up the mail from the green box across the road, there were three things in it: a Sears catalogue, a gardening catalogue, and a university calendar sent by a friend. I looked through them all. The Sears one was full of stuff I couldn't afford and didn't really want; the gardening catalogue was full of seeds and ideas for bigger and better gardens. Just looking at it made me tired. The university calendar was from the University of Victoria. They offered a degree in Creative Writing. I had been considering going to college to take a course in forestry or welding, anything with which to get a job. Now all those fine practical ideas went out the window.

It took me another two years on welfare to save the money to get there, but I finally did it. I loaded up my truck, and my children wailed for their grandma, for the farm, for their home. After arriving in Victoria, we found a basement apartment, and I started school.

♣ On the day my poetry class was scheduled to workshop one of the poems I'd submitted, I drove my ancient pick-up through two red lights on my way to university, The cop who stopped me was laughing. He walked around the truck. "You've got bald tires and no brake lights," he said.

"I'm going to school," I said. "I can't be late. It's my first class. We are talking about my poem this morning."

He shook his head. "Well, I'll let you off with a warning, this time."

When I arrived, the professor shuffled papers around until we got started. Finally, he held up a poem that I recognized as my own. We had been asked to submit them anonymously.

He sighed deeply. "This is just a really bad T.S. Eliot imitation," he said. My breath stuck in my chest. The other people chimed in with their criticisms, but I couldn't hear anything. There was a roaring in my ears, a red mist in front of my eyes. What did he mean?

Eventually, the red mist began to clear, and I began to listen. He was going over my terrible poem line by line, pointing out its strengths and weaknesses. I looked at my own copy. He was right. There was a way of thinking here, a language that I didn't understand. Somehow I would figure it out. When I went home, I picked up my youngest son from his new daycare. I carried him down the block to our new basement apartment. The sun was shining and anything was possible. Finally, I was going to learn how to be a writer.

My two years at UVic were extraordinarily happy. My children loved Victoria, and I loved UVic despite their philosophy at the time that, if you were tough enough to survive their program, you were tough enough to become a Canadian writer. They also told their mostly female students not write that "women's stuff," that touchy-feely "confessional" writing, as it was then termed. It was 1979. UVic had just started a Women's Studies program. I took Women's Studies and Creative Writing and ran happily through the halls.

I also had met a wonderful new man. After two years, he and I loaded up our ancient white van and drove back up the mountain passes to the house he was building in the Kootenays. I had a folder full of poems and stories; I had even been offered a job at a magazine, but I had spent two years in the city dreaming of going home, back to the Kootenays, so I turned my back on the city. At that time, my friend Julian Ross, who wanted to start a publishing company, offered to publish my first book of poems. His company, he said, would be called Polestar Books.

♣ When we moved back to the Kootenays, reality hit hard. Our new house, which Len had been working on for a couple of years, had a floor, four walls, and a roof. We had no jobs and only a bit of money that disappeared like magic in one visit to the building-supply store. Len could always make money surveying, but jobs for women in our small town were specific. Women were still confined to being secretaries or cooks or nurses or teachers. Homesteading, house building, acquiring tools and animals, even planting a garden – all took immense amounts of time. And we had four growing, eating, demanding children who wanted more than anything else to live in a real house with normal parents. Yet I was still determined to be a writer. My first book came out; I went to Victoria for the book launch, had a wonderful time, and then crawled back into the mountains.

Although I loved our fortress oasis, I couldn't make my restlessness go away. Words and stories and poems came and, just as quickly, went. Sometimes I wrote in the mornings after the kids left, but the house was such chaos – spilled milk and cereal dripping off the counters, at least two loads of laundry to be done every day and hung out to dry, dishes stacked on the still unfinished counters, beds to be made, flies and dust and sawdust and piles of paper to be gotten rid of, the woodstove to be filled, wood to be split and carried in – that I could only steal a couple of hours or so before my conscience took over. Outside were the chickens, the horses, the garden, the lawn, and the flowerbeds. My mother phoned every day to see if I wanted to come for coffee. She was so lonely, she said, but my mother had always been lonely.

I wrote at night, or I wrote in the bathtub. I put things in the mail – poems and stories – and sometimes they got published. I began writing a column for the local paper. Whenever I went to town for groceries, I always went back to the bakery. There was something about the irresistible combination of coffee and sugar and the hum of conversation that would let me write. But I could only steal half an hour away – there was always much to be done, and usually some kids needing to be picked up from hockey practice or music lessons or soccer. I watched the trucks and tourists race by on their way to somewhere else. There was always somewhere else. And despite having a book of poetry published, I still didn't know how to be a writer.

On every trip to town, I went to the library where I kept a list of books on order. The nearest bookstore was two hours away, and whenever possible I went there and bought books and magazines I couldn't afford. Books spilled over onto the floor, climbed up the walls, threatened to become compost on the floor. I read and read into the night

There were no jobs in the town. Occasionally I was hired for a few part-time jobs, but they never lasted. A reporter's job came up at one of the local papers and I sent in my resumé. The editor called me to come and see her.

I went in her office and sat down.

"You know we can't hire you," she said. "I think you understand why."

No, I didn't actually. I was the only person in town with an actual degree in writing and journalism. Was that what she meant? Until then, the paper had only hired a succession of journalism students who stayed a year or so and then moved on. I stared at her. She wouldn't meet my eyes. I left.

The other newspaper in town was dying. I worked there for a while. I threw out all the whiskey bottles stashed in various drawers and stayed up all night writing the entire paper on the ancient phototypesetter that spit out long strips of paper that were then waxed and laid on the layout sheets. Eventually I added up the revenue from the few ads that were still coming in and the cost of actually printing the paper. They were far apart in the wrong direction, and that was the end of that job.

✣ Eventually, around the time I obtained a computer, our home finally had running water. We had hand-dug our way through a quarter mile of rotten granite and dirt, laid the black plastic pipe in the trench, covered it with sawdust and filled it in. It was a miracle – no more heating water on the stove in the mornings so the kids could wash their hair, no more hauling water in plastic buckets, no more trips to the outhouse in the middle of the freezing night.

At a conference I organized on women and words in Nelson, I read some of my own poetry. After I finished reading, the audience all stood up and applauded. I fled the stage. I ended the evening wandering drunk around through the empty rooms of the college where the conference was held, struggling in a drunken daze to remember how to lock everything up, going to my room, and doubling over with anguish and nausea and fear. Who had those people been applauding? One of the women at the conference was a well-known writer – she had congratulated me on my poetry, held my hand, looked into my eyes and said, "Send me some work. I'd like to read it."

When I went home, I tried to return to walking and doing laundry and making dinner, but a new person was looking out of my eyes. A new person lay in bed every night, reading, turning over, restless, sometimes getting up to go downstairs and read by the fire.

❧ Years later, I was teaching at a First Nations college in Merritt. I decided to rent a cabin on Nicola Lake and come to Kamloops to be with my family on weekends. My husband was studying nursing at the college in Kamloops, my daughters had fled to Vancouver after finishing high school, and my sons were still in high school. After I moved into the cabin, I realized I had never lived alone before. In the evenings, the silence filled the room like fog, making it hard to breathe. No stereo, no TV, no children's voices calling from room to room, no fridge door opening and closing and opening and closing, no cat or dog to feed. I sat up late at night and wrote into the silence. I was teaching full time, but I kept writing poems and stories that I threw in the mail. I started another novel and, this time, kept going until it was done. No one interrupted me. The silence broke around me like black water. I struggled to keep my head above it. Was this the cost of becoming a writer? Two years later, after receiving some money from Canada Council, I quit teaching and moved back to the farm to keep writing.

I finished the novel and sent it to a publisher. They accepted it almost immediately. While I was waiting for it to come out, I started another one. I continued to throw things in the mail – poems, stories, anthology pieces – and they kept being published. I missed my children. I hated the silence. I wrote and wrote to keep from drowning.

My grown kids visited, but they now had busy lives and careers of their own. Every week I threw one or two envelopes into the green mailbox across the road. I compared it to buying lottery tickets. Some envelopes came back, some disappeared. Every once in a while the phone would ring and something else would get published.

But I had very little money. Day after day, despair and depression sunk barbed hooks into my soul. One day on my way home, I stopped at the grocery store. I bought $20 worth of groceries to get me through the week. The woman at the checkout counter in the grocery store said, "Are you writing another book?"

I mumbled something.

"Well, you just keep writing them, and I'll keep reading them," she said cheerfully.

Over the years, I kept writing books and sending them to publishers and they kept appearing. But things were not going well at the farm. I couldn't keep doing the level of physical work I was used to because of painful swollen joints, an illness that after a couple of years, was diagnosed as rheumatoid arthritis. My brother and his wife, who had always been part of the farm life, fought with my parents and then moved away. My mother was deeply depressed, terrified that she was losing her memory. It was obvious to me that if I was going to keep writing and stay alive, somehow, I had to find a way to make more money. I applied to the UBC master's program and was accepted. So I moved away from the farm, yet again, back to Vancouver, yet again, returning to UBC to go to graduate school, and to be closer to my grown children and grandchildren.

❦ After I finished the Master's at UBC, I did a Ph.D. For the doctorate, I wrote a memoir about my life. One night just after it was finished, I had a dream that the university was next to the mountains at the farm. In the dream, I realized I could walk from the university and back into the trees anytime I wanted or needed to. Somehow, the two halves of my life, writing and living in the mountains, had come together and healed a deep split in me.

Books are still heaped beside my bed, in the bathroom, on the table beside my computer. But now when Louis, my four-year-old grandson, wants to play, I stop what I'm doing and we do whatever he wants. My old impatient irritation at being interrupted by a child has been replaced by joy. I never did make a choice between writing and children. I made a commitment to them both and whatever the cost to me, to the writing, to the children, we paid it together and somehow, miraculously together, we all survived.

Once, when my daughters were teenagers they asked me a difficult question. "If you had to do it over again, would you have had children?"

I looked at them and gave them the only truth I had. "No, I wouldn't, but I would have had you. I can't imagine my life without you guys in it."

My children and I grew up together and they seem to have kindly forgiven me my many failings as a mother. They do tease me. One of their favourite stories is about the time they built a pile of furniture around me while I was reading. I didn't notice until I finished the book!

For most of my life, becoming a writer seemed an unattainable dream, and some days it still does. My head is stuffed with ideas for poems and stories. I make lists of the books I will write someday. I dream my way into another story. And then I turn on my computer and begin.

Elements

FIONA TINWEI LAM

earth

"Where are we going?" my mother kept asking in the car, her eyes darting with anxiety.

"To the cemetery," one of us would answer. "It's Father's Day."

In the pauses, I imagined my mother's tangled neurons, thought-sparks arcing into emptiness. My family had habitually visited my father's grave every Father's Day and Christmas since his death in 1976. But four years ago my mother's dementia had progressed to the point that she would become disoriented when away from her immediate neighbourhood.

"My husband died," she said finally. A sudden bleakness came over her smooth brown face. Although she was in her late sixties, her face had a childlike quality. "He was very sick."

At the cemetery, my brother and sister placed chrysanthemums in the underground vase in front of my father's plaque. Then we all stood side by side to bow three times to pay our respects.

Unbeknownst to my family, my parents' first grandchild was growing cell by cell inside of me. I silently pleaded for my father's blessing and aid. It seemed fitting that the man I'd mourned most of my life would be the first one to receive the news. I wondered how to inform my mother. Would she be alarmed, excited? Or oblivious and blank, as she invariably seemed in her current condition, no matter what I said.

WOOD

Years ago, as I'd prepared to flee the matrimonial home for good, my husband at the time had scoffed, "What makes you think you can write?" I'd grown up in a non-literary household where writing was never considered more than a weird hobby. So I'd repressed my desire to write for years, forcing myself through law school, lawyering, and nonprofit work with community organizations. After years of being buried in a stultifying career and marriage, I'd finally let everything explode in order to be and do what I had always wanted – I'd lit the fuse myself. Having been born in the year of the Wood Dragon, I was prone to leaping boldly and impulsively into the unknown. In Taoist astrology, the dragon is associated with dynamism, leadership, and benevolence. The element wood represents boldness and initiative. Dragons born with the element of wood are supposedly particularly imaginative. Whereas dragon sons are seen as a blessing, dragon daughters are not: their headstrong nature makes them resistant to submission to men.

Despite my sense of urgency, the return to writing was tentative, if not outright excruciating. I anguished over each word I squeezed out. It wasn't until I came back to my hometown of Vancouver to take on a small share of my mother's care that I began to write in earnest. My brother had been living with her, assisting with the driving and cooking after her retirement from the medical profession due macular degeneration. Although her cognitive difficulties had started long before the Alzheimer's diagnosis, she'd refused to see a doctor. She'd managed to fake recognition of friends and relatives but was steadily losing her ability to communicate. One afternoon, she stood staring at the contents of the fruit bowl.

"What's that?" she asked.

"They're mangoes. You've had these before." I sliced one up and offered it to her. "It's a fruit. You used to buy boxes of them in Chinatown for us when we were growing up."

"*Ho sic,*" she nodded, chewing thoughtfully. "But I've never had it before."

Another time, she pointed to the sock on her foot, "What is it?"

When she was finally ready to admit something was wrong, I took my mother for doctors' appointments, tests, and scans. During this time, although we'd never been close, I found myself stroking her arm, even embracing her, trying to soothe away her panic and bewilderment. This was not the raging, suicidal mother I'd fled from as a child, but a woman facing the loss of her mind and her life. Compassion made me the daughter my mother needed.

My mother's Alzheimer's diagnosis freed me to write about her. The subject no longer seemed taboo, or a betrayal. As I wrote about being raised in a home characterized by grief and isolation, I began to explore in my poems the generations of absent or disrupted mothering in my family history. In China, my maternal grandmother had been sold by her mother and later became a fourth wife to a businessman with three concurrent wives. She had rejected my mother for not being a son. My mother's childhood was also marked by the Japanese invasion of Hong Kong and then her own father's premature death. Later, my mother married my father, who transplanted the family to Canada, away from her colleagues and friends. After his death, she struggled through exhaustion and depression, trying to raise three children single-handedly while returning to the practice of medicine after an eight-year absence.

I had no idea that – much like my mother – I would also be entering a "dark wood."

water

I had been certain the red line forming on the pregnancy test strip was a mistake. I'd dipped the second strip, with the same result. Stunned, I'd started to take my usual morning shower, but as the hot water rained down upon my back, a mixture of exultation and terror had inundated me. My body had been claimed, and everything in me and ahead of me had altered course.

Prior to my pregnancy, I'd been overcome with envy and ardent longing whenever I'd seen a pregnant woman or a baby. Over the years, with each period, another viable egg, another possible child had gone down the drain, while my age had crept up the statistical charts for birth defects and my mother's mental abilities continued to decline. When I became pregnant, I was afraid to rejoice during the first trimester, concerned about a miscarriage or birth defects. I was too worried about how the pregnancy would affect everyone else to even consider how it might affect my writing. When I told my lover of five months about the pregnancy, he sat back, as stunned as I was. He was unsure at the time how involved he'd be, but clearly I was going to be a single mother. The jury was out with my siblings.

During my pregnancy, extreme and unexpected fatigue and nausea had made writing sporadic until my second trimester, although my senses and instincts were on high alert from the start. But by the third trimester my mind became sludge. With my new bulk, I felt both solid yet utterly vulnerable. So I felt gratitude toward any person who offered me the least bit of kindness or assistance – offering me a seat on the bus, letting me jump the queue at a public bathroom, refilling a glass of water unasked. Those small gestures inhabited me, crystallizing later in poems as an understanding of the possibility of goodness or beauty in the slightest of acts. Meanwhile, with his feet imbedded beneath my left ribcage just under my heart, the baby kicked me awake night after night, preparing me for what was to come.

Finally, I had to inform my mother of my pregnancy. Her eyesight and inability to follow conversations had prevented her from noticing it until then. I sat beside her on the couch and brought her hand to my belly.

"Mom, two months from now, I'm going to have a baby." I paused. "You'll be a grandmother."

She said nothing for a few minutes. I worried that it was already too late for her to comprehend me, despite her obstetrics training. But then she looked me in the eye for the first time in years and said, "You're ..." She struggled to find the word "pregnant," then gave up. "Who's the father? Is he going to marry you?" she asked in alarm. It was as if the mother I'd lost to dementia had suddenly been dredged into consciousness.

"You don't need to be married or even have a partner to have a baby nowadays, mom," I said flatly, trying to reassure both her and myself.

After half an hour of fuming and hand-wringing over my future and that of my child's, she was taken home. But from then on she would notice I was pregnant and repeat the same questions. Having raised three children alone as a widow, she still had enough of a memory to know what lay ahead.

Two weeks before the due date, I wrote for two days and through the night to write a short story to meet a deadline. Then I rushed around to set up the baby's room. With the help of a girlfriend, I heaved a crib back to the store to replace it with another one. That night, my water broke early. I ran to the bathroom, laughing and crying. I thought it would be over by morning. I was in labour for three days.

meTaL

The last day of my labour, the resident anesthetist spent almost an hour ineptly poking at my spine with the epidural needle, forbidding me to move during my contractions. The baby had turned to the wrong position and become stuck in the birth canal, requiring a forceps intervention and an episiotomy. The inexorable sound of metal clipping through thick muscle and membrane preceded the sudden whoosh of the birth.

Afterward, I tried to suckle my son, but I had no milk. It took four days of trying with an increasingly dehydrated child, pleading with nurses and midwives. But suddenly on the fourth day, mired in desperation and helplessness, I felt as if myriad doors had flung open in a dim network of corridors. Behind the open doors were mothers, across time and continents, who had striven and suffered at whatever cost to keep their children alive. My milk finally came in. It was the true start of my journey into motherhood.

FIre

For months after coming home with my son, my brain smouldered. My nipples were chafed and stinging. I kept looking down to see if they were about to fall off my chest. I hadn't slept in months for more than two hours at a time. I'd put the baby in bed with me, but he'd wriggle me awake. I'd put him in the bassinet next to me and he'd still groan and writhe, pulling his knees up to his chest in pain for no reason the doctors could discern. I'd watch and watch him, praying he'd eventually sleep in peace. I read articles, consulted experts, took out dairy products, wheat, cruciferous vegetables, onions, garlic, and spices from my diet, gave him gripe water and chamomile, gulped down herbal tinctures. Nothing worked.

Soon after his birth, a publisher accepted my manuscript of poems for publication. I had a deadline of a few months for my first book, the one I'd been working for years toward, poem by poem. But my child cried inconsolably for hours during the day, no matter what I sang, no matter how I rocked or cuddled him. Shattered, I couldn't think, let alone write. Words disintegrated before they reached my mouth or my hands. Nouns were elusive; verbs wouldn't conjugate. By month four, the colic disappeared by itself. But sleep still didn't come. I lost my keys, my train of thought, my library card, my grocery list. A few times, I left the house with the stove on. Once I returned home just after the fire engines had left. Huge fans were blowing streams of acrid white smoke out the doors and windows. My breast pump had melted to a black lump in the pot where it had been sterilizing.

Those days, when he was napping, I would put him in his car seat on the floor beside my desk chair, draw the blinds, stifle coughs, try to breathe and type quietly to the metronome of his breathing. Stale words would venture from my fingers, stuttering out only to scuttle back in. I'd end up making lists in my head: read last week's paper so I could feign adult conversation; try to nap, too, and fail; remove all rice grains stuck to the floor from yesterday's lunch; open the week's unopened mail. The bone-white screen of my every day would blink, wiped clear of who I was or tried to utter.

In order to write, I coordinated a complex patchwork of childcare with my long-suffering sister, my child's father, babysitters – anyone who could give me three or four hours alone every other day. I'd chastise myself about time lost with my child while also lamenting the time lost to be with my mother while she still recognized me, let alone time sacrificed for precious sleep. But on a few occasions, when my mind cleared, my maternal "milky eye" became "crystal"[1]: the words would come, as would a portion of radiance, that would give both me and the poem a glimpse of that seal-sleek, bright-eyed perfection that was my child. Here at last were the poems that would enrich and complete my book, shifting away from the stark early poems about loss and alienation, toward plenitude and connection.

After submitting my finished manuscript when the baby was six months old, I didn't write for a long period. My urge to write had become stronger just as my ability to find time and energy to do it diminished. The book had just been the start: I wanted to move forward with whatever I had in me, to reach for the transcendent and luminous. But to be able to function even as a household drudge, let alone as a writer, I needed sleep. For over two years, my son refused to sleep until late and would awake every two to three hours at night, then be up at dawn. Successive bouts of teething, colds, flu viruses, ear infections impeded every strategy to persuade him to sleep through until morning.

It was supposedly a productive time for me: a poem appearing on local buses as part of a public transit program to promote poetry, the launch of the long-awaited book, graduation with a master's degree, stories published that I'd written during the pregnancy. But those achievements seemed surreal, disconnected from the reality of motherhood. There was delight at hearing my son's first coos at the tinkling of his mobile, the first laugh of delight after a long nursing, the time we sat in a patch of sunlight and I stroked the warm globe of his head until we both melted into a luxurious catnap. But too often there were those long, gouging hours when he wouldn't stop crying or whining, when I had to cradle him even while perched on the toilet. I'd expected a docile child who would be soothed by a cuddle: I'd given birth to a spirited boy who constantly grabbed, pulled, pinched, bit, kicked me even in infancy.

Yet I also felt separate even from the concrete maternal world: confident, cheerful mothers with their swinging pony tails, their clean clothes, their jaunty strides to the park, their chatter and laughter in coffee shops. Mothers with partners, and with able-bodied, able-minded parents to grandparent their children. And of course, there was the professional world going on around me, with writers networking at festivals and book launches, discussing authors and books I hadn't had time to read.

One week, my child and I were both sick again. After days of continuous nursing, the baby had depleted me down to the bone. I would nurse him for an hour. He'd fall asleep. I'd put him down in his crib. He'd awaken ten minutes later. I repeated the cycle all day until it was dark. My son's father, who at the time would spend a few weeknights with me, came in after 11 p.m., barely looked at or spoke to me, and went to sleep on the far side of the bed. The baby then awoke to nurse, and an hour later awoke again. And again. I went to his room, positioned him on my lap, raised my t-shirt and relinquished myself to his avid parched mouth. I started to weep. It had been days without any substantial sleep. There was no respite ahead and no one to turn to. I couldn't take care of my son, I couldn't take care of myself. A kind of animal panic rose from my belly to my throat, beginning as a wail that became one sustained guttural scream that led straight into another and another.

The baby's father rushed into the room to seize him from my arms. "Please," he said in a charged whisper, "please get a hold of yourself." He left the room, soothing the baby.

I sat a few moments in shock. When I emerged from the room, I made a move to resume nursing.

"Go to bed and sleep," he said. "We'll stay out here in the living room."

A few hours later, when I awoke, I had changed, the father of my child had changed. He would still leave me, but I would know I could turn to him when in crisis; that he would be the father my son needed.

air

My publisher arranged for me to give a reading in Toronto, my first outside of Vancouver. I would be separated from my child for twenty-four hours, the first time I'd be away from him. My sister and my child's father would care for him while I was gone. I left detailed instructions and stocked the fridge with dated and timed bottles of breast milk.

As I left, I felt lighter, more myself than I had since giving birth. I walked unencumbered through the airport and sat at the gate, amazed to be able to read a whole newspaper at one go, not a few paragraphs spread over a week. Not having the baby carrier strapped to my chest or a stroller to push, my arms dangled weightlessly from my shoulders. With my shoulders no longer bunched over my chest, my body straightened. It felt like I'd shed twenty pounds – my child had become so much part of my body. My breasts, however, reminded me who I really was: it didn't take long before they were throbbing boulders. Assembling, disassembling, and washing the inefficient plastic hand pump was a nuisance, so I expressed thin streams of milk by hand into the tiny airplane lavatory sink every hour.

I arrived late in the afternoon a few hours before the reading. I'd been parachuted into another life: I could actually chew my food at a leisurely pace in a fine Italian restaurant. I even finished my meal. I talked without interruption with friends I'd not seen in years – although ironically mostly about the baby. That evening, I read my poems, and people listened and nodded, sighed, applauded, bought books. Meanwhile, every hour or two throughout the evening, I ran to the bathroom to frantically squeeze out what milk I could to relieve the unbearable pressure. Afterward, both ela- tion and physical discomfort kept me from sleeping. I returned to Vancou- ver the next afternoon, painfully engorged but somehow victorious. When I arrived at the doorstep, my son who was examining the flowers in the front garden, looked up at me as if he suddenly realized I'd been gone. He ran soundlessly into my arms. We hurried into the house, where I nursed him until we both fell into a long, blissful sleep.

earth

I started teaching a few words of sign language to my son when he was seven months old. Language acquisition snowballed after his first year, beginning with his signing back simple words, then gradually with lengthy streams of phonemes addressed at adults, other kids, animals. I heard every sound from every language mashed together into almost coherent speech rhythms but making no sense except for the accompanying hand gestures and facial expressions. Soon enough though, words emerged in clusters as he named everything he touched or saw. Meanwhile, my mother was slowly losing her ability to communicate. Her dementia whittled away her vocabulary in English, then Chinese, eventually leaving only tangled and mostly nonsensical shreds of words in either tongue.

"Hi, *poh poh*," my son would greet my mother. "How are you?"

"Hi hi hi!" my mother would sometimes be able to say in return, bending down and clapping her hands. But nothing more.

I would bring the two of them together for weekly family dinners at my home until she started trying to grab or even slap him after the meals if he was jumping around. Then we went to her care facility instead. Her room was full of instruments to keep her amused – an electric keyboard, some recorders, wooden clackers. One time, my son spotted two harmonicas on the counter. He quickly took one and gave the other to my mother. My mother blasted out a chord and grinned. My son laughed and tooted out a response. Back and forth, louder and louder, both of them giggling. It would be the first and only sustained conversation they'd have before his visits would have to end.

My son's vocabulary grows daily. Now three, he talks all the time, asking where God is, why forest fires happen, questioning homelessness, war, car accidents. He no longer fights for up to forty-five minutes getting into a car seat, wriggling out in the middle of a ride, or does the old "scream, arch, and slide" when placed in the stroller. Now, he just leaps into my bed at 6 a.m. for a prolonged and vigorous tussle. I have tried to capture in poetry his delight and exuberance – but it's like taking photographs of the solar system with a point and shoot camera. Meanwhile, he still frequently comes to my bed at 3 a.m. to knead and grab at my breasts for the milk he still remembers. He'll flail around and pedal his muscular feet against me all the night. He'll knee me in the neck or face. If I try to rearrange his limbs, he rotates his body around the bed until he lies across it horizontally, an emperor seizing territory, so that I'm forced – just like my writing is – right to the very edge.

I've fantasized about those miraculous children who soon after birth sleep through night from 7 a.m. to 7 p.m., with daily two to three hours naps, who can be buckled into a car seat or stroller without struggle. There'd have been all those luxurious hours to shower, cook, eat, clean the house, read a novel, write a novel, and be fresh for my child, without having to ask favours or owe anyone anything! Unimaginable. But then I wouldn't have a child who runs as if he were flying through a hundred finish lines and somersaults on every lush green patch of lawn he sees.

To write, mothers have to combat the continual erasure and submersion that mothering entails: the submersion of needs, ambitions, identity, and the erasure of privacy and personal boundaries. To reappear as a writer required a carving out of a mental and emotional space for oneself through time away from mothering, to be free to dream, read, and then eventually write, eventually building the kind of momentum that will drive a project to completion. But days without childcare can be a relentless marathon of attentiveness and giving, especially if a child is sick. Those are the days it is a challenge to even answer the phone or wash the dishes. I don't try to sneak away to the computer because my son will eventually follow. "I miss you, mommy," he'll call out plaintively from the doorway. I'll turn off the computer and go downstairs to play trains.

A young poet/mother once asked me if I had been worried about becoming a mother given my fraught childhood. I was taken aback by the question. I hadn't, but I couldn't articulate the reason until recently. My son is an emblem of love and continuity. He loves purely, simply, outside history. He represents both the child my mother could have been and the child I could have been: a child deeply cherished by both parents and extended family, who is nurtured and nourished in every way. Both my parents and I, as well as my son's father and I, are united in my son in a way we could not have been otherwise.

My son is coming into his own, just as my mother slips irrevocably away from me, neuron by neuron. He teaches me the beauty and resonance of each word he learns. Despite the tedium, drudgery, and intense sleep-deprivation, having a child has allowed me to become a witness to the infinite tiny quotidian miracles unfolding all around me. I will likely always feel that I am gestating as a writer, but my child has been a crucible, bringing me into and through my deepest passions and fears, past petty ambitions and desires to connect me both to the Earth and to the sublime.

♣ It is Christmas Eve. After being shown some old photographs, my three-year-old son has particularly requested that he accompany us to visit my father's grave. I've told him a few stories – the few happier memories I had of my father from my childhood. He's asked questions about heaven I'm often unsure how to answer.

"I miss my grandpa," he says in a serious tone. "I never knew him. He was a good doctor, you know."

He helps pick out a vivid bouquet of fuchsia and orange gerberas at the florist's shop, clutching it protectively during the drive to the cemetery. When we arrive, he insists on carrying it to my father's plaque. My siblings and I unwrap, trim, and arrange the flowers in the underground vase, then stand in a line facing the grave. In this crowded Chinese community section of the cemetery, the plot next to my father's is still vacant – my mother purchased it for herself soon after his death.

"Now we must think or say some good thoughts about grandpa," I tell him. My siblings cast sidelong glances at me, surprised. Until now, I've never uttered my thoughts aloud here. "Dear Dad ..." I pause. I try to distil all there is to say. "Your grandson, Robbie, is here with us today. You'd be proud of him. We all miss you this Christmas and hope you are at peace." We then bow three times together once again, hands clasped like knots against our hearts. My son follows suit, his air solemn and pensive.

When we return to the car, his smile returns. "I hope grandpa can see my flowers!"

Through our eyes, my father does. And one day, my mother will, too.

notes

1 Wilkinson, "Lens," *The Collected Poems of Anne Wilkinson*.

& in our languages, mother is the land

sнarron proulx-turner

sand under pure
clear water
her underwater sound
the sound of life
her heart a drumbeat
certain & ancient[1]

I'm a word woman. I love to write. my métis grandmother gave me a dictionary, an old giant webster's, for my fourth birthday. on the rare occasion
when she visited us, she'd sit on the phone chair where my mother kept the
dictionary, in an open area between the kitchen and the front door, and
she'd hold that dictionary on her lap, point to a word and tell a story long
as your arm. I thought the dictionary was a story book for the longest time,
and I was so excited when I learned to read. I was planning to read that
whole darn book. but it wasn't a story book at all, and even though I was
disappointed, that's where I first learned to love words and to know that
even powerful, mean-spirited adults used words incorrectly sometimes. I
have dyslexia, so my introduction to the dictionary was fortunate in that
way too.

in a way, I read to write, and though my experiences with writing weren't
always encouraged, I've been a writer of sorts since I can remember. I wrote
on bits of napkin and slips of paper and I would write out long passages

from my favourite books. I still do that. language fascinates me. as a small person, I read every book I could get my hands on at the local library. I could tell that there was a whole world out there that was very different from the one I lived in, and in many ways that's one of the main things that kept me going and kept me able to hold my silence and maintain a sense of peace in the face of the utter chaos that defined my early years.

some family stories are too painful to tell, and even if they can be told, where and to whom do you tell them and who can sit still long enough to hear/read them? how many of the stories even get told? I live with post trau-matic stress symptoms every day. I'm a survivor of severe childhood abuse, including sophisticated torture over a period of several years: having my hands and/or feet flattened in a device causing unbearable pain, being put in a cage where I was unable to sit or lie (only squat), hung by my wrists, confined in a small, cold space and left without food or water – all of these often for days. I received severe, repeated beatings, I was raped by multiple adult perpetrators, I was exposed to long-term isolation, and the list goes on. by some miracle, I'm what's referred to as a "high functioning" survivor and I firmly believe that without reading and writing, I may not have sur-vived so well.

in many ways, my story as a writer began as a story of speaking silences, a healing story that began with my mother's family and the foster "care" system that scooped my mother and her brothers and sisters during the 1940s. métis children who were living in among the urban and rural folk were routinely taken from their homes and put into white homes with a goal of assimilation/genocide. when my mother was fostered out, she spoke french and was sent to a french-speaking urban home. the man of the house had just left for the second world war and the woman ran the house where she lived with her daughter, her dog and my mother for four years. when the man returned from the war, the foster family put her back into the system.

at her request, my mother was placed in the same home as her sisters, the twins, who were six years younger. this one was an english-speaking home in a farming community. I can only imagine my mother's horror when she discovered that, among others, punishments for her baby sisters included days and nights on end with a dead, decomposing chicken tied around their necks, being tied with thick rope to a wooden kitchen chair and lowered into a well in the summer kitchen, alone, with the trap door closed over her head for hours or days on end without food or water. these children ate at a separate place from the family, at a wooden crate. they were given rusted aluminium pie plates to eat from, rusted tin cans to drink from, and they waited each meal while the rest of the family and guests finished what was on their plates. the foster children were then given the scraps from the table and a very limited time to eat them.

I didn't hear these stories from my mother, but from my aunty, and she prefers to keep most of her stories between her and me. it's better this way because, as she says, two wrongs don't make a right, and she doesn't want to hurt her foster family's children – their children – the way she was hurt. to this day she doesn't know why as a very small person, one day a stranger picked her up at her home, brought her to a room in an office building, moved her into a car and drove her away from the only life she knew. her stories are so painful to tell that my aunty has taken years to disclose what little she has. my mother, who died of cancer in 1986, told me nothing about her childhood. my aunty, however, plans to tell as much as she can so's to help the ones who follow to know the bravery and courage our roots grow from. she tells me it's my duty to do the same. we have miracle roots, she says. all us métis and indians. we have miracle roots because it's a miracle we're still here.

yet enduring so much violence, living in poverty and keeping down two or three jobs, didn't prevent my mother from expressing herself in so many important, creative ways. she went back to school when I was about twelve, and being I was the one considered to be patient and to have a gift for words, I was assigned to help her with homework day after day, year after year, while she upgraded her entire elementary (in english this time around) and then high school. she continued on into what was called business college, where she trained to be a secretary. I learned shorthand and I learned how to juggle her learning and my own, and I absorbed a lot of her personal strength and integrity. my mother was caught between the worlds and caught inside a myriad of binaries – the native and the non-native, the anglican and the catholic, the french and the english, the tender and the tough. she didn't talk to me about her childhood because she couldn't. my aunty talks about hers because she can. different people, different personal thresholds. this may be the first time much of this has been written down – by anyone, and certainly by me – and writing on a computer makes the process easier for me, if such a word could ever be adequate. I find when I write longhand, I can feel my emotions move from my heart, to my head, to my arm, to my fingers, and I'm a slow writer on top of that. when I write with a computer like this, the words come quickly, and I have to take breaks to process what I'm feeling.

> & now the words
> have left the soft sensitive skin
> of my fingers
> their long cool touch
> left lonely for that talk
> slow & lazy
> talk that can be heard
> between the tips of my fingers
> & the skin of my children
>
> the intimacy of bark growing
> inside quiet rain
> & graham
> to name my feelings for you
> would be to fly into the heart of a flower

my métis grandmother used to say, the kids will follow their mothers. go to school, my girl, you've got what it takes. your great granny was a poet, like you, my girl, she'd say. the years when my children were young I was an avid writer, yet I didn't start either keeping my writing or publishing until my son, graham, was eighteen, both of us graduating the same month, him from high school and me from a degree in english literature, something I did for my late mother and grandmother, for my kids and grandkids. then I graduated from a masters degree in english literature at the same time my daughter, barb, graduated from junior high, three years after graham finished high school. it was during school – as a single, two-spirit parent in my thirties – that I began to view myself as a writer. I started out in fine arts, and only after failing the university writing requirements did I take an english literature and writing class. it was either that, or be expelled from university. during the first few weeks of my first english class, the prof, an alberta writer named aritha van herk, handed back a batch of essays to the class. she was cross. she said only two people in the class passed. to my utter amazement, I was one of the two. when she handed back the essays, she included a recipe card. her bold, large, red handwriting read, this is no essay, but you sure as hell can write.

yet, even at that, I learned to write an essay because of the patient teachings of graham, who could pass any writing test with ease, and who, as a young adult, attended the all-native creative writing and fine arts school at en'owkin, in penticton, b.c. I knew graham would be a writer from the time he was not yet three years old. as he sat on a chair in the early morning kitchen looking out the window at the dawning day, he asked in his still-baby voice, is frost frozen dew? how does it make pictures like that? at six, for him, it wasn't a gift of a dictionary, but a gift of a book, *charlotte's web*, given to him by my mother. I'd been reading the book to graham nightly and we had a few more chapters to go when early one morning he woke me and crawled into bed beside me, crying so hard he couldn't talk. I cuddled him and spoke softly to him until he could catch his breath. between great gobbling sobs, he said, how can a book make you cry? it's just words on a page, mom. how can words on a page make you cry? when graham learned to write, we often wrote stories together, each of us putting down a paragraph or a sentence until we decided to move on to another story. we got this idea from puzzles where images were buried inside images, like frost or clouds, he'd say, and from stories where some of the words were hidden inside pictures. when graham grew from a boy into a young adult, he was a role model for me, a sure and fluid writer, a fine-tuned people reader with a sense of humour to match. yet, my own writing was done in secret, then burned or tossed into the trash. not too surprisingly, graham doesn't remember me as a writer in his growing years, but barb does.

hers was the hand of a woman

I woke up the other morning with an image of a dragonfly hovering not six inches away from my eyes, directly in my field of vision. *&* my vision there, in dream world, unlike here, is perfect. I could see into the eyes of that dragonfly *&* I could hear her tell me, today is your lucky day. today is a day of miracles.

& right away I thought of you
of blue on blue
& barb

to name my love for you
would be to
step outside the bounds of the ordinary
& into a place of miracles

barb's quite a bit younger than her brother, and she says she especially remembers the richness of the stories I told at bedtime when she was small, particularly stories of the little people who followed us through our day to day lives and took us to the water at fish creek, hopeful we'd encounter those little people in their homeland. when barb learned to read she'd ask me to put little notes into her lunch box for her to read and that marked the beginnings of a ritual where I'd draw an image accompanied by encouraging words on her paper napkin each day. as a young adult, barb surprised me by placing some of these napkins – her favourites – in a gift bag and wrapping them for me as a gift. to this day, those napkins hang inside their bag on my cork board, waving at me as I write. but probably the most remarkable mother-daughter collaboration between barb and me that coaxed me toward my present certainty as a writer was a book barb created during her early teens as part of a language arts assignment. her idea was brilliant, and far too much work for one person, so barb asked if I'd help her by drawing the illustrations in a choose your own adventure book she titled, *gates to the unknown*, which later appeared in a cross-country book show. barb tells me our work together on that book influences her as a word woman more than any other of her life experiences to this day.

I spent my mothering years in calgary. before that, I lived close to the bush in ontario where the seasons are well marked and the river water is as wide as a lake, creating in me a lingering wish for river and a respect for the land, for mother earth and those who rely on her as their true mother. I learned to aspire to that understanding myself and to infuse my writing with mothering in mind. if there was a way to express my feelings about writing right now, I would become the sound of the water I am. I'd mingle with the river in a way that was unavailable to me in my early years. my fingers have touched the softest down on my babies' backs and felt the centuries of ancestors waiting – those who've gone before us and those yet to come – their stories open moments inside a rainy day.

just as my daughter barb tells me our work together shaped her future relationship with language, métis elder maria campbell's comments in *con-*

temporary challenges: conversations with canadian native authors have influenced me in a most profound way as a word woman. in this interview, maria campbell said an elder told her it's one of her (and, by extension, our) responsibilities as indigenous writers to put the mother back in the english language.[2] I like that statement and I agree with it, and since that moment that's what I try to do every time I write. I could never thank the elder enough for his words to maria campbell and I could never thank maria campbell enough for sharing them in such a public way. reading those words in the early 1990s changed my life and since then, I've had dreams where the women are cree and speak to me in cree, and, though I understand them, I constantly ask them to speak to me in english and they just laugh and say something like, in dream world we can speak to one another across language with clarity and understanding. in my waking world, I understand no indigenous language that I know of, but when I write, I know I'm part-way into my spirit self and I'm able to hold onto the english language like she's a gift held out of herself, unrestrained by prejudice or fear.

english is noun-driven and is sometimes considered rigid and unyielding by speakers of native languages when it comes to expressing movement, and movement is motion, growth, life. for example, I remember teaching grammar classes in an all-native setting, and trying to convince folks that, in english, fire is a noun, river is a noun, air is a noun, earth is a noun – trying to articulate, even in english, how that can be – is a tremendous challenge. I'm not going to say I've ever been successful. language is very personal to me, one of my closest friends, and it just so happens that I write in english. so, yes, I love english. there. I've said it out loud in my head.

at the same time, language *is* culture, and I'm of a mind that it is paramount to do whatever is needed to keep the native languages going. in my own little life over the past twenty years or so – my writing years – I've spent a lot of time in métis, cree, lakota and blackfoot ceremony. those who speak the languages – and there are many children and teens – communicate in the way of their ancestors. when they express a concept in their language, when they tell a story, it's often in its original form. being a part of traditionally oral cultures makes language-learning all the more important. if I or my children had learned one of our cradle languages that's not french or english, we would be different people today, I'm sure of that. we would see and hear and smell and taste and laugh and cry and pray in a completely different way. but, because we speak in english and write in english and love in english, that doesn't mean we're any less "métis." I can't speak for my children, but my métisness is not separable from my me, from my body or my mind or my heart or my spirit, any more than the language I inhabit is separable. the two aren't mutually exclusive.

same for my writing. my writing is a reflection of my body's water, my hair braided straight down my back. mothering, like writing, is time-consuming, and, like a waist-length french braid, requires tremendous patience and calm. these are good preparations for writing. the strands of a braid represent body, mind and spirit. when a person braids her hair, she creates balance for herself, like a braid of sweetgrass, cleansing and gathering good things around the holder of the braid, burning beauty and peace and creating a space for solitude and calm, like creating a space to write. if I could expand on the metaphor of the braid, each strand of hair is considered sacred, just as each word uttered, each word brought to thought, is meant to be carefully considered. thought is real, as solid as a table top, its matter not of a visible nature, but the matter of creation – not unlike children.

until my early thirties, I had very little privacy, and everything I wrote I burned. I'd take those pages and offer those words, those feelings, to the fire spirit, the winds. the water. the smell of words on fire, their distant relatives rekindling inside the ashes into a rebirth witnessed only after centuries of thought, settling themselves around the roots of a cedar, expressing a love of girlhood during a warm, flash rain. there's so much that can't be expressed through words, not words on a page and not words burned into forever. I was thinking about that last night when I was standing close to the water and all I could hear were the waves, loud and laughing, all along the shore, meeting with my toes and spreading themselves into the womb of the mother.

> tiny fingers
> cold inside my hands
> leaving marks
> around the margins of a page

the other day, I had my little grandbaby overnight. before I dropped her off the next day, I took her to swing on the baby swings, something she loves to do. the weather was mild and it was the first time since the fall that I had her out on a swing. I just pushed her and pushed her and she just smiled, open mouthed, and occasionally said, "fun, nokomis, fun!," in her monotoned, excited baby-voice way. when I'm writing, that's how I feel: fun, nokomis, fun!, only for me, nokomis is both the great spirit and the language itself. my first language was french, as my mother was french speaking. when the men weren't around, my mother spoke in the language she felt most comfortable with. she prayed in french to the day she died. my métis grandmother spoke french, and if she were here today she might joke about the fact that we don't even know our own languages, but instead we speak the languages of the squatters.

the ideal is, we respect our children as the gifts they are, given to us by the great spirit to guide into adulthood. I aspired to that ideal, and though I'm sure I failed in many ways, I did manage to pass along a tremendous respect for all creation, for the power of the word and the importance of choosing words and actions carefully. both graham and barb are writers now, and both love language. both respect creativity and both are very creative. we attend one anothers' public readings and performances and we read to one another, from our own and from other writings. we tell stories. barb beads and acts, and graham paints and dances. I sew a bit. my métis grandmother taught me to embroider, to work with ribbon. my work is nothing like hers was, but I'm still learning. my mother didn't live long enough to expand her creativity much beyond her early fifties, yet her sense of beauty and grace is reflected in every movement my baby granddaughter makes, and in every ribbon her mommy braids into her hair.

this certainly wouldn't be true for every mother, but for me? coming from severe violence and alcoholism during childhood, my children taught me to love in ways I only imagined happened between the lines of books and between the acts of a play. my kids, graham and barb, my son-in-law harold, and now my grandkids, willow and jessinia, are my learning place. from them I've learned to love myself, to braid balance into my world. the other day my granddaughter was watching a dvd of a children's cartoon. there was this one section she kept rewinding and watching, rewinding and watching, rewinding and watching. here it was a section where this little guy throws his head back and lets out this huge laugh. after a few rewinds, she started to imitate his laugh, throwing her head back and letting out a good belly laugh.

my water
learning from the water here
learning to laugh out loud
& hear that laughter as if on the wind
a crow call caught forever
& passed from one generation
to the next

notes

1 All poetry in the text is copyright the author.
2 Maria Campbell, interview with H. Lutz in *Contemporary Challenges: Conversations with Canadian Native Authors*, 49.

mothering first

A Mum's Guide to Outer Space

CATHERINE KIRKNESS

Check out that pregnant woman: beneath the taut skin of her belly beats the heart of an alien life form. The creature waits, growing more independent of its host with every passing day. Soon, it will burst out of its fleshy prison to feed and excrete, wreaking havoc with the life its host once knew. You've been there? Then you know how it feels to go boldly forth into motherhood, even though each of us has a different experience every time. Each baby has to be learned, like a foreign tongue. Experience, intuition, research, interviews, groping in the dark: you do whatever you must in order to figure out the unique being with whom you now live.

There are plenty of decisions made only one time, but many others which must be made again and again. My choice of motherhood over all other careers is one of the latter. However many times I revisit, question, or struggle with this decision, I always end up making it again. Sometimes it doesn't feel like a choice but an inevitability: I want my family to flourish.

When my partner John and I were in graduate school, we lived in a tiny rental apartment and neither of us had a permanent job. Looking for a way to meet people in our new city, we chose babysitting. I wrote on topics like "False Death and Rebirth in Shakespeare's Comedies." After graduation, our next project was conception. I was fed up with intellectual exercises, and, after arguing in my thesis that readers need passion as well as reason, I felt ready to throw myself into the emotional challenges of parenthood. We planned that I would be home with the baby for the first two years and

John would be home for the next two; at this point, life with a five-year-old was inconceivable.

Pregnancy quickly ensued but ended painfully after ten weeks. I carried home a stack of name dictionaries from the library one day, and the next day I started to bleed. This loss swept away any doubt about whether we were ready to become parents, and made me wish that we had started trying a lot sooner. What if this miscarriage were the first of many? What if I were never able to have a baby? I could easily conjure up a baby in my head, but creating one in the flesh was a more difficult assignment.

Establishing a career at this stage seemed like a terrible mistake; why would I devote myself to something that I knew would matter less than having a child? My day job as a library assistant paid the bills, and my temporary sideline as a babysitter gave me valuable experience. I devoted much of my emotional energy to yearning for motherhood and seeking out books and stories that would speak to the intensity of my longing. I could tell that I would want to write, someday, the kind of stories I now most wanted to read but, at this point, I felt overwhelmed and underqualified; I lacked authority.

I was lucky. Just over a year later, I gave birth to Rowan. A.S. Byatt, whose romance *Possession* was at the centre of my master's thesis, has said that having a baby was the first time she felt fully engaged with life as opposed to art. I felt the same way. Entry into motherhood transformed my understanding and priorities. With Rowan's arrival, life took over.

❧ It is hard to know, without having tried it, what breastfeeding is like. In the moments after Rowan's birth, when I first offered him my nipple, I was taken aback by the intimacy of the act and also the strangeness of it. I had cared for many infants before but never in such a direct, physical way. Why had I not read more during pregnancy about how to do it? How come it looked easy yet seemed so hard to get right?

I admit that I am rather an intense person, with passionate beliefs about moral issues. Once my strong emotions are evoked I can be a bit extreme. Breastfeeding hit me hard. When my new child was latched on, drawing nourishment from my body, I felt newborn myself, as a powerful mammal. The mere idea of him wrapping his tiny lips around anything but me was appalling; I didn't want anything or anyone to interfere with the intimacy of our bond. Responsibility for Rowan's survival rested with me and me alone. Oh sure, there were others involved. His dad (apart from being our sole bread-winner) changed all the early diapers and carried out an elaborate bathing ritual, while my own mother ensured a constant flow of sustenance from the kitchen and less tangible places. Both of them were loving and attentive caregivers, but only I was his nursing mother. I gave myself up to my child out of necessity: I couldn't do it any other way.

Sleep deprivation is often part of a regime of torture. Disorientation, paranoia, anxiety, irritability, obsessive thoughts, muddled reasoning – these problems will affect anyone who goes long enough without adequate amounts of sleep. Some babies sleep more than others, and mine was one of the others. He took ages to fall asleep, never seemed to stay asleep for longer than about two hours at a stretch, woke up relentlessly early, and did I mention breastfeeding? I felt an unearthly fatigue all the time. I went to bed, exhausted, when he did, and got up, still exhausted, in the morning. My own insomnia made matters worse; once he woke me up, I often stayed awake for hours, waiting for the next round of nursing, craving sleep and unable to leave the bed. I felt strongly that it was my job to meet his needs, day and night, and Rowan confirmed my primary importance with amazing feats of wakefulness at times when others stepped in to help.

The public library offers numerous books with titles like *Solve Your Child's Sleep Problems*, but I could see that the sleep problem was mine and not his. No amount of get-tough rhetoric can transform a high-need infant into a big sleeper, and I resisted suggestions from anyone who believed that locking my kid in a room and letting him scream would somehow enhance our relationship. I talked tired the way the Inuit talk snow, but that was the extent of my creative output. I poured all of my energy into being a mum and felt deeply satisfied. I didn't plan to care for my child with such reckless abandon, but it happened anyway. Why would I write when I could live?

♻ As Rowan grew into an energetic toddler with a strong will and a short fuse, I felt more ready to take some space for myself. But where does space come from?

John's mother warned me that once kids start to talk, they never stop. At first, I thought this revealed a lack of empathy on her part, but Rowan more than proved her right. John once asked two-year-old Rowan if he would keep his voice down so that I could sleep: "I can't do that, Daddy. Talking is my specialty." All of Rowan's waking hours were like an endless cocktail party for me. I listened and nodded and said "mmm hmm" and asked interested questions. Why didn't he ever run along and play?

Research into temperament makes it pretty clear that some people are born extroverts and others are born introverts. Some people are closer to the middle of the continuum than others, but whether we derive energy from being with others or from being alone is not something we can change. Many writers are introverts, although extroverts outnumber us three to one in the general population. Rowan clearly fed off his interactions with others, while I longed for quiet so that I could recharge. His thirst for stories and information was insatiable; he sucked up new words and made them his. I imagined that while his brain grew, mine was shrinking. Whenever I could, I read compulsively. Text flowed into me like cool water down a parched throat, but, even though I had some time, I found myself completely unable to write. When I had to produce a "thank you" note or a shopping list it was like wringing blood from a stone. My thoughts raced, but I felt mute and strange around other adults.

The demands of motherhood are clearly metaphysical, but childrearing is easily reduced to a set of purely practical concerns. By the time Rowan was ready for preschool, things seemed easier. Our family was settled in a two-bedroom condo, within blocks of two sets of eager grandparents, and John's work was stable and enjoyable (as if I would demand that he quit the dream job to stay home with Rowan while I went back to shelving books for half the money – so much for that plan). Rowan was eager to be with the other adults in his life, and I was able to look longingly at mothers with established careers returning to and enjoying them. Now that we were a family, money seemed to matter more. John had found a way to get paid to read and write, and every day at work he honed his skills and broadened his connections. Meanwhile, I was mired in the unpaid work of homemaking; the more I did it, the more it felt like the only thing I could do. Important people were waiting for John's reviews and articles, and each piece attracted a cheque. I focused my efforts on the only audience who clamoured for and rewarded me: Rowan.

One day, a close friend invited me and Rowan over to play, and her daughter announced that a little brother or sister was on the way. John and I wasted no time. Rowan's little sister was born four months after his friend's little sister. Now that I thought I knew what I was in for (disappearing into a black hole), I was keen to get childbearing out of the way before

I got any older (this work took all my strength). It was easier to follow the same orbit than to gather the force required for a new trajectory.

Guess what? Having a second child means a lot more work, and even if you read *Siblings without Rivalry* when you are pregnant, your children may not get along very well and you will have to live with their conflicting sets of needs forever. Maybe you will need not one but two separate caregivers in order to have time to yourself.

With one child, I often felt like a reasonably competent parent, even though I no longer had much truck with the world beyond our home. With two children, my hard-won confidence ebbed away completely. When the three of us were alone, I felt like a bad mother. Rowan's stream of talk and play washed through my ears. I tried to listen, but often I was just making listening noises without engaging in what he said. At the same time, I was carrying Skye or jiggling and joggling her and barely looking at her. I didn't have enough senses to do the job well, and the stress of their discontentment weighed heavy. Both of them seemed to demand something from me all the time. Sometimes when I was trying to do a chore while holding Skye – turn over laundry, prepare food, set up something for Rowan – I had an urge to hand the baby to him. I needed my hands free and there he was just hanging about, talking and waiting.

I never knew when Skye's night sleep would begin. Or by the time I knew, it was too late to prepare. I never got her into a double diaper at the right time. Or almost never. When I put her down I hardly expected her to stay asleep because so often she woke up and I had to pick her up again before her screaming woke up Rowan. I felt triumph when I laid her down and she stayed asleep. I felt resignation and failure when I laid her down and she didn't. She was a night owl and he was an early bird; at this point their sleep cycles only overlapped by six hours at the most. If I had been a real writer, maybe I would have found a way to work, but motherhood had subsumed all of my other identities.

When people ask if your baby is a "good baby" what they really mean is "does your baby sleep for long, uninterrupted periods, fall asleep quickly and without effort on your part, and lie around even when awake without needing any human contact?" By that definition, my babies were far from "good." What do you call babies like my two? Evil? You can't really call yourself a good mother if your babies are "bad"; what proof do you have of your own efficacy?

The day Skye was born, she screamed whenever I put her down. When our few visitors had gone, she screamed and screamed and screamed even though I was holding her. Over her first few months, I figured out that if I held her all of the time, she would not spend the evening screaming. Until she was able to sit up by herself (about seven months) I wore Skye strapped onto my body. I don't think I left the house without her until after her first birthday. I quit my four-hour weekly shift at the library because I couldn't imagine how John would be able to manage both kids for that long without me. I didn't go out in the evening alone until she was two and a half. One night I tried to write in bed with Skye sleeping on one side and Rowan sleeping on the other, but the shifting light of the flashlight disturbed Skye and I had to stop.

❧ Mothers have always had influence on an individual level – we create the places where children find out who they are and we encourage them to temper their temperaments. Our children learn language from us, and they take their words and thoughts with them into the world when they go. In this way, mothers shape children, and children shape the future. At the same time, our work involves many activities to which our society attaches little value.

My hands and brain are seldom free at the same time. Lots of childrearing tasks give time to think and compose but take over my body. Changing diapers, nursing, feeding, wiping, carrying, shopping for food – mothers are often too busy cooking supper or waiting in the dentist's office to be out changing policies or fighting political battles or even writing our memoirs. But we are not too busy to think; our job demands a constant evaluation of priorities and a steady awareness of what it takes to sustain human beings. I now feel kinship with women who care for children throughout the world, and I have a more nuanced understanding of how and why patriarchy happens. I know far more about backhoe loaders and ear infections and the shape of the moons of Mars than I did before. I know more about rage and pain and empathy too. Being intimately connected with where babies come from leads to an interest in other kinds of origins (another reason to buy organic); mothers have daily opportunities to wish we might leave the world better than we found it.

Doris Lessing has been quoted as saying "there is no boredom like that of an intelligent young woman who spends all day with a very small child."[1] I quite agree, and I thank her for having the courage and taking the time to say it. Yes, if mothers could just get away from the crying and the crapping and the physical constraints of breastfeeding, then we could get something done. But I also question the way my feminist foremothers seem to have thrown the baby out with the dishwater. I would never burn my nursing bra! What does our longing for escape do to our kids? What are the social implications of paying others a pittance to raise them? Maybe it's the sleep-deprivation paranoia talking, but there just aren't a lot of people I trust to handle my kids. (If I find it so challenging, how will someone who doesn't love them fare?) I want to be there when they say: "I'm running as fast as my little legs can carry me."

Once, I stood in a doorway and wrote about Skye (one year old):

She loves a vinyl toy tape measure. She wraps it around herself: up over her head, round her waist. Somehow around her ankle. She watches the process in the mirror. After long explorations she decides to involve the ride-on car as well. She climbs on, tape measure in hand, and begins a more complex wrapping process that goes around the car too. She pushes astride, backs into the mirror, checks over her shoulder. Climbs on and off. Slips on the toy-strewn floor. Gets up again. Calls out "hello" to me.

As Rowan (five years old) said, "me and Skye are very vivid." They have their work to do, and it is the process that matters, not the product. As a mother, I have to remember that my work is all about process, too. I have had a hand in creating my kids, but I can neither choose their characters nor direct them to my selected happy endings. I can make art flow from motherhood, but my children belong to life and they keep happening around me. Skye (five years old) says: "Mummy, we love each other more than we can explain, don't we?" She is right. Stories I might make in my own image, but the children belong to themselves.

🦋 The details of daily life demand my surrender. If my mind is keen to be busy with other things, then it is harder to endure the pace of children patiently. My particular children call for a level of engagement beyond anything that I had imagined. Rowan (six years old) put it well: "I am so highly strung that I cannot be plucked. If you pluck me, my cord will snap. Every cubic inch of me is highly strung." There are plenty of kids out there whose special needs push their parents to far greater extremes of self-sacrifice than mine; it is no coincidence that their stories are seldom told.

When I read books from the library about ramps and wedges or spend two hours of every evening lying in a dark room and waiting for someone to fall asleep, when my only adult conversations involve who will do which chore when and how, when the children bicker and squawk: at these times I long to walk calmly out the front door or lock myself away with a book. Yet I always manage to convince myself that watching life unfold from nothing, seeing personalities emerge and develop, sharing experiences with those who matter to me most, that this is all grist to the mill. There are days when, as soon as I wake up, I know that I am not interested in motherhood. My kids seem so tedious; their hunger is endless for meals, books, conversation. I want them to be quiet and elsewhere. I want to be alone for long enough that I can comb my thoughts smooth.

How long will that take? John has taken both children to the beach. Any minute now they will burst in. I'll hear them from outside our door. They'll be hungry and keen to tell their tales. I will get up and remove their shoes. John will be harassed and grumpy as he was before they left. I should make food. I should tidy the house. I should always do everything but write a book. I don't have time and any minute I will be interrupted. Sentences must be short and structure formed moment to moment. Commit to nothing. Oh, here they are ...

Virginia Woolf understood, even though, mercifully, she did not have children. The ensuite bathroom is mine. In here, with the door shut, I am free. At least until I hear shrieking elsewhere and rush off to attend. Until someone bursts in to say look at this thing or where is that thing. I long for a room with a window and a door. A room empty of items screaming sort me discard me fold me mend me read me.

Motherhood presents many opportunities for ambivalence to rear its head: imagine saying "shut up" to a three-year-old so fresh and smart and loving that you get tearful just thinking about the meanness you have perpetrated. But what about the glory of snuggling children close and feeling the benefit of their quick forgiveness? What about the thrill of their questions? *Why are eyeballs round? When will you die? What was the most embarrassing thing you did when you were my age? Are spiders ever called "cobs"?*

They need human brains and hearts to feed on, and I am honoured for some of them to be mine.

I get frustrated, but I never regret cherishing my relationships with my kids. I want to get them launched properly before I travel in a different direction. Even as I write those words, I know that I will always be drawn by their gravity. The stories of their lives interest me more than any of the tales that I might tell in my spare time.

NOTES

1 Lessing, *Under My Skin: Volume One of My Autobiography, to 1949*, quoted in Davey, ed., *Mother Reader: Essential Literature on Motherhood*.

The Sun Knows What It Does

DEIRDRE MAULTSAID

In Northern Spain, the women make Chantilly lace on their porches. The men plough corn in their small holdings and put out rafts in the quieter harbours onto which mussels latch by the thousands. The famous wind is harvested by giant white windmills standing in long rows on the ridges above the harbours. I taste these muscular orange mussels; I hear, in the town of Camariñas, the noisy criss-crossing and clacking of bobbin-ended white threads that grow rapidly into delicate lace in the hands of skilled young women; I feel the wind, everywhere the wind. However, I am no poet of travel narratives. As with the constant and merciless wind, my some-times churlish, sometimes impish, sometimes sweet sons are with me. For several years, around school and work schedules, my family traverses Spain and Portugal, from Gibraltar in the south, through to Galicia in the north, through Lisbon to northern Portugal. I labour to make meaning of my journeys, to confirm my dual consciousness, mother-writer-writer-mother. I tolerate the silencing of my imagination. With children, nothing seems lyrical. Nothing is illuminated but them. I spend money. I make porridge. I. Am. So. Busy. Trying. To. Keep. Their. Hands. Clean. And. Keep. Them. From. Falling. Off. The. Cliff.

One hot fall day in 1998, I stand beside my young sons on the highest cliff of Gibraltar, in the relentlessly buffeting, gritty desert wind blowing from Morocco, and tell them to look up through the haze to the dark blue humps of the Atlas Mountains of North Africa. I want the boys to sense that they are standing on one of the pillars erected by Hercules looking across at his other pillar and beyond to the end of the world. My sons glance for a moment before running away to the other side of the platform. The ode-worthy moment is muffled by the usual family acrimony, created when, down at the cable car stop, I won't let them get too close to the mangy yellowish Barbary Macaques.

The mythic moment, the recognition of what Hercules built is further spoilt because I harshly encourage the boys to keep on moving through the 370 feet of dim tunnels, tunnels first dug through the solid limestone by the Company of Soldier Artificers in 1782 and finished by the British Corps of Royal Engineers with sledgehammers and gunpowder, tell them to keep moving because I do not want them to be awed by the batteries of guns and barrels of gunpowder in the musty munitions rooms – war-glorifying museum! – nor be impressed by the Victorian sixty-four-pound-cannon in the Upper Galleries, nor to set off the motion-detector device, which makes the life-sized statue of a British soldier evoke the four-year Great Seige that started in 1779 because the soldier, to the boyish thrill of my sons, shouts out from his tape in the ceiling, "Halt, who goes there?" Instead I bark at the kids, "Let's go, let's go!" and guide them quickly through the tunnels.

I have waited long for motherhood to have a presence in my literary imagination. My imagination is a wild place. There is a hiss of ancient steam; a shriek of dying bats, briny water, moral ambivalence, and rage. To write of motherhood is to be ruminative and nostalgic, to make Chantilly lace of my feelings, to quarter my heart as if it were nothing more than a sweet orange, to be sense-imbued, a dumb animal, a mother. What is there to say? Motherhood is complicated. I would have to pretend that my children don't fiercely hate and love me in turns. I hate them, too, for the fear they create, for giving me the impossible task of keeping them safe. My sons are pirates, rampaging through the Mediterranean, Barbarossa ("Redbeard") and his mate, making slaves of Christians, corsairs of my heart. My sons cherish not what I cherish, despair not over war, gore, history, or dying cultures. My children are themselves, other people, *others*.

In the *Museu do Chiado,* Lisbon, there is a life-sized smooth white marble statue, *A Viúva* (the widow), by Antonio Texeira Lopes. The widow sits. The baby in her arms tries to nurse but the milk drips wasted from her mother's unwrapped breast as she gazes away to the horizon, bereft. I see the statue;

my heart breaks for this maternal ambivalence. Contemporary, overheated children, my children, gawk not at the widow but up the three-storied narrow staircase of the museum, which is an old biscuit factory. The boys want to go up themselves. Can they poke in those old ovens? "No." Can they go up to the rooftop terrace? "No." These children are inviolable, with stout legs and custard-tart-crumbed shirts. Nothing could pass me and get to these children whom I love fiercely. "Halt, who goes there?"

In *Sheep's Vigil by a Fervent Person*, the Canadian poet Erín Moure translates herself into Portuguese[1] and calls up her Northern Spain Galician roots, her Eirin-ness. She says: "How can people think of reasons and conclusions /when early morning opens rays of splendour, and among the trees / a slow golden glow dispels the darkness?" [*É como pensar em razó efins / Quando o começ da manhã está raiando, e pelos lados das árvore / Um vago ouro lustroso vai perdendo a escuridão*].[2] Moure talks of trees and sun. Her senses are open. She seems to find mysticism. What a poet! She invokes Fernando Pessoa, modernist poet of Portugal. In *The Keeper of Sheep*[3] Pessoa said, "Because the light of the sun is worth more than the thoughts of all the philosophers and all the poets. The light of the sun does not know what it is doing."[2]

Erín Moure can invoke Pessoa. I cannot. His bronze statue – up in the hilltop Lisbon neighbourhood of Chiado, outside the *Brasileira* tearoom, with his oversized jacket and smallish head – is unattended, certainly unworshipped. My family eats at *Martinho da Arcada*, the restaurant Pessoa used to frequent, to make coffee-inspired poet's talk across the broad, white-clothed table. My children do not want to taste anything from the tureen of fish stew; they will have only crusty buns and individually wrapped strong white cheeses and leave a stack of crumbs and empty packages. I take them across the *Praça do Comercio* ("don't step in the pigeon droppings") until we can see the Tejo River, even in the dark. I tell my sons that Fernando Pessoa is a well-admired national poet. They don't even listen to me. They give no credence to this, to poets, to the scruffy mustiness of urban Portugal, the hills and narrow alleys of Lisbon. All these children care about is buns and pastry.

My children clamber around the marine-themed playground at Belém where the Tejo River joins the Atlantic. One piece of equipment is a hollow whale into which children can climb. After lunch, in a maritime museum, and in the waning daylight, the boys, naturally, and without any prompting, linger over models of Portuguese caravels, from the days of Portuguese imperialist conquests. Does Erín Moure think that I could use my children as inspiration to write a poem that evokes the Portuguese fleet, Brazil when it was wild, Goa, Angola, Pessoa himself, children, trees, parks, and sun? "I taste the iron of the Atlantic mist. My son climbs a metal whale. I eat a whole white *dorado* / while through the window; winter sun illuminates its bones." That is the only poem I can write.

Instead of Pessoa, or Moure, would it be wiser to invoke some acorn-fed Celtic princess, and have her journey to Galicia to one of those enclosed circle *citānias* (villages) and be buried there? I do not see any of those granite statues of wild sows, the Celtic fertility statue, called simply a *porca*. I drive on the narrow roads, through the small stone-housed streets, up over the hills, past the cabbage and corn patches, past the ancient black-clad Portuguese farm women, to the baroque eighteenth-century, archbishop-commissioned *Bom Jesus do Monte* Church with its vast decorated outdoor stairway and many cultivated hedges. After running up the stairs of *Bom Jesus* – not penitents crawling on their knees – my children are too tired and hungry for Celtic villages. They doze in the back of the grimy Renault. They do not care for primitive fertility rituals. They take turns shaking a fridge magnet, a half globe inside of which a *meiga* (a Galician witch) flies on her broom in glitter-filled water. I am making that up. They do not rally or play with the magnet, still in its shopping bag, stuffed in a suitcase pocket. The children whine incessantly until I shout at them, as usual, and all hope of wooing poems into my mind is gone.

Despite what Moure says, I think of reasons and conclusions. An overwhelmed mother cannot exalt the life of the senses. As soon as I say to my children, "Find your soul! Experience the world through your senses! We are all poets!" I am mothering, evangelizing for how to be human. Moure wants to keep it simple? Sun. Golden glows. Trees. Things. I am not enough of a dumb mother or a mystic for poetry. Moure abandons me to be sense-addled, to hear the susurration of the wind in the pines, to smell the salt brine, to hear the clickety-clack of the bobbins as the girls make lace on their looms. For me, to see the lace is to know that this lace absurdly, superstitiously dresses statues of the Christian Virgin Mary for Holy Week processions. To see the *mejilloneiras* drift in the waves in the Atlantic harbour of Muros is to know about the declining Spanish fishing industry. To experience any stimulant through my senses is also to remember my stunned midnight dumb animal nursing, the smell of my own sour milk and, later, is to hear someone I love with my life, run away saying, "I hate you."

What artist wants to know that a child's presence can overwhelm all other sensations? Always there, at your elbow, trying to have their own private life in your public world. A skin you cannot get out of, even if you scrape it off with a dirty bayonet.

Erín Moure can get away with her refrain: "sun" and "nothing thinks nothing." No duty-bound essayist, no workaday writer like me can do that. How can I write about my own ambivalence? I have no words for that dangerous duality – mother-writer-writer-mother. Maybe for this ambivalence, they, the Macaques, Redbeard (with his one arm shot off by a Spanish cannon), the ghosts of British soldiers, the unrelenting wind should shove me through one those gun embrasures, and out and off the rock of Gibraltar.

Moure wants to say, "I see [the world around me] and am heartened"? I say, "I see a red-faced, listless, midnight-awakened, too weak to cry, sunken-eyed baby, and I am frightened." I am so frightened that I am furious. I defy anyone to make a poem of that. I could try to write a poem about childbirth myself, but who would read it? Who wants to know that tale of natural gore, pain, and the inexhaustible, strong sinew of love? The pain and energy of birth could blast through 370 feet of limestone, grow a thousand acres of corn, or make Redbeard weep. The discipline of motherhood is more arduous than that of any Catholic penitent. Like most mothers, I am solemn with my love. I don't need Chantilly lace to decorate it. I don't need a journey through it. I need better representatives who can portray my maternal ambivalence.

This is, therefore, a requiem for marble widows, and Eiren-ness, and the lace makers, and the fertility sows and the old Celts, and Fernando Pessoa who cannot help me, and Redbeard, and mussels, and the Atlantic, and mangy monkeys, and for Gibraltar, that controversial protectorate. I can't surrender to these experiences, or to my reason-withering senses. To write is to go down inside a dripping grotto, every rock, and every saved shell on the grotto walls an ancient barnacled overanalyzed resentment, every bat blind, waiting, breathing. There is so much danger. I can hardly navigate the dark, tide-shifted caves, and I must always go alone.

There is also so much danger in not feeling the intensity of maternal love. This love will silence the shrieking bats; it will bring such bright sunshine into those fetid menacing ancient unrecognizable places. Children are not "among the trees." They are everywhere and my own skin. Children shine not with the "slow golden glow." They are the sun. They know what they do.

If I climb the high cliff, I can see through the gap to the end of the world beyond the Atlas Mountains. Hercules held these pillars up once. I could hold up those pillars now, for them, those pirates, my sons. Pass through. We could venture beyond the end of the known world together.

My son laughs, "Redbeard had his arm blown off!" My son is someone I recognize.

In the tiny northern Portuguese village of Paradela we are the only guests, crammed into some small overfurnished, overdraped rooms, with narrow balconies below which a black-kerchiefed woman leads her cow through the sunny meadow. The children's voices echo in the hallways. I have nowhere to take the children in the evenings; I have nothing to show them but the old woman and her cow. It is so truly silent up in this *Serra;* we can hear the cow bells peal across the whole mountain. The owner of the hotel, Aurora, is like a widow; her husband is away working. When we come into the silent dining room, Aurora begs me to let her prepare any special food my sons want. She fetches large salads of dark leafy greens and fresh tomatoes, and steaks as big as my son's thigh. She sits right down at our table, sighs and stares out the large window at the treed mountainside. We say *"Obrigado"* over and over when she bustles about, bringing coffee, then sticky buns, then chocolate bars, and asking us, "More, more?" We don't know how to refuse. We come back from a hike late one evening, and Aurora greets us in the hallway and escorts us into the silent, dark dining room. She brings the huge salads and steaks again. Although we have had the same menu at lunch down in the valley, we say only *"Obrigado, obrigado."* Aurora sits down, rubs her face tiredly and, to my surprise, says, "I live New York. Here – nothing. Work. Work. My daughter. Braga for the *escola.* I go to there and then happy." She stares out the window at the night.

When we pack up to leave the village, Aurora stands in the hallway, hugs the boys hard to her and almost starts crying. She adores my children. "I pray you," she says, and I believe her. The pretty blue tiled floor of her front hallway, the cobbled streets, the sun on the vines, the lush red tomatoes in her garden, the generative tranquillity of her undiscovered river valley and her forested *Serra,* the fascinating religious beliefs of her neighbour who has given us the evil eye from beneath her black kerchief, none of these magical sounds and sights are felt by the hotel widow. She misses her daughter. One day the hotel widow might walk all the way down to the city of Braga. Aurora is someone I recognize.

notes

1 Erín Moure calls herself the both the "translator" and the "trans-e-lator" of *O Guardador de Rebanhos,* in other words, interpreter and writer. Her poems are different from Pessoa's.
2 Moure, *Sheep's Vigil by a Fervent Person, 17.*
3 Ibid, 14.

Wearing Different Hats: Mothering, Writing, and Keeping Your Sanity

THeresa sHea

1. THe romanTic myTH

It is tempting to buy into the romantic myth of the writer who is so driven to produce work, no matter what her circumstances, that she sacrifices everything in order to do so. After all, the general culture admires such devotion and believes the spark of genius is fanned by an obsessive need to create art. Even *I* believe it at times, especially when I'm not writing and when mothering is demanding all of my energy. Didn't I feel guilty when I read about Margaret Laurence rising in the early morning hours in order to write, sometimes by candlelight, before her husband and kids woke up? Or when I read of her late-night bursts of creativity *after* she'd put the kids to bed? How on Earth did she have the energy? And what about Alice Munro, who often lied to protect her writing time, telling her suburban housewife friends that she was busy sewing curtains – a domestic enough reason to seclude herself?[1] And didn't I feel like a poser when I read how Sylvia Plath "was capable of the most rigorous discipline, the most productive concentration in making use of the time she allocated for writing"?[2] These women writers, and so many others who were also mothers, were *driven* to produce their art. My attempts to write seem feeble by comparison.

In my childhood I read obsessively and wrote poems and short stories. I was convinced I saw the world differently than others, that I felt more deeply and was more attuned to the subtle nuances of human relationships.

Yes, I had all the ingredients to be a great writer. I would be famous one day. I would be generous with my riches.

I first began publishing when I was in my twenties at university. The McGill literary publications accepted several poems and one short story. I remember walking around campus, collecting copies of the glossy magazine *The Pillar* that had printed my dystopian story about a world in which eating disorders were a natural part of culture. I sent copies to all the members of my family to *prove* I was a writer. When I graduated, I crossed the stage and, in addition to receiving a diploma, I accepted a cheque for $1,000.00 for winning a poetry award. Yes, I was well on my way. The creative fires were stoked.

2. PLANS TO WRITE

Eighteen years later. It is three in the morning, and I am wakened by my youngest. He has just turned three but still wants to nurse his way through the night. I know if I simply give in to him he'll have a wee nosh and quickly fall back to sleep, but at the moment I resent his needs and I want to be left alone. "Go to sleep," I tell him. "My boobies are tired." "Please?" he whimpers, "just a little bit." I ignore him, hoping he'll give up. Instead, he begins to cry, not the soft "I'm not too committed" cry, but the "I'll wake up everybody in the house" wail that indicates he will persist until he gets what he wants. Despair, anger, and hopelessness battle for supremacy in me. Anger comes out on top. Sometimes it catches me entirely off guard and explodes like a train from a tunnel. I am afraid of this rage, yet I'm often powerless to keep it at bay. It's not my son's fault, however, that I've nursed him on demand, nor is it his fault that we've always had a family bed. I believe in these things. But he's wakened me once already, and at three in the morning all I want is a good night sleep. I had plans to write in the morning and a sinking despair kicks in. How will I write if I'm exhausted? How will I parent? How will I possibly go on?

Experience has taught me I do my worst mothering when I have other plans. It seems the children demand even more when they sense I've removed myself from them rather than surrendered to them. But experience has also shown me that I parent better when I'm writing, because then I don't feel like I'm "just a mother." It's a dicey combination, juggling the needs to care well for my children and to write. How have other mothers done it? With great difficulty. Alice Munro, for instance, talks about the baggage of guilt that continually accompanies the mother who writes. "I don't think in terms of a female life without children," she said in an interview. "So what it means is that you are doing these things all the time that are psychologically terribly, terribly hard on you. You're always failing somebody. Even when the children are grown."[3] Yikes. You mean, it doesn't get easier once they're adults?

Knowing the inherent difficulties women writers face, and *feeling* the guilt when I head off with my laptop to create something that I'm not even convinced will be any good (or plump the bank account), I sometimes wish I didn't have the desire to write. Why couldn't I simply be happy tending to my kids and keeping house? Life would be easier. My kids would be happier. *I* would be happier. We would eat better, wear cleaner clothes, have better hygiene.

3. ON BEING "JUST A MOTHER"

When my second child was six months old, I suffered a moment of insanity and started writing a novel. I was thirty-seven and still clinging to the hope that I'd *be* somebody one day. Too late, I discovered the fictional world of a novel is a large beast to keep in one's head, along with all the other domestic details accompanying the needs of small children. What possessed me to begin a novel? (And it *was* a form of possession.)

My husband and I had somehow survived the first three months of our daughter's colicky life. I was feeling particularly trapped by the incessant needs of our demanding baby, in addition to those of our two-year-old son. I desperately needed some identity separate from that of being a mother. During that time, I recall getting the children to sleep and racing to the computer in the back room, only to have my daughter wake up crying an hour later. The rage was almost uncontrollable. *Why couldn't they leave me alone to write!* My husband often had to talk me down from my cliff-top heights of despair. Obviously writing at night would not work. I devised a new routine.

It was winter and dark when the alarm sounded in the morning. I'd quietly sneak out of bed, trying not to waken my daughter, and then stumble outside into Edmonton's snow and −30 temperatures with my laptop. The bus stop was at the end of my street and took me directly to the library downtown. Once there, I'd buy a coffee and muffin and plug in. I put myself on a rigorous regime, like the crazed dieter I was in my twenties, and wrote a thousand words a day. I did this every day for months, sometimes slumped over my laptop with exhaustion, fearful that a missed day would upset the entire routine. One day I had a draft done.

When the writing went well, I had a difficult time returning to the bedlam of my home. When the writing did *not* go well, I had an even worse time returning to my children. I had three hours a day to write, including travelling time. The bus ride home from downtown was only ten minutes, not nearly enough transition time to get me back into the parenting mode. Margaret Laurence wrote in her memoir, *Dance on the Earth*,[4] that she stopped writing two hours before her kids returned home from school in order to make the necessary transition from her fictional world to her domestic world. She painted a pretty picture of writer turned mother, baking cookies as she waited for her kids to barge through the door from school. In his biography of Laurence, however, James King paints a different picture of a mother who, "even when present, often wasn't present."[5] As any writer knows, coming out of the "zone" of creativity isn't always easy. Often there's a huge hangover period during which everything else is merely an annoyance to deal with (especially young children). Alice Munro's daughter, Sheila, wrote about returning home from school to find her mother "in a morose state of inactivity" when the writing hadn't gone well. This state would last for the remainder of the day.[6]

Too often I resented going home after my writing time. I had "worked" all morning, and now I had the "work" of childcare to face in the afternoon. Worse yet, it was now my husband's turn to head off to write. The afternoon loomed large: just me and my kids and a frustrated creative spirit. How could I be good to my children?

That was six years ago. I learned that a novel written in exhaustion and haste, with the desire to *prove* something, makes for a poor book. However, maybe that was exactly what I needed to get me through those early years of mothering. I was floundering, searching for a new identity. I was no longer the university lecturer or graduate student. I was a stay-at-home-mom, and, despite the inroads of feminism, a social stigma remains attached to that particular label. Even though I'd consciously chosen the life, honestly believing that my children had saved me from a workaholic career in academe, I didn't yet know how to live it.

Weeks before my third child was born, I waited anxiously for news from a literary agent about my novel. As it turned out, she chose not to represent it, and with good reason. I was reaching too high too fast. I was too anxious for recognition. Disappointed, I put the novel in a drawer and felt a deep shame for the amount of time I'd taken away from my kids. All for a poorly written novel. To paraphrase one of Munro's titles, who did I think I was? Knowing I'd have to leave the writing behind for some time, I focused on my family and made preparations for another birth.

4. SOMETHING HAS TO GIVE

When I was younger I wanted everything: to be a writer, to complete a Ph.D., and to have a family. In the process of attaining all my wishes, I learned that I *can* have everything, just not at the same time. And I learned that being a good mother and a good writer, *at the same time*, is for me an impossible undertaking. They're both full-time jobs, and the demands for each are too high. When I devote myself to being a great mother, I inevitably feel resentful for not being able to write. And, conversely, when I give all my energy to writing, my kids suffer from both my mental and physical absence. I can be a writer who does not write, but I can't be a mother who does not mother. Wherever I choose to put my energies, I am *always* a mother. Not writing causes me less guilt than not parenting well. Something has to give, and in my case it's usually the writing.

5. LOSING IT

I didn't have my first child until I was thirty-five. Had I become a mother in my twenties, I think the creative ego would not have subordinated itself to my children. Alice Munro married and had children when in her twenties. She confessed to having experienced a "monomania about being a writer." Two decades later, however, Munro had a different relationship to writing. In an interview she stated: "I think up until the age of forty, I would have done anything to be a good writer – really, *anything* ... And then all that changed ... [W]riters, it seems, have an enormous faith in the importance of art, and then you lose it."[7]

Can it be that I have "lost it" before I've even really begun? And is that necessarily a bad thing? Thankfully, I am no longer burning the candle at both ends to write a novel. I look back with quiet sadness on the days when my daughter was a baby. I remember the frustration, the exhaustion, the burning *need* to be recognized through my writing. At that time, the romantic myth of "art at any cost" sat like a devil on my shoulder, urging me to see my children as an impediment to creating "art."

I would like to take full responsibility for my newfound maturity in "choosing" to put my children before my artistic ambitions, but in reality it's likely a happy accident of time. I have matured. I no longer possess the youthful *need* to publish and to be known. The years from thirty-five to forty were a blur of childbearing and childrearing. Don't get me wrong, I still write, and I still *want* to write, but writing isn't my primary focus. It's something I do when I can, and often it's something I desperately want to do when I can't. In a culture that continually rewards self-realization, it goes against the grain to give one's self over to others.

6. on being "just a stay-at-home mom"

I never imagined I'd be a stay-at-home mom. Yet, at forty-three, the majority of my time is spent with my children who are eight, six, and four. My husband makes his living as a writer even though he is basically a stay-at-home dad. As Margaret Atwood once said, "A family and writing is OK, even a job and writing is OK. But a job, a family, and writing is not OK. Only two out of the three is manageable."[8] We have managed, for the most part, to sidestep "the job" in order to focus on the writing and family. We tag-team parent, jockeying for position to see who goes out first to write. Because we have great flexibility with our schedules, most days I can get out on my own. I am rarely left alone with the kids for eight or nine hours at a stretch. If the children are sick, my husband doesn't write. After the birth of our first son, he took a month off. When our colicky daughter cried for three months straight, he did not work. When our youngest son had six ear infections in less than a year, Tim spent many a night sitting upright in a chair with him so we could all get some uninterrupted sleep. Still today, Tim doesn't need to be out of the house early. In fact, nobody in our house wakes up to an alarm clock. We are living exactly as we want to. But we have also chosen a life in which we have time and little money, and we pay a large economic price for our freedom. Somehow we cobble together a living. Somehow we write. Somehow we have become more secure with our insecure lifestyle.

Although I can "have my time" every day to work, because we live off the proceeds from Tim's writing, the role of primary caregiver falls to me. I am the one who takes the children to the doctor, the dentist, who buys them clothes and footwear. I am the one who handles most of the children's social interactions. And this means that less of my brain is available to create. I can resent this fact, or I can accept it. My reaction depends entirely on the day, on the amount of sleep I've had, on how much caffeine I've consumed, on how well the children are getting along, on what I am writing. I am coming out of a seven-year cycle of profound sleep-deprivation and exhaustion. My energies are only now returning.

Give it a few more years, you might say, because then your kids will be in school and you'll have at least six hours a day in which to work. Carol Shields had five children and spent twelve years in a zone of frenzied domesticity before her youngest was in school. Then she had the day at her desk. Oh, it's so tempting. But that's another story.

7. HOMESCHOOLING

As I write this, the "Back to School" sales have hit with a vengeance. I feel the all-too-familiar seasonal urge to buy new clothes and sharpen pencils. Like most folk, the majority of my childhood was spent going to school. Sure, I turned out okay. But what if I hadn't gone to school? What might I have done instead?

As writers, we're always concerned with issues of freedom and escaping the constraints of society. We have consciously chosen an unconventional path to give *ourselves* this freedom. Isn't it therefore natural to want to give our children as much freedom as possible? If we really believe in freedom, we need to understand it as a process within which people can work and live.

When our eldest turned five and it was time to send him to school, we decided we didn't want someone else to have him for the best hours of the day. Similarly, shuttling him to and from school five days a week and separating him from his siblings was not a selling feature. We wanted our children to learn how to read and write when they were ready, not when some arbitrary age-linked curriculum determined it was best. We didn't want school to put blinkers on our children by deciding what was most important for them to learn.

As luck would have it, when we moved from our walk-up apartment to a small house nearby, the next-door-neighbour was a Waldorf homeschooling mother. She, and other longtime friends, made the homeschooling life appear attractive. We liked the flexibility of waking up slowly and living together more fully as a family. We don't follow any set curriculum, so our learning comes about through daily experiences.

Most people believe sending their children to school is easier than keeping them home. One would think that daily separations would help to replenish the supply of patience, but it doesn't work that way. Like creativity, parenting has its own "zone." One doesn't step in and out of it seamlessly. Surprisingly, I have discovered that the more time I spend with my children, the easier it is to be with them. School creates a whole host of problems that people are willing to accept to procure their own "freedom." Because of the way we've chosen to live, Tim and I both have "freedom" within our homeschooling regime. If either of us had chosen a career that took us from home five days a week for eight to ten hours a day, I'm not convinced we'd have the patience and commitment to keep our kids out of school. But as I watch them on a day-to-day basis and observe how they interact in the community and with one another, I'm committed to another year of their freedom, even when it means curtailing some of my own.

8. making peace

I've been a mother for eight years now, and I've grown into it. Spending time with my children is much more joyful now. Early on, I realized I needed to talk with mothers, who were also artists, who had found some peace, however turbulent, with the need to subordinate one's own ego for the sake of others. Often I *needed* these women more than I needed to read good books or attempt to write them. I am grateful to these mothers for the many fabulous conversations about who we are, who we'd like to be, and where we're going. They've given me the strength to write and, perhaps more importantly, the strength to *not* write. As a friend of mine said, "there's a difference between quitting your art and stopping your art." During my years of mothering, there have been times when I've had to stop writing altogether because it was the right thing to do. But I've never *quit* writing.

Fall is here. For me, it's the most productive season. I entered the "zone" to revise my novel and have put it into circulation again. Now I'm enjoying a fallow period, having learned that I cannot sustain the rigours of constant artistic productivity. Somehow, between the music lessons, the dental appointments, the childhood sicknesses and celebrations, the words get written and revised.

But it's not easy. Even though I believe the most productive years of my life lie ahead, I expect I will always feel some tension between my roles as a mother and a writer. It is difficult to be pulled in two directions simultaneously. Sometimes I wish I believed in the romantic myth that would have me sacrifice everything in order to write. But then I ask myself, what is the purpose of art? Is it simply about self-realization, or is it an attempt to participate fully and creatively in a world of freedoms and values you passionately believe in? Mothering three children outside the box of social conformity, I've come to understand, is no less creative than writing a great novel. At least, on my best days, I'm willing to believe this. On my worst days ... let's just say the learning curve is still curving.

notes

1 Sheldrick Ross, *Alice Munro: A Double Life*, 55.
2 Middleton, *Her Husband: Hughes and Plath – A Marriage*, 157.
3 Sheldrick Ross, *Alice Munro: A Double Life*, 55–6.
4 Laurence, *Dance on the Earth: A Memoir*.
5 King, *The Life of Margaret Laurence*, 200.
6 Munro, *Lives of Mothers and Daughters: Growing Up with Alice Munro*, 86.
7 Sheldrick Ross, *Alice Munro: A Double Life*, 71.
8 Sullivan, *The Red Shoes: Margaret Atwood Starting Out*, 322.

Transformations

STEPHANIE BOLSTER

A decade ago, I visited the National Gallery once a week all winter, then walked back to my small office at the back of our apartment in Ottawa's Lowertown and wrote about what I'd seen. Among my subjects: Lucas Cranach's chaste "Venus," Gustav Klimt's pregnant "Hope I," and a vast, explosive canvas by Jack Shadbolt, called "Transformations No. 5." The final poem in the series, about Shadbolt's painting – the vibrant wings of which suggest a newly hatched butterfly – began: "Yes, she is here, she is real – / she smells of iron afterbirth" and ended: "I would want / her every colour for myself and she would laugh / with her worm-mouth she will devour / the world as she must."[1] "She" was imagination, but also the child that, after two years with my partner, I was working up the courage to conceive.

For the moment I was too busy in front of the computer screen, writing new poems in which Johannes Vermeer painted still women in quiet rooms, while his own house filled with children and his town with strife. While I was finishing the series, a dear friend died, then her daughter was fatally struck by lightning. Art offered no answers.

Yet still I wrote, about train stations converted to museums, plants gathered from around the globe and set into botanical gardens, and, especially, endangered animals residing in the tidy frames of cages. As a child I'd seen zoos as life, a chance to witness the vital, strolling mass of the elephants that patterned my bedroom curtains. Now they were something else: a desperate and probably necessary attempt at preservation, yes, but also a sad replica, differing little from the taxidermied dioramas in the Museum of Nature. I was still stuck on (or was it "in"?), as one poem put it, "the difference between life and imagination."[2]

❧ I grew up certain that I wanted children. If I couldn't have a sister and if soulmates existed only in books, then as a mother, at last, I would find the bond I sought. As writing began to fill my life (and as I found a partner), the desire for that other person, that self/non-self, muted – my life was rich and full of love, friendship, intellectual and creative stimulation, travel – and practical considerations loomed.

"Every child is a lost novel," quipped a well-known, childless novelist, chatting with a group of writers in the bar at a literary festival. The time and energy devoted to raising a child would, certainly, amount to far more than that poured into a single novel – but could one even compare the two? Apparently, yes. Over a decade ago, a friend said that nothing, not even seeing one's own child for the first time, could compare to the first glimpse of one's own book. "No one else could have written that book," she said. She'd published three, and given birth to two children. I, having neither book nor child, simply nodded, thinking, Could anyone else have given birth to that child?

But then there was work. I'd hoped for a stable income before embarking on parenthood. Now – after years of freelance contracts, grants, and study – that my husband and I both found full-time teaching jobs meant that we'd be spared the financial anguish that plagues so many artist families. But "freedom from" such worries meant a lack of "freedom to." Once I began teaching, I realized what a colleague had meant when, during the job interview, she'd said, "This isn't just a job." Through the academic year, and often well beyond it, our jobs were full-time in a sense that no one outside our household could entirely understand. When I wasn't critiquing student manuscripts, I was emailing students about appointments. When I wasn't in appointments, I was in department meetings, or attending readings, or arranging visits by writers, or reading essays on craft, or writing grant applications. A pile of portfolios from prospective students teetered on the bedside table. Oh yes, and when I could manage it I wrote poems.

Students regularly told me that I was the most devoted, patient teacher with whom they had studied, that no one else gave as much time and individual attention. Colleagues praised my commitment to departmental service. My husband, also overworked but with a healthier sense of balance, joked, not jovially, about the need to schedule appointments with me. Clearly, I hadn't listened to the acquaintance, herself a writer, who had said, upon learning that I'd been hired, "Maybe it's not such a bad thing to not be a great teacher." Meaning that it was better to be a great writer and an adequate teacher than the other way around. I agreed in principle, but once faced with the students – real minds, real lives – and with the institutional pressure to perform, I let my inborn perfectionism run rampant. Was this life, or just work?

Each May, the students to whom I'd become half-mother, half-friend, headed off for magazine internships, tai chi workshops in China, backpacking adventures in Australia. I sat down at my desk to write, often about what I saw out my window: the blank slate of a backyard, visited by squirrels, crows, and the occasional rabbit and presided over by one white pine. The next year, the students (a new batch, mingled with a few returning faithful) were the same age, and I was a year older. Would life continue like this until 2034, the retirement year proclaimed on my annual pension statements? And then what?

❧ While arguments for art and for life chased each others' tails, I never planned *not* to have children. Just not yet. In each apartment into which my husband and I moved, I imagined myself pregnant, imagined where the child would sleep. But there was that manuscript, that teaching gig in St Petersburg, that tenure application to consider. My husband, who had, when we met, said that he wanted five or six children and was ready to get started at any time, pressured me only gently; after all, he was busy, too. I echoed my parents' unprying silence. My husband's parents hinted about grandchildren and the passage of time, but eventually, after my husband had a word with them, they stopped peering expectantly at me each time I declined wine.

Meanwhile, our friends and colleagues – nearly all writers, artists, or academics – were having children. Leisurely dinners became noisy, messy brunches, if we even got together at all. Talk of daycare waiting lists replaced talk of manuscripts-in-progress. I stood on shore as these bustling families headed off into choppy waters. They waved for a while, then headed for the buffet or the swimming pool, or simply watched the horizon. I was still there, waving.

For years I'd feared that, if I had a child, I would lose control of my life. But I was finally acknowledging, in my mid-thirties, that I didn't *have* control of my life. How many more times did I need to hear that parenthood would change my life – even my writing – for the better before I believed it? "You just become more efficient," said an award-winning fiction writer. "Sure, I write less," said another, "but my son's not going to be young forever. I don't want to miss anything." How many times did I need to remind myself that "Life is not a dress rehearsal" before I lived differently? If this went on much longer, waiting would resolve into a decision and childless would be the default setting.

If I didn't have a child, I would, I knew, often regret it. If I did have a child, I would, I believed, sometimes regret it. But the former would be a deep, insurmountable regret and the latter temporary and always overridden by love. If I had a child, I wouldn't lose the ability to write (would I?), just the time, and even that loss wouldn't be permanent. If I didn't have a child, that was it. Advice, read or heard, abounded: *You can't have it all.* But also: *To have a child isn't a rational decision. Better to regret something you did than something you didn't do. Feel the fear, and do it anyway.*

♣ Real-life turning points lack the resonant clarity of those in fiction. There was no sole epiphany but a series of small affirmations over several years, none startling, all serving to edge out doubt. As I was flying alone to Mexico City for several readings, my plane dipped alarmingly. After a moment, it began to ricochet. Some passengers gasped. A voice proclaimed, in swift, urgent Spanish, the locations of the emergency exits. I gripped my armrests and shut my eyes. This was it. I did not think of my unfinished manuscript. I did not think of the students whose work lay half-critiqued on my tray-table, nor of my colleagues. I thought of my husband, my parents, my brother. I thought of the child I had been trying – at last – to have.

When the halting English announcement finally came, it said simply, "The captain has switched on the seat belt sign." Panicked by the Spanish passion of the flight attendant's voice, I'd misunderstood. The turbulence passed. We were, and would be, fine. But I resolved – as I had resolved before, and would resolve again – to live by the priorities I set in my heart.

♣ Soon after, I learned that I was pregnant during that flight. After two years of plotting ovulation cycles, of tests and appointments and pills, the child I feared would never exist was with me during those moments. Two years of crushing, monthly sadness – and over a decade of waiting (first in trepidation, then in expectation) – had ended.

And yet, when the test confirmed my pregnancy and my chest lightened, giddy with good fortune, in some sliver of myself I still wondered whether this was really what I wanted. Had my it's-okay-if-you-can't-get-pregnant-life-is-easier-this-way pep-talks been too convincing? Or was this just the old doubt stirring? I delightedly researched the histories of names, examined paint colours, and emailed ultrasound images, even as I mourned the passing of my present life. Last time coming home alone on the bus at 1 am after a reading. No, not the last time, but the last time without guilt or worry. Last time writing alone in utter silence. But who was that squirming in the space where my lap once was? I had finally made the decision upon which I couldn't turn back. Not that I wanted to. But would I, later, want to?

As news of my pregnancy spread, former students sent emails, many of which mentioned that no one deserved the "break" of a maternity leave more than I did. Others, usually those with children, asked if my manuscript would be finished before the birth. I doubted it. I had plenty of poems, but they weren't, I felt, the right poems. The manuscript needed something else. Perhaps motherhood would grant that something, perhaps not. Perhaps I wouldn't write for a year or more. The young writer I once was possessed a Rilkean need to write and a fear that, if neglected, "It" would vanish; the writer I was becoming was just a little less intense, a little more patient, a little more balanced.

♣ During the first weeks of my daughter's life, that balance tipped. I believed, sometimes in desperation, sometimes in grudging, exhausted acceptance, that I would never be lucid again, let alone write. But by the time Madeleine was two months old, I'd turned the couch into my office. While she nursed, I scribbled revisions – often illegibly, with my left hand, while my right held her – onto a stack of poems I'd promised to submit as a chapbook. Oblivious, she fed as I read, reread, crossed out, added, ordered, reordered. Creatively focussed in a way I hadn't been since the last few days before her birth, I was doing good work. Suddenly, without any stagey entrance, my old self was here; I was her, she was me, and I was mothering, too – writing and mothering as simultaneously as one can.

Two weeks later, the poems hovered on the computer screen, beside which lay that ragged heap of revisions. At my feet, Madeleine cried out from her activity mat, the elephant that had entranced her a second earlier having become frightening, or frustrating, or dull. The word I'd crossed out now seemed better than the one I'd replaced it with. Or perhaps they were both wrong. The third word lurked somewhere ... just there ... I could almost see it but all I saw was her crumpled mouth, real tears in her eyes now, and oh that pinch between my shoulder blades, from turning from screen to floor. I saved the file and rescued her, but who would save me?

❧ Madeleine is now six months old, and I'm still here. As I soon realized, it's simpler if I don't try to do anything else during her waking hours. She is enough: wide of smile and eye, she's survived (as have we) the agonizing first few months and is now the wonder all those baby cards promised. My life is quiet and simple in ways I longed for during the hurly burly of teaching. My husband, meanwhile, teaches classes, meets with students, flies to Boston to present a conference paper. Is there a word that means both blessed and resentful? He's striding down the driveway – heading off to lunch meetings in restaurants, classes during which he'll talk to students about ideas – while Madeleine and I wave goodbye from the window. (Here I am, on the other side of that gulf, still feeling like the one left behind.) Yet while he treks to the train in –30 winds, I get to read her *One Fish, Two Fish, Red Fish, Blue Fish*; I'm getting paid for a year to be her full-time mother. I should be grateful. I am grateful. A graph of my daily emotions would resemble that of a chaotic day on the stock market, soaring and plummeting between gleeful and grim.

Nap when the baby naps advise all the books. Instead, I write. For periods of almost exactly forty minutes, during which sleep takes my joyful, noisy, curious daughter and replaces her with a mysterious, still doll, I do something that is mine as nothing else is. As she is not.

Having found the solution, poet resumes writing happily ever after – except that once those initial revisions are done and the chapbook submitted, the blank screen returns, and all the new insights the poet has had – that everyone on this planet, my God, was *born*; that your child's childhood is your child's, not your own; that you can be a daughter and a mother simultaneously – are clichés. Once the writing about writing and about not writing – this essay – is done, what next?

❧ Writing lyric poetry is selfish. For me, anyway. Though I'm moved when someone likes what I've written, that pleasure remains shallower, briefer, and less interesting than that which writing itself gives me. As Seamus Heaney wrote, poetry is "a revelation of the self to the self."[3] These days that self urgently needs to talk to itself. But, faced with the responsibility of raising a child, can I justify this glorified daydreaming? Can I take advantage of my husband's good nature and cooking talents any longer? Leonard Woolf (childless) claimed that the world would be no different if he played ping-pong rather than writing books. But the fact that I know this proves him wrong. However selfish the writing of poetry may be, the poems, once published, are the world's.

My first poems date from adolescence, that most self-absorbed of times, and are Plath-inspired bursts of anguish and despair. As a writer I remain most at ease in the minor key, in that which is melancholy, pained, bittersweet. Though I'm loathe to admit it, I believe that darker, more difficult emotions are deeper. Over the years, this predilection has troubled me, but never enough to prompt any real transformation. I preface the second reading I've given since Madeleine's birth with an apology, something I've told my students should never be done. "I've realized recently," I admit, "that my poems are far too depressing." All these animals in cages. A colleague has recently died, and reading these poems, I realize as I'm up there, is an affront. Where is the life about which my colleague was so passionate, the life that fills my daughter's face when I present her with a clementine peel to sniff? Where is the delight at the fact that an armadillo exists, the fascination of a day spent among such varied living creatures? The joy of a day spent alive oneself?

❧ A decade after I wrote "she will devour / the world as she must," my daughter rages on her stomach at the ball just out of reach; her openmouthed leaps shriek the springs of her Jolly Jumper; she pulls each new, bright thing into her mouth. An acquaintance, on seeing us together during those first weeks, warned, "A child like that will take everything. You have to put yourself first." Some days I feel myself receding, my powers of conversation diminishing. Forty minutes is not a wide enough door into imagination. To write the melancholy poems of my past feels false; to write the happiness of my present feels trite. I have seen in others' work how the gush of the newly parental poet turns all edges sticky.

I don't have new lines of poetry with which to end this essay. That worries me. The thought of returning to work sometimes terrifies me. And yet that sliver of self that was once uncertain about having a child has winnowed to nothing. This, I confess, surprises me. Maybe this is how all parents cope, by blotting out internal resistance. Or maybe I was right to wait this long – I've published three books, won a few prizes. I have a career to build upon, and no wasted youth to regret.

Several years ago, in a poem about my household's calm relative to that of the teeming Vermeer household – yet another poem in which I tried to convince myself that I was ready for a child – I wrote, "I haven't spun enough / to find the centre."[4] Perhaps in a few years, when Madeleine rages at us rather than at her toys, when we dash from office hours to daycare, when to even think about writing new poems from September through April is impossible, I will laugh bitterly at that romantic metaphor of art as diamond, forged under pressure. For now, despite my worries and fears, I still trust it. Bringing a child into the world was a rare act of optimism for me, and a transformative one. As years of writing have taught me, what is most worthwhile is rarely easy. And as motherhood is teaching me, art – exhilarating, audacious, exquisite, demanding, chaotic art – is only part of life. These days, my life is all these things, too.

notes

1 Bolster, from "Three Goddesses, III. Fear of the Twenty-First Century," *Two Bowls of Milk*, 75–6.
2 Bolster, from "Biodôme," *Biodôme*, unpaginated.
3 Heaney, "Feelings into Words," *Preoccupations: Selected Prose, 1968–1978*, 41.
4 Bolster, from "Vermeer, Impoverished Father of Eleven Surviving Children, Paints Our House," *Pavilion*, 10.

THE muse

Mama's Voices

susan OLDING

PLAY

When my daughter, Maia, was twenty-one months old, I left her for ten days to attend a writers' conference in Vermont. Maia stayed at home with my husband, who took some time off work. From the moment of her adoption at the age of ten months, Mark had been a full partner in caring for her. True, I prepared her bottles and cuddled her and played with her more often; I planned her days and spent more hours in her company. But, if she woke with a cry in the night, Mark went to her as often as I did. As the father of three older children – by then, young adults – he knew how to change a diaper, when to sneak a tickle, where to look for the missing blankie, what to do for an owie, and whom to phone in an emergency. Yes, I was her mother. But her dad was the more experienced parent.

Also in the house with us all that spring and summer was one of Mark's older children, Noah. Early evenings, he'd perch on the steps of our west-facing front porch, a Corona in one hand and a book in the other. Maia followed him there, clad only in a diaper, her skin still damp and smelling of the baby oil we squirted in her bath. She plopped down beside him, grabbing his book with clumsy fingers and losing his place in the text, calling out to every dog that ambled past. Noah taught her how to blow across the beer bottle to produce a sound. From the kitchen where I stood preparing supper, I'd hear first his bass blast and then her fainter, eager echo.

Most weekdays while I was away, Maia spent several hours – my writing hours – with her regular babysitter, Sue, just as she would have, had I been home. At Sue's, the air smelled like flowers and lemon furniture polish. Sue wore denim overalls and a big silver cuff and silver necklaces and earrings, and on sticky afternoons, from the deep recesses of her freezer, she produced juice popsicles, translucent as jewels in the sun. Maia sucked on them and then rolled on the floor with the dogs or splashed in the cool water of the swimming pool, supervised all the while by the woman who, over the years, had cared for each of Mark's older children in their turn, and many other children besides.

None of that could make up for my absence. A toddler needs her mother. A toddler who has lived in an orphanage for most of her first year needs her mother even more. Convinced of this, and concerned, even frightened about how our separation might affect Maia, I planned for my departure with the diligence of a general preparing for battle. I read the experts, most of whom declared that she would manage just fine, with support, and emerge from the experience stronger. I played countless games of hide and seek – *Mama goes away, Mama comes back* – and then we practiced – *one whole day apart, one night apart* – and I gauged her reaction on my return. I gave her a photo of the two of us, my high-beam smile turned on her, my arms protectively curved round her body. I searched the library for kids' stories about mothers who travel for work. I gave her an old red plaid shirt of mine and watched as she sniffed it and claimed it. And I gave her a basket of gifts – one for each night I'd be gone, a tangible calendar – each present wrapped in brightly coloured tissue, and all of them placed in a big basket. She still has some of those toys. A plastic tea set. A clock with hands that move, for teaching time. And the biggest gift, the most extravagant – a Little Tykes tape recorder.

Mark set up the machine that first night and turned it on. Maia watched, solemn and apprehensive, as the homemade recording crackled and hissed. Then she smiled. "Who's that?" Mark asked. "Mama!" she crowed, swaying back and forth in her excitement. "Mama's ... *voices!*"

FAST FORWARD

Four years later, I am on my way to the famous writers' conference for a second time. The day of my flight, I meet with an agent in Toronto. He has read an essay of mine in a literary journal and wants to discuss it with me. He likes the piece – likes it a lot – and over coffee at an outdoor café, he asks whether I'd consider expanding it into a book. If I write that book, he would very much like to see it.

Light hits the green leaves of the vines growing up around the patio trellis. Light dances over the spoons, the knives, the porcelain cups. I sip my black Americano, savour its bitter brightness.

The encounter is an emerging writer's dream come true. Or, as my instructor at the conference will put it: "The Schwab's Drug Store fantasy."

STOP

"The Schwab's Drug Store fantasy" *is* a fantasy. Lana Turner, said to have bewitched a talent scout with her beauty while sipping a cola at the soda counter there, was actually discovered at the Top Hat Café.

The Top Hat sits across the street from Hollywood High School, where Lana, then known as Judy, was an indifferent student. She may have been drinking a Coke, as the legend goes, but more likely she skipped out of class to sneak a cigarette.

PLaY

The tape I made for Maia included nursery rhymes – traditional favourites like Wee Willie Winky and Banbury Cross and Baa Baa Black Sheep, and modern-day versions by Eric Carle and Sandra Boynton. I recorded stories she already knew, like *Goodnight Moon*, and *Runaway Bunny*, and stories that were new to her.

Maia hadn't warmed to any of the commercially available books about adoption, so I wrote and read onto tape a version of her own story, explaining how she came to be our daughter. I told anecdotes about my childhood and about her grandparents, to strengthen her sense of history and connection to our family. I read Chinese legends, to strengthen her connection to the country and culture of her birth. I read Blake and Coleridge and Keats. I read Lear and Lewis Carroll. Words for counsel. Words for encouragement. Words for information and education. Words for the pure, sweet beauty of words.

FaST FORWARD

In the years between visits to the famous writers' conference, I have written little. Little for publication that is. Instead, I've filled out dozens of doctors' forms, responded to psychologists' questionnaires, and recounted increasingly bleak descriptions of my life as a mother to parent support groups on the internet. In the years between visits to this conference, my active, delightful toddler has disappeared and been replaced by a raging, resistant, impulsive changeling. Maia's violence has to be seen to be believed. She picks up chairs and throws them. She pokes her fingers into our eyes. She kicks. She bites. She scratches.

I have tried to understand. I have tried to find help and therapy. I have spent a small fortune on parenting books and have tried, fruitlessly, to follow their recommendations. I am getting used to the disdain or pity of strangers. I am getting used to feeling lonely. I've lost friendships over this; people think it's my fault, that I must be doing something wrong; people, understandably, get tired of my complaining.

The essay the agent likes is the story of our struggle. It is dark and ambiguous and does not offer answers, easy or otherwise.

STOP

Lana Turner described her life as "a series of emergencies."[1] That's an understatement. The first emergency was the murder of her father. John "Virgil" Turner gambled at cards. Once, he boasted too loudly about the tricycle he planned to buy for his only daughter with his winnings. His killer took the money and Lana never got her bike. Instead, she and her mother moved to Los Angeles, where a decade later she began her career, eventually appearing in fifty-four movies, as well as performing in radio, on television, and for the theatre. She became one of the highest-paid women in America. Yet for all her outward success, she never garnered much respect for her work, and at least once, depressed over a box-office flop, she attempted suicide. A life-long alcoholic, she was married eight times to seven different husbands. One marriage was annulled, and the rest ended in divorce. Her love affairs with famous men – Tyrone Power, Howard Hughes – were similarly unhappy and short-lived. Inherited Rh-factor complications ruled out the large family she had dreamed of, but she did bear one child, a daughter, who was only saved from death at birth by an immediate blood transfusion.

FAST FORWARD

Famous names, clever classmates, gold clapboard buildings, wine and cocktails on a wide veranda overlooking stubble fields and the rumpled shoulders of Robert Frost's fabled Green Mountains: this is the conference. Every morning, in a converted, whitewashed barn called the Little Theatre, over a hundred of us gather to hear faculty and fellows talk about the writing life. *Follow your obsessions*, they say. *Write about what matters to you. Write what bothers you, what you can't get your head around. Write what keeps you awake.* Later, in class, we critique one another's efforts and our instructors advise: *Bring authority of significance to your own stories.* Afternoons, we hike in the woods and pastures. New York agents and editors come to call. Every night, the moon ascends over the mountains and two hundred of us leave our rooms in the clapboard dorms and file into the Little Theatre again, and the screen doors swing shut and the lights go down – all except for one light at the podium, like a campfire glowing in darkness. We angle ourselves onto folding chairs, pull our sweaters tighter against the chill, and listen as one after another the authors take the stage, and above the trilling of crickets, above the din of our own minds, their voices rise – whispering, beseeching, correcting, caressing, complaining, explaining, shouting, persuading, teasing, berating, comforting, lying, and laying it on the line – a symphony of sound, resonating to the rafters, leaving enduring echoes, weaving indelible magic.

PLAY

Every morning, I called home. I woke early, still on toddler-time. Mist shrouded the mountains. Dew dampened the hems of my jeans as I crossed the lawn to an old-fashioned phone booth that stood in the field next to the laundry compound. I dialled the number, waited for the ring.

"I love you, Sweet Bean."

"Mama. I went to the park. I throwed a ball. I swam in the pool."

"The pool! Was the water cold?"

"A tiny tiny tiny bit cold."

The sound of breathing. In the background, Mark walking past, heavy-heeled on our creaky wood floors. A cupboard door closing. Then, "Mama. Where are you?"

I drew faces on the booth's foggy glass. A smiley face. A puzzled face. A frown. "How's she doing?" I'd say to Mark when he came on the line.

"She's fine," he assured me. "She's happy. She loves the tapes."

STOP

If Lana Turner had hoped for an easy child, her daughter, Cheryl Crane, must have proved a disappointment. Spoiled and sullen-looking in her early photos, Cheryl later became rebellious and unruly. She had her reasons. At ten, she confided that her mother's current husband, Lex Barker, or "Tarzan," had been sexually abusing her for the past three years. To her credit – considering how desperate she was for male attention and approval – Lana defended her daughter. In a performance worthy of one of her films, she withdrew a gun from a drawer next to her sleeping husband's bed, nudged the muzzle to his ear, and said, "Get out."

Four years later, Cheryl assumed the role of avenging female. For some time, Lana had been trying to extricate herself from an abusive relationship with a small-time hoodlum named Johnny Stompanato. Stompanato refused to leave. One night Cheryl overheard them fighting in her mother's room and became frightened. As their voices rose in anger and Stompanato began threatening to cut her mother's face – the family's livelihood – and to hurt her grandmother, she ran to the kitchen and grabbed a carving knife, which happened to be lying on the counter. Returning upstairs, she begged her mother to open the door. Stompanato stood with his back to her, leaning over her mother, grasping something in his hands – a weapon, Cheryl believed, or so she later said, although in fact he held a bundle of his clothes, still clinging to their hangers. Over her mother's frantic protests, Cheryl lunged and stabbed him.

Fast Forward

One of my obligations as a scholar at this conference is to give a reading in the Little Theatre. I think about reading from the essay about my daughter and my stomach clenches. That piece is too long, too personal, too difficult to excerpt, too domestic, too dependent on all its parts for a true effect, I tell myself. What I mean is, that piece is too revealing, too raw. Or maybe it's just too real. I scroll through the documents folder on my laptop, looking for something more suitable.

But walking out by the river one afternoon, reflecting on the history of this place, counting the names of writers who've come here in the past – Anne Sexton, Truman Capote, Toni Morrison, May Sarton, Ralph Ellison – I am overcome by an ideal of literature as life-changing. *Write your obsessions, write what matters to you, write what you can't get your head around.* That's what those writers did. They wrote about sex and madness and death and childhood and loneliness and race, and their stories came from their own lives, and they didn't play it safe. I'm playing with the thought of a book. When else will I get to test this material on so large an audience? Suddenly, it seems cowardly not to read from this essay, the essay that I might – or might not – expand. After all, what's the worst that could happen? Nobody here knows me. Nobody knows my daughter.

I approach the podium, peer into the lights, pretend to look at an audience that I can't see through the glare. Leaning hard onto the surface of the wood to prevent myself from shaking, I read. And – surprise! – it's over almost before I know it. Afterward, I look up from my pages to find myself surrounded. Editors of journals press their cards into my hand, inviting submissions. Faculty members offer congratulations. Days later, participants collar me in the cafeteria line or sidle closer under the shade of those wide verandas. *My son was like that. My wife works with kids like yours. My cousin just adopted a kid like the one you wrote about. My sister-in-law has two daughters like that.* Everyone, it seems, has a similar story.

Everyone wants to know more. I try not to become too inflated with self-regard.

STOP

An exciting new voice. A bold, authentic voice. A stylish, urban voice. A raw, unvarnished voice. A mature voice in full possession of its powers. Loved the voice! Sorry, we didn't like the voice. I've found my voice. I've lost my voice.

FAST FORWARD

With my instructor's permission, I substitute this piece for the one I'd originally submitted, and ask my classmates to consider how it might be expanded, opened up, for a book. I don't know what I expect. Probably more of what happened at the reading. Most of my classmates are working on books themselves. Some of my classmates were in that audience, some were part of the group that later surrounded me. So what happens comes as a rude surprise.

Here are the things my classmates say:

Hard to say how you could do this; you're still in the middle of it.
It's not your story. It's your daughter's story.
You shouldn't write this. It's too risky for your child.
You'll ruin your daughter's life.
Can't see this as a book.
It's wrong to write about a child.

Don't worry. You'll find other subjects.
If you must write this, put it in a drawer.

Here is what our Teaching Fellow says (she's a girl; she wears ankle-strap wedgies in dark red kid, the kind that Lana Turner might have worn, and I want a pair):
Ethically, this is wrong. It would represent a huge betrayal.
Writing it would violate confidentiality, and would irreparably damage your relationship with your daughter.

Here is what my instructor, the famous memoirist, says:
Renunciation is also a part of the writing life.
I would worry about you as a person and a writer if you pushed yourself into the limelight with this material.
Save yourself as a writer.

STOP
Lana Turner died in 1995 of throat cancer.

FAST FORWARD
My Canadian reserve collapses. Tears gush from my eyes, trail down my cheeks, and trickle to my chest. I think of Niagara Falls. We always knew that our side held more water. My classmates pretend they don't notice. They keep on talking, saying again what they've already said. Nobody offers me a break. Nobody offers a tissue. I wipe my face with the back of my bare arm. The woman beside me, a therapist in her regular life, fishes in her bag and retrieves a thin paper napkin, the kind you find on the tabletops of diners in aluminium dispensers, the kind that Lana Turner might have dabbed to her lips when a stranger approached her in the Top Hat Café with his card. My classmate hands me this napkin before resuming her arguments against my project. Her eyes are soft and brown but something in their expression reminds me of a puppy you might find digging up your garden. He's sorry. But only because he's been caught.

At the mid-point of the workshop, after they are done with me and ready to move on to the next victim, I try to get into the bathroom. But someone has beat me to it, so I spend the next hour piggy-eyed, blotchy, and silent throughout discussion of my classmate's submission. My tears continue to flow. I have never cried this much in public. I can't remember the last time

I cried this much, period. Maybe when I was a teenager? After class, my humiliation complete, I retreat to my room, where I lie face-down on the bed. Like the schoolgirl I've been reduced to.

STOP

The symptoms of cancer of the throat, or larynx, depend mainly on the size and location of the tumor. Most cancers of the larynx begin on the vocal cords. These tumors are seldom painful, but they almost always cause hoarseness or other changes in the voice.[2]

FAST FORWARD

I wear sunglasses to my meeting with the instructor. I apologize for crying in class.

"Oh," she says. "No need to apologize. We all come here for professional validation and advancement. I *expected* you to break down. I just wasn't sure when."

Behind my glasses, I blink, grateful for their protection.

"You know," she muses, "your story reminds me a bit of one that I have wanted to write for a long while, about a friend of mine who is a priest ... and a pedophile. Nobody wants me to write this story. People don't want to hear that he might not be evil, or that I might want to know him anyway."

She's been wearing sunglasses, too. She takes them off. Her face, round, pale, and unlined, does not betray her age, does not reveal a thing about who she might be. "I haven't written that story," she says. "It makes people uncomfortable."

STOP

I've promised my family that each may pass on the book. I've promised to take out anything that anyone objects to — anything at all ... I don't believe in a writer's kicking around people who don't have access to a printing press. They can't defend themselves.
– Annie Dillard[3]

Writers are always selling somebody out.
– Joan Didion[4]

Writing ... is like rearing children.
– Annie Dillard[5]

rewind

Write about what obsesses you. Write what bothers you, what you can't get your head around. Write what keeps you awake.

My daughter is what obsesses me. My daughter keeps me awake.

record

Once upon a time there was a writer who could spin words into gold. She was as gentle as she was gifted and as kind as she was keen, and growing up she paid close attention to her unusual and unhappy family and to her feelings about them – as most writers do. Her first book, a collection of pellucid autobiographical stories, won the acclaim of critics, the admiration of readers, and the agony and ire the family members she had drawn upon in creating her "troubled" characters. The writer smiled modestly for the cameras and took her bows in public, winced and grieved and repented in private, and then, like all good writers, she sat down to work on Book Number Two. But before she got far into it, the writer married and bore children, and the children needed nursing and then their noses needed wiping and then they needed clothes and books and college funds, and the writer took a job, because Book Number Two wasn't finished yet and not even the strong sales of her first collection could feed her ravenous family.

Nighttimes, in her basement office, the writer wrote. But having used her family for the first book she was shy of doing so again. She worried that her work was too purely personal. She worried that she was nothing but a navel-gazer. She wanted to make a difference in the world. But between calls from the school and Halloween treats and dentist appointments and doctor appointments and nightly tuck-ins with her kids, the words came in fits and starts, jerky and then slow – so slow, so cryptic sometimes, that they felt almost like semaphore. So one day, on a tip from a good friend, the writer decided that she needed a change of genres. She would forget about writing stories for a while. She would take her gift for telegraphed images and write for television, write scripts that brought attention to serious political problems, scripts that showed she was more than a mere "domestic" scribbler, more than a navel-gazer.

Sure enough – because she was a good writer, a writer whose touch could turn anything to gold – success followed. Awards, articles in the press, offers of more work. The writer felt happy. She'd produced something that had reached a wide audience – a much wider audience than any literary book could reach. Something that might help others. Still – in the darkness of her basement office, her desk lamp beaming onto her brown hair, if she was honest with herself she had to admit it: she missed words. She missed language, her first love, and she longed to dive deep into a narrative. She was, after all, a writer.

One day, after a long dry spell, a story occurred to her. The story concerned a journey she had taken with her children. It touched on all her most pressing obsessions. Family *and* the world. Domestic *and* political. Not either/or. Both/and. Feverishly, she wrote up a proposal, thinking it through, checking it over, making sure it was the best that it could be. Then she printed it and left it on her desk for one last revision before sending off to her agent. For the first time in many years, she felt excited and hopeful. This was her *real* material. She knew it.

That afternoon when she came home from work, her son – now on the verge of manhood – stood at her desk. His feet, a shoulder's width apart, seemed rooted to the floor. His face – that nose she'd wiped, those teeth she'd paid to straighten, those lips that had lisped his first words of love to her – was dark. He held the proposal in his hand. "Am I in this story?" he said.

The writer said nothing. She shivered, as at a sudden gust of wind. She watched the pages of her manuscript fly out of her son's hands and skirt the walls. Some of the pages sped out the window, scudded through the yard, and flapped against the trees and the telephone wires. Some of the pages soared up, up to the west, swooping and darting like seagulls until they disappeared in the wide dark. Some of those pages sped toward her open mouth, surged down her throat, gagged that scream that struggled to rise, wadded themselves into a lump, choked her.

"I don't want you to write about me," her son said.

The writer said nothing. There was nothing to say. She took the pages from her son and rent them to bits. Book Number Two did not appear.

STOP

Surgery to remove part or all of the larynx is a partial or total laryngectomy. In either operation, the surgeon performs a tracheostomy, creating an opening called a stoma in the front of the neck. (The stoma may be temporary or permanent). Air enters and leaves the trachea and lungs through this opening. A tracheostomy tube, also called a trach ("trake") tube, keeps the new airway open.

A partial laryngectomy preserves the voice. The surgeon removes only part of the voice box, just one vocal cord, part of a cord, or just the epiglottis, and the stoma is temporary. After a brief recovery period, the trach tube is removed, and the stoma closes up. The patient can then breathe and talk in the usual way. In some cases, however, the voice may be hoarse or weak.

In a total laryngectomy, the whole voice box is removed, and the stoma is permanent. The patient, called a laryngectomee, breathes through the stoma. A laryngectomee must learn to talk in a new way.[6]

FAST FORWARD

I do not talk much to my classmates outside of workshop. But one day one of them spies me in the lunch line. "I've been thinking," she says. "People *do* write about their kids. They write about them all the time. Maybe we were a bit hasty in class."

This is generous of her; if anyone has reason to feel threatened by the essay I wrote, she does. She was once a foster child. Her story, while not identical to my daughter's, echoes those themes of loss and longing and violence.

She's right, of course. People do write about their kids. But mostly they write print versions of those bare bum on the bear rug photos. Gee willakers! What a little dickens! *Kids Say the Darnedest Things.* Their kids may hate them later, but more for lapses of taste than for any serious revelations about their lives.

STOP

Voice in writing, identified variously as style, persona, stance, or ethos, has never been very clearly defined, and, as a consequence, there has never been a consistent methodology for how to use it in the teaching of writing. Although these definitional and methodological problems have frequently been chronicled in the journals (see, for example, Hashimoto; Leggo), the voice metaphor, which emerged in the 1970s, remains extraordinarily popular ... and has a strong presence in contemporary discussions of writing.[7]

REWIND

If you must write it, put it in a drawer.
Put it in a drawer? Who am I, Emily Dickinson?
Tell the truth. But tell it slant.

Fast Forward

I meet on the grass with our Fellow. She, of the pretty shoes, of the dire warnings and grave predictions. She, who looks so beautiful and so serious and so exhausted on the jacket photo of her first book, a memoir about her heroin-addict mother.

I ask the question that's been bothering me. Was it something I said? Was there anything in that first essay – the one I brought to the class – was there anything in the *writing*, that led her to believe I might treat this material in an exploitative way?

No, she says. It wasn't the writing. The writing was fine. The writing was good. The essay was "beautiful." But the situation is inherently exploitative. My daughter, I'd said, had been traumatized by her history of abandonment and orphanage neglect. To write a book about my daughter's trauma would be to reinscribe it. It would be a huge betrayal. "To a non-writer, a book is the truth."

"Suppose I wrote a book of poems?"

"Oh." She pauses. "That would be okay. That would be different."

But why? Because nobody would read it?

STOP

Lana Turner was fifteen (according to her) or sixteen (according to most sources) on the day that Billy Wilkerson, a journalist with the Hollywood Reporter – a writer, not a talent scout – spotted her at the Top Hat a Café, gave her his card, and told her to give him a call. Lana had no acting experience.

rewind

I would worry about you if you pushed yourself into the limelight with this material. Bust foremost, like Lana Turner, the Sweater Girl. All flash, no substance.

Save yourself as a writer.

Save myself for what?

Having come to writing late (too afraid, too unsure, too concerned that I couldn't find my voice), having laboured already for nearly my full complement of "ten years in the cold" once prophesied to apprentice writers by Ted Solaratoff, having published a long string of short pieces that may win awards but don't win me recognition or respect, I don't *want* to put aside my own ambitions. Not once I've found my material.

Renunciation is a part of the writing life.

I am no stranger to renunciation. I love my child without expectation of return. Must I love my work the same way?

Save yourself as a writer. It smacks of saving myself for marriage. There is something illicit, even something erotic in the idea of telling truths about the people we love.

And everybody knows this: mothers must eschew the erotic.

FAST FORWARD

Later, much later, I read my classmates' written comments. They do not sound like what got said in class. Sometimes that happens in workshops. A ball starts rolling and nobody can stop it. It picks up momentum, and so much gets left behind. Now I can see that my classmates liked my writing. They thought I had an important story. They just didn't know if it could be, or should be, a book. They didn't know because they weren't experienced. None of them had written a book. (The instructors had written books, though, and they thought I should not write this one.)

Later still, I think about the people in that class. Most were daughters. Not one, as I recall it, was a mother. Not one.

STOP

Cheryl Crane was arrested and charged with the murder of Johnny Stompanato. Despite confusing evidence – including a lack of fingerprints on the weapon and an absence of blood at the scene – a coroner's inquest ruled it "justifiable homicide," and Cheryl went free. But she and Lana Turner remained alienated for a long time – according to some accounts, for almost forty years, or until her mother's death.

REWIND

Writing this will irreparably ruin your relationship with your daughter.

I've often wondered whether I'm to blame. Whether that long separation for the first writers' conference was the cause or at least the catalyst for Maia's later anger and anxiety and violence. Her reactions at the time had seemed normal. She had welcomed me home. We'd slipped back into our routines like otters returning to water. The problems hadn't surfaced until later. They had seemed complex, so complex that the psychiatric labels couldn't cover them, so complex that no one cause could be found. But what if the reason had been staring us in the face? What if it was all my fault?

Your story reminds me of one that I want to write, about my friend, the priest who is also a pedophile. When is a child like a pedophile? (You can't portray a pedophile as good in any way. You can't portray a child as bad in any way. People want the simple story.)

Maybe the writer is the pedophile. Abuser. Exploiter.

PLAY

As Maia matured, it became clear that she has what teachers call an "auditory learning style." That is to say, she learns primarily by listening. She also shows a gift for words. Her puns startle and amuse. Her vocabulary rivals that of children twice her age. She reads aloud with enthusiasm and intonation, mimics newscasters and our guests, and can retell a story as told to her, exact in all its parts.

How great a role did those tapes that I made for her play in the development of these strengths?

FAST FORWARD

It takes me almost a year to write this essay. To say that I compose it would imply a calm deliberation I don't feel. Writing this feels wrenching. But it's not like pulling teeth. Pulling teeth is a lot easier. At least you know what you are going after. This is more like pulling at entrails. Or untangling a knot. Looking for a thread that I can't find. And every time I do find it, every time I get a purchase, feel a loosening, something interrupts me. So I start. Stop. Start again. Go over what I've already done. Change it. Stop. Change it back.

Sometimes, I am the cause of these interruptions. Me. My own fears. My own worries. My own process and problems and angst. But often my daughter interrupts. She falls from a fence, needs stitches, and her hard-won calm shatters. So improved over the past months, she begins to rage and hit again, so each morning I sit at the computer with bruised forearms and a sense of discouragement. Then she gets a virus, and I have to give up my writing hours to care for her. Then I am volunteering in her classroom; then it's her gym day, and I need to pick her up early; the next day, she has an appointment with her therapist. That's what it's like.

PLAY

Listening to those tapes, I am struck by the energy in my voice. I'm no actor. But I read with expression, verve, gusto. Individuating each character, from Mortimer, who takes such glee in annoying everybody else, to Shy Charles, who doesn't like to talk. I'm the witch, the princess, the fairy godmother, and the wolf. I sound happy on those tapes. Even when impersonating a growling ogre, my sense of humour is audible. What I hear in those tapes is pure, uncomplicated, unconditional love. And that's what my daughter listened to, every night. The nights that I was gone and the nights that I was home. During the day, I may have sounded – *must* have sounded – irritated, exhausted, sarcastic, judgemental, disappointed, even despairing at times. But at night, Maia heard a different mother. At night, she fell asleep to joyful heteroglossia.

STOP

Stoma. Stompanato. Eerily similar sounds, the one an abbreviated other. Perhaps this irony occurred to Lana Turner as she lay, those last months, on her deathbed. She was known for her sense of humour, so the thought might have tickled her. Tickled – then lodged in her throat, and become an irritation, an annoyance, maybe a sore. Unvoiced.

PLAY

Before my second trip to the conference, I made a new recording. Instead of a tape, I burned a CD, using the soundtrack on the movie software that came with my computer. It was rough, patched together, but passable, although the built-in mike kept cutting out on me and I had to rush through several of the stories. After recording forty minutes or so – poems I'd written for her, songs, a funny story about a boy who calls himself "King of the Blahs" – I realised that, this being a CD, there was lots of room for more. So I downloaded some Robert Munsch books from the web. Authors as popular as Munsch apparently can afford to give their work away. Maia loved the CD. But later she told me, "I wish it was just you on the CD. I like

Robert Munsch, and I like his stories. But I like your stories better. And I really like to listen to *your* voice."

STOP

Literary critics often speak of "presence" and "codes" and "intertextual discourse" when discussing voice, but writers can scarcely afford to be so theoretical or lofty in their approach. Voice is, to paraphrase Flannery O'Connor, the mud that we use to write.[8]

rewind

"Mama's ... *voices*." Charming mistake, or startling insight? Even on a cheap kids' tape recorder, you can always hear more than one.

record

Like any curious child, Maia liked to play with the buttons on her tape recorder and to experiment with the amplifying feature on its microphone. Parts of those old tapes are blank now, where she has erased them. Parts of them sound with her own words. In her own voice.

notes

1   Lana Turner official website: www.cmgww.com/stars/turner/biography.html.
2   www.medicinenet.com.
3   Dillard, "To Fashion a Text," *The Fourth Genre: Contemporary Writers of/on Creative Nonfiction*, Root and Steinberg, eds, 276.
4   Didion, *Slouching towards Bethlehem*, Preface.
5   Dillard, *The Fourth Genre*, 278.
6   www.medicinenet.com.
7   Bowden, "The Rise of a Metaphor: 'Voice' in Composition Pedagogy," *Rhetoric Review*, vol. 14, no. 1, Autumn 1995.
8   Schwartz, "Finding a Voice in America," *Bringing the Devil to His Knees: The Craft of Fiction and the Writing Life*, Baxter and Turchi, eds, 46.

The Joshua Stone

anne SImpson

> You who were darkness warmed my flesh
> where out of darkness rose the seed.
> Then all a world I made in me;
> all the world you hear and see
> hung upon my dreaming blood ...
>
> "Woman to Child," by Judith Wright[1]

Between Dunn's Beach and Monk's Head in Antigonish County, Nova Scotia, lies a bracelet of sand, one of a string of barrier beaches. I call it the Joshua Beach. Everyone else calls it Boy Scout Beach, which makes me imagine freckle-faced boys handily pitching tents, gathering wood, and roasting hot dogs over campfires. In the distance, to the west, the headlands of Cape George seem ghostly, and, to the east, the blue headlands of Cape Breton fade into the horizon. This is a wild place, dunes laced with marram grass, on the shelf of the Northumberland Strait.

It was there, one late July afternoon a few summers ago, that I picked up a small, round stone. The clouds were low, and the ocean was grey-green, with loosely rolling waves, each one feathered white. My sister was scheduled to have a C-section that day, and I was worried about her. I found the stone and rubbed it between my thumb and fingers, hoping she'd be fine. Was the stone a kind of talisman? Perhaps it was. The birth went well, despite a few complications: a healthy child, my nephew Joshua, came into the world that afternoon. His parents were thrilled, intoxicated, delighted.

For any birth there should be a resounding crash of waves, a piping of plovers, a flight of arrow-sharp terns over the ocean. Banners of blue should be unfurled from east to west. Nothing comes close to the explosive, fecund energy, the sheer force, of birth. One thing takes shape within another; when it is ready, it gathers itself, pushing its way out into the bright glare of the world.

When I was pregnant, host to a life that was not my own, there were times when I thought I had nothing to do with the squirrel-like quickenings, the *making* that was going on in my body. Nor did I have much to do with the delivering of a new life. It was out of my control, and all I could do was give myself over to it. It was body doing what body does so well – generating life.

In my second novel, *Falling*, one of the characters, Ingrid, talks to a man, a stranger, about the birth of her son. She tries to articulate the enormity of it, and the man recalls the birth of his own son. She says, "Then you know what it's like. That moment, at the beginning of things. It's as if you can see further."[2] The work of writing is not only seeing again, in the sense of remembering, or re-envisioning, it is also seeing further. Seeing into things.

❧ I went back to the Joshua Beach this past autumn. It was windy, cold; the tide was up and the sky was the colour of slate. I was there to gather things. Our Labrador dogs, one golden-brown and the other black, raced back and forth along the shore. I found red stones with seams of quartz, heavy rocks flecked with black, a crab claw, ribbons of seaweed, a shard of green glass, broken shells. I lost one black stone. It was flat, but not quite round. I dropped it while slipping on a bit of slick, clay-dark mud that had been washed down from a cliff by the recent storms. I was carrying too much; things were spilling out of my hands. A tiny, pastel-coloured crab shell dropped and smashed. It was then that I saw an eagle lift up over the wetlands behind the ridge of dunes and into the spruce trees. The marram grasses of the intertidal marsh were gold, tinted with orange. Everything else seemed to be shades of silver, grey, or charcoal, but the grass was fiercely bright. And the eagle swept overhead, swerving gently away. It was a moment of seeing into things, as if I were seeing into the wildness of the place and taking it up, carrying it with me, bearing it inside my own body.

♣ I have my collection of gathered things on my desk as I write. There are six stones: one is flat, another is egg-shaped, and three are striped with quartz. I have the crab claw, from which sand trickles out. Almost all of the thick, ropy, very damp seaweed was tossed out by a well-intentioned cleaning woman who comes into my office a couple of times a week. She overlooked one delicate twig-like bit of inky black, sharply branching against the pure white of the clamshell in which it lies.

What do any of these things have to do with motherhood? Maybe not that much, except that my own mothering has grown into a mothering of my children as well as my writing. It has also grown into a mothering of the place in which I live. The whole undertaking has grown larger than I would ever have thought possible.

I pick up one broken mussel shell and run my fingers over the mauve lines in the hard shell. These ridged lines describe its age, as rings tell a tree's life. I think of my son, a newborn child one minute and a young man the next; I have to look up at him when I'm asking for help with the dishes. My daughter, once a round cherub with a fuzz of golden hair, is now slender, dark-haired, and tall as my son. Learning to mother them meant steep learning curves for me as well as my husband. Motherhood, like fatherhood, is passage. Others pass through us. We pass through them. For every change in my children, there was a comparable change in me, just as there was in my husband: from the beginnings of birth and onward to adulthood, there has been a stretching to meet their transformations.

As for all mothers, there is a literal widening and shaping of the body, which translates not only into birth but into a new relationship with the world. I felt flickerings of it in the snow that spun through the blackness of a mid-April night the first time I went into labour. I felt it in the ferocity of labour pains slamming into my body, especially after a venomous green liquid was fed into my arm by IV when I was induced. I felt it when I held a small bundle of a son and, later, a daughter, swaddled in hospital-issued, striped flannel. After such monumental effort, privilege consisted of simply basking in the warmth of love, meeting these children for the first time.

Immediately after my son was born, it struck me that we had not been separated. We slept and woke and slept again. When I felt pain, I was certain he felt it, too. In those dreamlike days, I sensed myself underwater with him. I wrote about this in a poem shortly afterward, trying to convey the watery world we inhabited, where both of us floated, "newly born / tipping from one side to the other, / between water and air."[3] It is intriguing that this sensation of being between worlds is one that approximates creativity. There is the *beginning-to-be* of any work, whether it is a painting or a poem, as it yearns towards being. It moves, flashes, dips. It is on the surface of the ocean for a moment, and then it flips under the waves. It is all a writer can do to catch glimpses of it.

This fragile time of being between worlds didn't last. I had gone through the threshold of becoming a mother; my son was becoming a separate self. The complex, layered difficulties of learning to master things was becoming plain to me. Fatigue to the point of tears. Fear when he lost weight, instead of gaining it. Confusion about feeding. Terror about colic. When my son was only a couple of months old, I remember seeing an advertisement in a parenting magazine. It showed a pretty woman in a white dress, frolicking down a daisy-covered hillside, an infant in her arms. I wanted to rip the pretty woman into pieces. I wanted, savagely, to sleep; I wanted my son to sleep. For some unfathomable reason, I kept a journal, to track the patterns of the unpredictable creature that was my child. One day I flipped back through the pages. Feeding, sleeping, and napping were meticulously logged. The time and length of each screaming bout had been duly noted. I threw out the journal. What had I been thinking? The screaming didn't stop for months, but I wasn't going to record it anymore. As for the white-clad woman dreamily dancing with her baby, I hoped that both of them had gone rolling down a hillside somewhere, tangled up in daisy chains.

There are two sides to motherhood: light and dark. For me, there was the utter contentment of running a finger over the velvet softness of an earlobe, or over the dip of the fontanelle as my child sucked at the breast, mouth aquiver. But there were times when my wailing newborn had me in tears because I couldn't calm him. This is why I am fond of Sylvia Plath's poem "Child," which reveals the stark contrasts of motherhood. It crows with delight: "Your clear eye is the one absolutely beautiful thing. / I want to fill it with colour and ducks, / The zoo of the new." At the same time, the poem doesn't shy away from misery: "... this troublous / Wringing of hands, this dark / Ceiling without a star."[4]

In the middle of our son's colic, on a humid June night, my husband and I saw fireflies outside. It had been a long, hot day with a squalling infant, but my husband called me to look out the screened door of our rented house. There, in the dusky hills beyond the backyard, where the wild roses and a couple of ancient apple trees had not yet fallen to a bulldozer, a miniature light show had begun. I watched the fireflies tracing what might have been messages in the darkness. It was magical.

I could get through it. We could get through it. Was it then that I understood how much I had stretched to meet what had come to me? Was it later? I don't know. But I must have begun writing, because sometime in those early months I sent a poem to *The Malahat Review*. It was the poem I'd written just after giving birth, one that I'd revised in the fragments of time I had to myself. It wasn't the first thing I'd written, but it was the first I'd ever sent out for consideration.

It was accepted.

❧ There was a two-and-a-half-year span between the births of my two children. At some point during that interval I started to paint again. I asked if I could set up an easel in the Art Department at St Francis Xavier University; for at least three mornings a week after my son was about eight months old, I worked there. On those mornings, I took my son to a babysitter who took care of her own child as well. Perhaps because time was so limited, those hours were furiously productive. Some of the paintings weren't successful, but some of them were: I wasn't sure how it happened that there was a convergence of an actual birth with a creative outpouring. It wasn't just an impulse to paint, it was as if I were compelled to do it. A surplus, an over-abundance within me, needed expression.

Annie Dillard writes about fecundity in *Pilgrim at Tinker Creek*. She talks about nature not knowing when to stop. It is generative; it is multiple; it knows no limits. Certainly creativity can arrive in such spillage that it threatens to disturb balance. As Dillard points out, "the driving force behind all this fecundity is a terrible pressure I also must consider, the pressure of birth and growth, the pressure that splits the bark of trees and shoots out seeds, that squeezes out the egg and bursts the pupa, that hungers and lusts and drives the creature relentlessly toward its own death."[5]

To have children is to be vulnerable to having them die, even as we witness the energy of their vitality. No wonder the very act of making can be feverish. We are up against it. The children we bring into the world are up against it. Yet, backed into a corner, we go on making.

The winter after my daughter was born was a time of snowfalls. One upon the other, the blizzards hit our house on Hawthorne Street. In the nighttime, when I was up with her, the wind howled, rattling the windows. During the day, I looked out to see the drifts made by the snowplough growing higher and higher. There were spellbound joys in that quiet time: my daughter was a gorgeous, healthy baby, never more so than when I picked her up from the yellow-lined bassinet where she napped. But it was winter outside, and the drifts grew into a nearly solid wall of white. I didn't go out much. If it happened that both children were sleeping, I tried to write. I had set aside the work of painting because it was impractical. How could I manage such big canvasses now? How could I get out of the house to paint? I stopped painting and set myself to writing instead, because I could do it at home. And I could send it out, which I began to do, over and over.

❦ Motherhood is passage, and it is also, of course, relationship. One being carries and sustains another, so that the two are intertwined and interdependent. Yet the full significance of reciprocity, obvious as it is, only became clear to me lately. One summer evening, while I was walking with a friend on the Joshua Beach, I began musing about jellyfish. It was mid-July, and my friend and I were watching the small jellyfish pulsing in to shore. They weren't large; they were limpid and nearly transparent, except for their purplish domes and trailing tentacles. Because they were almost clear, the idea of things passing in and out of them was all the more obvious. They digest their food very swiftly to move more efficiently through the water. I was bound to air; the jellyfish was bound to water. Air went in and out of my lungs. I was partly air, just as I was partly water. Like the jellyfish, I wasn't separate from the world around me.

I began to think about my husband's description of the placenta. It was, he said, a purse-shaped mass of brilliant scarlet. For some reason, I imagined it to be as vividly red as the firebird, that magnificent creature of folklore. It was through the placenta that I'd given sustenance to another being. I wish I'd seen it. It would have allowed me to see the tangible link between my body and another one. But I didn't need to see it to know the fierceness I felt for my children.

We are part of the world, part of one another. We can't afford to stand back and merely observe. To be a mother is, essentially, to be a participant, a maker *in* the world. But it is more than this. To be a mother is also to be one of the makers *of* the world.

I see a long line of mothers like a set of Russian dolls, each containing the next. Women shaped my world: my great-grandmother, my grandmother, my mother, my sisters, my cousins. I stand within the intricate web of these relationships, drawing on the experience of others. What I've learned from them is how to mother and how to be mothered. In other words, I've learned how to create. I haven't just fallen in love with my own children, I have "fallen in love outward," as the poet Robinson Jeffers has Orestes say, at the end of *The Tower beyond Tragedy*.[6] With motherhood, as with writing, the boundaries of self are stretched to the very limit. We see into otherness.

❧ When I found the round, white stone that reminded me of a miniature Brancusi sculpture of a child's head, I picked it up. I rolled it in my palm. I saved it. I knew I'd write to my nephew Joshua one day about that beach, that wild, imperfectly beautiful place at the edge of the ocean.

Later I went to the local art gallery and had the stone put in a shadow box, against dark velvet, where it became a kind of luminous token. When I saw it in its shadow box, I thought, "It's a birth stone." It was a stone the size of an oversized walnut, containing its own making and unmaking.

notes

1 Wright, "Woman to Child," *The Penguin Book of Women Poets*, Cosman, ed., 379.
2 Simpson, *Falling*.
3 Simpson, *Light Falls through You*.
4 Plath, "Child," *The Penguin Book of Women Poets*, Cosman, ed., 356.
5 Dillard, *Pilgrim at Tinker Creek*, 164.
6 Jeffers, *The Selected Poems of Robinson Jeffers*, 112.

Motherhood and the Muses

noreen sнαναнаn

I clean houses for a living. I clean houses and while the rag swashes and the vacuum hums, my mind constructs moments of living, little stories, diamonds in the dust. Later, once the job is done, I take out my spiral-bound notebook and write it all down. Joining me on the path toward this birth of words come my lover, Heather, and my son, Toto, a boy who shares a name with the dog who trots along beside Dorothy on the Yellow Brick Road. (I actually named him Toto because it means "mother and child" in Swahili.) My son is my inspiration. He is the reason I clean and write and strain to keep our own home together and all bills promptly paid. He is the reason I carefully date and store my notebooks in a dry basement and remember to empty the dehumidifier. Not only do I enjoy our beautifully entwined lives, I also use my notebooks as a written testament. He is my inspiration, but is he also my muse?

Zeus slept with Mnemosyne. Three seasons later, on the snowy peak of Mount Olympus, Mnemosyne bore nine daughters: these were the Muses. The mother of the muses, Mnemosyne, is the personification of Memory. Her nine wee babes became her "Little Reminders" – reminders to be creative. As a cleaning lady, I don't do windows, but I spend many hours looking from them. I'm not referring to ticking-off the actual minutes while on a job. It's more as a metaphor for life. Like Chauncey Gardner, I like to watch. Life is perpetually interesting to me and becomes more – alive

– if I can write about it. The illustrator Edward Gorey, when asked in a *Vanity Fair* interview what was his favourite journey, promptly said: "Looking from my window."[1]

One morning, while spooning Shreddies into our mouths, Toto and I watch our neighbour Anna in her floral housedress pluck dead blossoms from her bounty; an old Ukrainian woman who lives alone with her flowers, silently in love with beauty and giving it to so many of us, her neighbours and passersby on Fermanagh Avenue in Toronto's Parkdale neighbourhood.

Early this spring, I ran into Anna at the corner of Roncesvalles, balancing a thirty-pound bag of fertilizer on top of a rusted shopping cart. Anna is in her mid-eighties. I am in my mid-forties. I parked my bike then pushed and tugged along with her. Anna speaks no English, not even hellos and goodbyes, so we sweated silently, smiling whenever we could. Arriving back at her place, Anna slid me a few coins. No, I said, I won't take your money. I walked away letting the coins land on the pavement between us. Anna picked them up, pocketed them in her apron, and began tossing manure onto the soil that feeds her peonies, roses, tulips, and sweet William.

Summer deepened. Wave after wave of heat scorched Parkdalians until one day Anna was felled in her garden by a stroke. An ambulance was called. She was admitted to St Joseph's hospital and six weeks later hadn't returned. Anna's garden ached for her watering can. For a few days, Toto and I watched her flowers wilt and droop then took up arms: we crossed the street and with Anna in mind latched ourselves onto not one but two hoses: front yard and back. While our own garden was forced into a slight state of neglect, we made certain that Anna's garden continued to flourish. Every day at dusk we were over there, caught inside colour just as Georgia O'Keefe was once similarly captured by her white camellias and blue morning glories. "Nobody sees a flower, really, it is so small," O'Keefe once said. "We haven't time." O'Keefe gave us beauty – and so has Anna. As with Thalia, the muse of "festivity, lyric and blooming," there's a literal sense in how Toto and I linked arms then linked ourselves to gardening hoses and encouraged more blooms from Anna's suffering flowers. Each night, I wrote the story up in my notebook.

My son insisted we remember this particular neighbourhood adventure. As a tangible reminder he placed a fistful of pansies in a slim vase on the kitchen table. ("Pansy" comes from "pensée": to think. The pansy's face is said to be a thoughtful one.) Very soon, my son and I will perch ourselves on the bench in front of our house and splash paint onto the palette to imitate the colours in Anna's garden. In flight, like a blossom, will be her get-well card.

Toto is my reminder that there is more to life than work, that once the cleaning job is finished I will be able to look from windows and write about what I see. A reminder that he is waiting for me, somewhere, if only to cook his dinner, monitor his homework, or quiz him for a French dictée. He is ever-present, and together we create memory. This other, the housecleaning, is another kind of ever-present, more about gooey stains on carpets and nasty grunge smeared behind table legs. Sometimes, when I'm struggling on my knees in the dirty homes of strangers, my cellphone will ring, and it will be Toto: "Can we order pizza for dinner?"

If Toto is *muse* and I am *memory* (Mnemosyne), it's worth examining ways in which we enact these roles. John Edgar Wideman, in an essay called "Looking at Emmett Till" had some powerful things to say about memory. "We depend on memory's capacity to hold many lives, not just the one we appear to be leading at the moment. Memory is space for storing lives we didn't lead, room where they remain alive, room for mourning them, forgiving them."[2] This makes me think of the nine muses, each embodying different spokes on the wheel of creativity; each inspiring her Mother/ Memory to make sense of life through art. When I examine this in light of my mother-work, I think about how I store memory for Toto, adventures like "Anna's Garden."

As a middle-aged mother, I also can't help thinking of the tabula rasa that my child was and how, in a sense, I get another shot at life, at childhood, through loving him. Like when he was a baby and I'd take him to the playground; we'd both get filthy in the sandbox before high-flying it to the swings. Although he is only one body and I am only one other body, I believe several lives dance around inside each of us. Through my writing, I hold the shared memories of our adventures.

Cleaning pays the bills and frees me up to write. I'm able to do predictable, mundane housework in these homes while simultaneously writing a story in my head then within a few hours lending it language. All this is fine. But what does it mean to my son? Does he inspire me in my cleaning work as well? It's a harder thing to examine, because it also raises difficult questions regarding identity, class, stigma, and shame, highlights the ways in which our particular mother-son relationship negotiates complex social and emotional terrain.

Is Toto ashamed of me for being a cleaner? Some details: I am a full-time lesbian mother with a child who lives with me half time. The other halftime he lives with his two dads. His homes straddle very different socioeconomic spheres: ours is a small rented bungalow in Parkdale; his dads own a large house on the Forest Hill ravine, just up the street from Casa Loma. Toto attends a private school where the average family has either a nanny or a housekeeper or both. Toto and his dads have Maria, a woman who has been cleaning their home since before he was born. I venture to guess that my son understands and experiences class and gender in a more complex way than the average child.

Toto occasionally joins me on cleaning gigs. Sometimes, for a few bucks, he dusts walnut what-nots or greases up piano pedals for me. If he isn't in the mood to work, I'll settle him in front of the TV, careful to click the door shut so the roar of the vacuum doesn't disturb him. It reminds me of Canadian novelist Adele Wiseman's *Crackpot*, which opens with a Montreal cleaning lady, circa 1920. Rahel brought her young daughter, Hoda, along with her to each job. In some ways, things weren't too complicated for this fictional child. Hoda only lived in one home with one mom and one dad. Her mother wasn't a writer and housecleaner combined. Hoda knew her place and stayed there – although sometimes only clinging by her toenails. My son, on the other hand, slides back and forth in terms of class and seems to manage the shifts quite well. For instance, he sometimes passes on cleaning tips from Maria, and assures me she wouldn't mind talking to me more about it. He also lets me know when his friends are looking for a new cleaning lady. His grade-5 parent newsletter once ran an ad for a housecleaner. "Why don't you apply, Mom?" he asked.

Alas, my sweet little boy became a teenager seven months ago, and so nothing is predictable anymore. For the first time in his life, he chooses *not* to out his gay parents; for the first time, he asks us *not* to pick him up at school; for the first time, he wants to know just *how much money* I earn as a writer and when the heck I'll be famous anyway. These days, Toto is more likely to greet me in the morning with a strongly worded command rather than a dreamy "Morning, Mom" spoken in a soft, pre-cracked voice. These days, as we settle into our routines, he's more likely to nudge me toward my computer by saying: "Finish your book, Mom!" I'm talking about his current role as a 6′2″, 185-pound nag.

Perhaps I made a mistake, a few years ago, in telling him I'm writing a book about my life as a cleaner and in sharing news of my writing. Perhaps he thinks his nagging is prompting or inspiring me toward my task. But he's not a book agent, or a publisher, or even a reader of my laboured words; he's just a lovely, awkward, teenage boy.

"How much more do you still have to write?" he'll ask.

"I don't know, eighty or ninety pages."

"Well, Mom, if you write a page a day, or even write that same page over and over again ten times, it would still only take you about three months to finish your book."

It's pointless to say: "Wait a minute, I'm the mother here – go do your homework!" because he does it anyway, without prodding. He's an excellent student. But maybe the ways in which our roles have shifted – beginning when he first towered over my five-foot frame – don't settle all that well on me. The muse that was my little tousle-haired golden boy has left the room and is replaced by a huge monster who twigs my writer's conscience daily, even if it's done in love.

I am no longer protected from the scorn of his more mature views; the ways in which he internalizes the limiting opinions of his enlarging world; the ways in which 'difference' is becoming a little bit more frightening to him. I've yet to discover how this will transpire in terms of my being a housecleaner. I suppose he might ask me to go back to university and get a *good job*, like his dads have.

I believe this is just one more step on the road to becoming less perfect in his eyes – something all parents must experience in one way or another, if their child is to successfully separate. Sometimes it feels like being unceremoniously booted from Mount Olympus, a god no longer. It also reminds me of a Looney Tunes cartoon I watched as a kid, where a cleaner quietly sweeps the spotlight away once the star has left the stage. I'm both the cleaner and the has-been superstar.

The nine muses are inseparable, writes theorist Nor Hall. They are aspects of each other in the way that inspiration, form, content, and performance are aspects of one event. "They are the great Awakeners," she writes, "the divine uplifters of our psyche's life."[3] Just like their mama, the muses are conduits of memory, passing stories back and forth in a kind of symbiotic dance.

My partner, Heather, and I went to an opening gala of the International Festival of Authors the other night. The event, held in Toronto, was called "Lives of Girls and Women." It began with Alice Munro reading from her early short-story collection and continued with a discussion on freedom of expression by Ann-Marie MacDonald, Deepa Mehta, and Dionne Brand. One thing that struck me about this evening was how deeply stirred each woman was by either her own children or other young writers. MacDonald spoke about being knee-deep in toddlers and gathering inspiration from their little lives. Both Munro's and Mehta's daughters have published books about their mothers. Dionne Brand read from "Baghdad Burning," a blog from Afghanistan about daily life at war, written by a twenty-four-year-old Baghdadi woman. I was also struck with how memory is simultaneously held by both the older artists on stage and the younger generation who inspires them or, indeed, writes its own stories. Mehta's daughter, Devyani Saltzman, wrote about what it was like working with her mother during a period of filming in India. Both women shared the experience of being attacked by Hindu Fundamentalists who disagreed with the stories they were telling. Mehta's film is called "Water"; her daughter's book is called "Shooting Water." Symbiosis indeed.

Regardless of the Greek origin of the word, can a child be a muse to an adult? While it's true that Carroll had Alice, and Rowling had her daughter Jessica, most of the muses I have read about were grown women who "a-mused" their men. In Francine Prose's *The Lives of the Muses*, she examines a range of such women: from Dante's Beatrice to John's Yoko. Tipping her hat to the myth, she selected as a subtitle *Nine Women and the Artists They Inspired*.

Prose writes: "Not entirely coincidentally, the various subsidiary activities included in the muse's job description – nurturing, sustaining, supporting, encouraging – are traditionally considered to be woman's work."[4] Traditional women's work? Like cleaning a house, for instance? Like mothering? It was indeed my hard work that got the pizza on the table for us that night he phoned. It is also my hard work, discipline, and dedication that puts the words on the page, regardless of whether we look from the same window or share many of the same stories; regardless of how often he is my inspiration. Yet, as a feminist, Prose dispels the stereotype of the muse as passive beauty put on a pedestal and oppressed by a male artist. She is almost entirely convinced that in order to be a muse, except for Alice, you have to be an all-grown-up woman.

So, is Toto my muse? Still pondering this question over breakfast this morning, I decided to go directly to the source.

"Are you my muse?" I asked.

"What's a muse?" he replied.

A hasty lesson followed, continuing as we grabbed our coats and left the house. "No," he concluded, "I am not your muse – Heather is." I got thinking a bit more about muses and souls and psyches and such while waiting for the streetcar. The boy had a point. It is my partner, Heather, who encourages me to write and supports this heady habit. It is she who remembers many of the stories I choose to tell; it is she who supports the flow of words and encourages me to send them out into the world on the wing of Pegasus. Even these words, for example.

"I really think you need to loosen up a bit. Otherwise the reader will sense that you're holding back and it'll piss them off."

"Yeah, but what if Toto reads it and feels like I'm using him? Like I'm telling too much about his life? I mean how many teenage boys want to be referred to as their mother's muse anyway?"

"But you're allowed to examine it. In fact you want to examine it, so don't shut yourself down so much. I mean let's face it, if he doesn't mind still being called Toto – and I know he doesn't – than he won't mind anything! Now, my darling, have a glass of wine."

It is Heather, not Toto, who stumbles under the weight of grocery bags, turning their contents into heavenly meals while I sit in the next room scribbling away in a notebook. The clatter of her stirring a pot; aromas melting toward me; that lovely *pop* of the Chardonnay.

These are some of the sensual delights offered not by my son, whom I love dearly and moment-by-moment gain inspiration from, but by my lover, who more often lends an ear to my celestial cries and almost always, like a pigeon pecking peanuts, cleans up my copy. And later – distancing us even more from Francine Prose's rather limited idea of muse – I'm the one who washes the damn dishes and sweeps the crumbs out the door.

notes

1 Edward Gorey, interview in *Vanity Fair*, from McDermott, *The Elephant House*. California: Pomegranate Communications, 2003.

2 Wideman, "Looking at Emmett Till," *In Fact: The Best of Creative Non-Fiction*, Gutkind, ed., 24–8.

3 Hall, "Channel A Muse," *Spring Journal: A Journal of Archetype and Culture*, Spring 2004.

4 Prose, *The Lives of the Muses: Nine Women and the Artists They Inspired*.

Dreams: The First, Irreplaceable Maps

ELIZABETH GREENE

(February 1977) I am trying to catch a plane. I manage to get to the airport, in spite of traffic, get through knots of people to discover that mysteriously there is no security, no one issuing boarding passes. Even so, I am afraid it's too late. Next I'm out on the runway; the plane is still there. There are other people in front of me, who may or may not be traveling. I am polite. I don't push. I stay in line. The door closes, the steps are pulled up. The plane leaves without me because I have been too polite.

I wake up shaken, afraid it's too late. Too late for what? My writing? I am on my first sabbatical in Toronto writing a short novel, a modernization of the Middle English Romance *Sir Orfeo*. Or maybe it's a baby? I'm thirty-three, newly tenured at Queen's. I love teaching. George and I have recently bought an old house. But I still don't have any presence as a writer. I have spent the past seven years finishing a novel and have spent this sabbatical year writing my second novel. An unpublished writer is only half a writer. But the dream recurs. Sometimes I'm missing a train, sometimes I'm missing a plane. I always wake up shaken. Whatever my conscious mind thinks, my unconscious contradicts.

That summer I become pregnant. I don't know I'm pregnant. I think I'm going to die. My breasts are tender; I've missed a period; I'm bleeding between periods; I'm weepy. I'm sure it's breast cancer.

"Nah," says George, "You're just knocked up."

When the doctor tells me I am in fact pregnant, I say to George, "I'm keeping the baby." He has a son from his first marriage, and I know he doesn't want another child. To my surprise, he takes me to the Firehall Restaurant, and we celebrate with white wine and salmon.

"Will you marry me?" he asks.

"Yes," I say, wondering if I'm making a terrible mistake. But I believe the baby, whoever it is, will want its parents to be married.

That baby spontaneously aborts at twelve weeks, jerking out of me in early September in a mass of clots and blood. I am about to start teaching; George and I are planning our wedding; I don't have time to grieve. But my body grieves. I can feel my cells drooping, directionless, as the whole process of growing a child suddenly ends. I wonder what the baby would have been like.

By the end of October I am pregnant again. This time I know I am; I feel my cells changing almost the minute it happens. I don't tell anyone; I am afraid I will miscarry again. I know my mother will make me frantic by telling me that anything I do is all wrong. I am haunted by the story of a girl in my high-school class throwing herself out of a window after a miscarriage, leaving a note, "I can't even do this." At this point I am not writing. I am just teaching, and I am exhausted. Sometimes I can't stand for fifty minutes in front of my first-year class. I sit and finish my lecture, trying not to look as sick as I feel.

In February, a year after my warning dreams, I feel the baby move, fluttering and playing, happy to exist. I don't know if it is a boy or girl, Alan or Sara, but I know this baby has a great sense of rhythm and a lovely touch. I have never felt as companioned as I do now, with this joyful being inside me.

(24 July 1978) I am inside Blake's painting "The River of Life." I swim serenely between George on one side of me and Alan, who was born yesterday, on the other. Suddenly a storm comes up, and we are blown apart. To my horror, I let go of Alan's hand. How will he survive, such a tiny baby? In the morning, I search the shore, not expecting to find him. But I do find him in a tide pool. He seems lifeless, but I hold him to my breast, warm him, and realize he is, by some miracle, alive.

I tell this dream to one of George's former students, who has a psychic streak. "Did you ever find George again?" he asks. He looks unsettled, though he says nothing, when I tell him I didn't.

Alan is alive, but he is having trouble nursing. My breasts are too big for his small mouth. I keep trying. On the advice of the nurses and pediatrician I give Alan formula to supplement my milk which hasn't come in yet. George is supportive. I have brought about twenty books to the hospital, but all I read is Dr. Spock.

Nursing is the hardest thing I have ever done. After ten days, my nipples are starting to crack but my milk is established; Alan has started to gain back the weight he lost, and we return home from the hospital three people instead of two.

The next months pass in a blur of exhaustion. Queen's doesn't have maternity leave, so I return to teaching three courses in mid-September when Alan is two months old. On Mondays, when I have an hour and a half between classes, George brings Alan into school, and I nurse him on my desk. I am so sleepy that I sometimes fall asleep in the middle of my first-year class.

(November 1978) I am looking in the card catalogue at the Queen's library. I see a story I haven't read in years, that I have forgotten. A little brown bear has always dreamed of Christmas. He asks his parents to celebrate Christmas, but bears don't celebrate Christmas, and besides, they are getting ready to hibernate. The little bear walks toward town and meets a magician in a red ski jacket who asks him why he is sad, and when the little bear tells him, the magician promises him a Christmas. It will be in a spruce grove near where the little bear lives. And the magician *did* decorate a tree that night with shimmery silver globes and stars and tinsel, and did put presents under it, but before the little bear could find it, the foxes came and took everything. On Christmas morning the little bear springs up and runs to the spruce grove, but finds nothing, except for bits of tinsel. He meets the magician again. "Did you enjoy your Christmas?"

The little bear tries to be brave. "I know you kept your promise," he said, "but the foxes came and took everything."

"Go back to the spruce grove," the magician says. "Your Christmas will be there." And this time it is. The tree is beautiful and silvery and there are presents under it for everyone: blankets for Mama bear; a jar of the best honey for father bear; and for the little brown bear, a wish, gleaming scarlet and silver, inside a crystal ball, which he hangs on the tree and saves, Christmas after Christmas, until years later, he gives it to his son.

I somehow find the time to write this dream down and read it to Alan on his first Christmas as he is in my arms next to the Christmas tree. I don't know if I will ever have any presence as a writer, but I know Alan has changed my writing. Five years later, I will send this story to the *Whig Standard* Magazine, and they will print it, the first story I will have published since starting to teach at Queen's in 1969.

October 1979: we are in Oxford. George has a sabbatical, and I have an unpaid leave. We have rented a house. I have finally found a good nanny who will care for Alan six hours a day. George has found an old typewriter at a second-hand store, and I begin my third novel, tentatively called *Strawberry Heaven*, planning out what I will write the night before as I lie in bed and writing uncharacteristically quickly in the mornings and early afternoons. Alan is walking now; he is meeting most of his milestones; he is fun to take to parks and downtown because he notices everything. He is easy to take to restaurants because he likes trying new foods.

By the spring, he is lying in his crib working out the songs I sing to him. He isn't talking, just pointing and going "Ah," but he is making himself understood and singing in tune. He likes books and knows when to turn pages. He understands puns. He knows that words with the same sounds can have different meanings, like "two" and "too." When I ask him to point to things in pictures, he can do it. I see that I can balance mothering and writing, if I have help, but I don't know how I can add the teaching. I tell George I want to take another year of unpaid leave. He says I shouldn't. We discuss it several times. He is an established professor, and I listen to him.

I finish a draft of my novel, except for the ending, send the other two out, get encouraging rejection slips, especially from the editor at Knopf who suggests that I try three agents. I do, and receive encouraging rejection slips, but I am still discouraged. I am going home to a hard and thankless year.

September 1980: the storm. I don't recognize it at the time. I only know that the days are filled with iron, the same iron I felt when my mother died the spring before. She had a brain tumour. No wonder she had a genius for saying the wrong thing.

We get back from England too late to find a babysitter. I snag the last available space at a daycare where there is a teacher who seems to get along with Alan.

Once teaching starts, I am exhausted. I get armloads of books on American Literature and somehow manage to limp through my classes. Tuesdays are the worst. I have to take Alan to daycare – usually he is screaming – teach my ten o'clock class, prepare for my first-year class, prepare for my three-hour night class, pick Alan up at daycare, feed him, get to my night class, come home around ten and put Alan to bed. I prepare my classes between two and four in the morning, the only really quiet time I have. I am not writing. The first draft of *Strawberry Heaven* is waiting for me in a stack, with all its problems: four heroines too much alike to carry the book.

Alan mostly sleeps in daycare. He stops liking books. He stops liking most foods. He stops noticing things. He stops singing. In January I say to George over tea. "I'm worried about Alan. Do you think I should take him out of daycare?"

"Alan is fine," he says. "Anyway, that's your problem. If you want to take him out of daycare and make other arrangements, go ahead." I can't. It is too hard to get through the days. I know I am cutting corners on my mothering. I am not writing. It is bad enough not to have a writing presence; now I no longer really have an academic presence.

I realize that I cannot teach, write, and mother. I ask for and am granted two years of unpaid leave. I leave Alan in daycare for six hours a day, three days a week. This turns out to be a mistake. By the time I take him out of daycare, after my father's death, in May 1982, Alan is withdrawn and inattentive. He can only say a few words. He won't look at books. He is not toilet trained. He screams when he sees other kids. He does not make eye contact most of the time. No one is saying "autism," but I suspect they may be thinking it. I have definitely let go of Alan's hand. He is almost lost. I don't recognize him as the same child who played inside me before he was born, who loved parks and ducks, and who was so sociable, curious, and interested. I only vaguely realize that I am inside the storm part of my dream, but I do realize that I need to bring Alan back to life.

What is the essence of a person? Was the real Alan the withdrawn, disturbed toddler or the charmer? I felt the "real" Alan was somewhere buried beneath his present surface, almost drowned. An archetype of motherhood is to search for your lost child. Alan was young, but that was the journey that lay ahead of me. If my dream was right, I could restore him.

November 1983: George and I move to an old stone house on a quiet street, a much better place to bring up a child than where we've been living at the edge of the student ghetto. George is doing almost all of the packing. Alan is screaming whenever anything goes into a box. I think he is afraid it will die, vanish, like his grandfather. He is in a therapeutic nursery school. He has just been assessed as having pervasive delayed development with autistic-like elements and an IQ of 64. I know he's been observed carefully for over a year. I just don't feel it's the whole story, even if it's true that neurological problems tend to surface between two and three, which is when Alan's withdrawal began. In 1983 any type of autism is a sentence of death in life.

While Alan is asleep, I put a few of my books desultorily in a box, without having much heart for them. I read some fairy tales in my *Orange Fairy Book*, saved from childhood, fall asleep on the guest room bed and dream.

Pale pink curtains flutter in the windows of a low-built summer house, the summer residence of a royal family of bears. The bear king is sick and his only hope is in his son, the bear prince. A woman, my aunt, and her daughter Tanya, about the same age as the bear prince, glide along the water in a flat bottomed boat and land at the bears' estate. This takes some courage, because the bears are said to be unfriendly to people. My aunt has brought flimsy costumes, and she and Tanya put them on. My aunt is so mesmerized by the beauty of the estate, the woods, the mosses, she doesn't realize Tanya has wandered off. Then she looks frantically for her daughter, calling softly so that Tanya may hear her but the bears will not. Finally, toward the end of the afternoon, she comes to a rose garden and sees Tanya and the bear prince playing, in silence, among the roses, near a waterfall. Tanya has become a little brown bear. But as they step into the boat, Tanya transforms back to her own self.

This afternoon is repeated many times through the summer. As the days start to shade into fall, my aunt knows the bears will go back to their palace. She comes on the bear prince and Tanya in the rose garden and sees the bear prince placing a gold bracelet on Tanya's arm. As always, they are silent. My aunt feels that Tanya is too young to understand what a solemn moment this is, but she says nothing, bows to the bear, and leads her daughter back to the boat. When they dock, her husband, Tanya's father, is waiting for them, furious.

He seizes the bracelet and sends Tanya to her room. He tells my aunt that he plans for Tanya to marry a forty-year-old neighbour who will give him five fields.

Five years later, the engagement to the neighbour takes place. But just before the wedding, a handsome prince, dressed in blue and silver, attended by six strong knights, rides up to my uncle's estate, and Tanya and my aunt ride away with them. The bear prince has been transformed by Tanya's love. They marry, and live happily ever after. My aunt returns to the estate. When I visit her, she seems happy too. There is no trace of my uncle, but a grouse flies here and there and picks juniper berries out of my aunt's hand. I ask after my uncle. My aunt holds out her hand and says, "He's thriving. Love can create enchantments, even as love can break them."

I hold this dream against heartbreak. The silence is obviously about the autism. The power of love is a message. My uncle's temper isn't so unfamiliar either, and I think it might be easier to live with a husband transformed into a grouse. It is easy to write the story, even in the small bits of Alan's nursery-school time. I send it to *The Whig Standard* Magazine, and it becomes my second published story since graduate school.

I don't have another dream this memorable for years. Instead, I start to set small goals: getting Alan to brush his teeth, taking Alan to playgrounds until he has the courage to go down small slides and then down large ones. When Alan reaches a goal, I set another one. The dreams were overarching guidance; the goal setting is like hiking following much more detailed local maps. I find friends with small children so that Alan can be with other kids without being scared of them or screaming.

When Alan is six, I buy him a camera and encourage him to start taking pictures. I buy him a blue bike with yellow wheels (and training wheels) and walk with him while he rides it. I find a school which is committed to integration of special kids. I work closely with the kindergarten teacher and Nancy, the aide. Often I cry. I still have Nancy's notes, and I reread the record of Alan hitting other kids, screaming, tearing pictures off walls, refusing to sit in the circle, refusing to take part, swearing. Gradually, over the year, Alan improves. He is sitting in circle more often. Occasionally he plays with other kids. He starts to enjoy recess. He starts to take part in the music. He learns to count to a thousand. There are still incidents, but they are less difficult. Alan graduates from kindergarten and is promoted to first grade. It is the first time since daycare, at the age of two, that he hasn't failed, hasn't been written off as hopeless. I continue to set goals for Alan (something his kindergarten teacher and non-teaching assistant encourage me to do). The next thing is toilet training. Alan is afraid of drains because of his grandfather's death – he thinks his grandfather vanished down a drain. I encourage him to use a mixing bowl, newspapers. The only thing that gets him to sit on the toilet is a promise of a pipe, a smoking pipe. (George smokes pipes.) By the spring of Alan's kindergarten year, he has quite a collection of pipes; he has started to smoke tea in them, and he is toilet trained.

When Alan is eight, in second grade, he has a bad teacher and starts to withdraw again. This time I know the signs. Also, I am getting the word from Nancy, who is still working with him. Toward the end of November, when I pick Alan up for lunch, he somehow makes it clear that he doesn't want to go back to school, and I keep him home until he is accepted into the co-op class, in the same school, with the understanding that he will start in January. Alan stops regressing, but he isn't learning, isn't connecting with the other kids. He is spending most of his time at the sand table, though he does make four lovely porcelain gold-trimmed Christmas ornaments, which we still have.

A woman in my aerobics class tells me about a really good principal, Jim Reynolds, as we jog around the room. I meet him, and Alan's prospective teacher, Faye Koshel who is just back from a year of travelling around the world, and make arrangements for Alan to change schools in the fall. Alan is wary, but during the next year, when he is nine, one of his classmates, Allison, befriends him, reads with him, plays with him, and includes him in her circle. He has people to lunch with. He goes to some parties. His educational assistant, Dan, is sunny and imaginative and writes a song, "Dare to Dream" with the chorus "Dare to dream and you can fly." So I am not the only one dreaming.

After a year Mr Reynolds is transferred to another school; Allison goes to a school closer to her home. Alan still has a few friends, though, and some very good teaching. He is bicycling to school (George goes with him in the morning; I pick him up after school). He is starting to read, really read, though he doesn't like it much, and he has so many book reports that he and I are reading several hours a day, before school, after school, after dinner. We somehow manage to get all the book reports done, the last one on the very last day of school. Alan passes fourth grade. But the new principal can't pull the school together. I arrange for Alan to go to a school headed by Mr Reynolds. Dan will be his educational assistant again. He doesn't have friends, but he does have the support he needs from grownups, something he still needs if he is to negotiate the school system.

In fifth grade, Alan begins piano lessons. At first he can't sit still for the whole twenty-minute lesson, but gradually he starts to pay attention. He has a good touch. His pieces sound good. His teacher is calm and patient. By the second year he takes his grade-1 exam. His teacher writes, "Congratulations, Alan! 82 is first class honours." Piano will anchor Alan from this point through high school. He will pass his grade 9 and start work on grade-10 pieces before he quits.

Over these years of putting mothering first, I am writing constantly, in the bits of time I have. I think I would sell my soul for a good night's sleep and an uninterrupted shower. I need to choose between writing and sending out. I write. When I do send stories out, they come back, usually with form rejection slips. I do not have the concentration to write novels. I gain seventy pounds.

When Alan is seven, I sign him up for pottery. (I sit outside in the car while he is in class, for the next several years, just in case there is an incident). He learns to skate and swim. By nine he is over his fear of drains and will swim in pools. We travel: to New York, to Florida, to San Francisco, to Vancouver and Vancouver Island, to England, to Banff and Lake Louise, sometimes with George, sometimes without. I have no idea if Alan is taking anything in, but he is taking pictures – he can look at where he's been.

In 1991 I sell two stories – one to *Quarry*, one to *Descant* – and in February 1992 I learn I have been accepted to the May Studios in Banff. When I am in Banff, Alan, now thirteen years old, and I talk about Latin grammar, about subjunctives of verbs and declensions of nouns. He sounds okay, but one of his sitters says he'll be glad when I return. George and I don't talk much. He doesn't even ask how I am until the final week.

Back from Banff, I tell him I want to separate. After we fight for the whole summer, he finally believes me.

(September 1998) Alan and I are driving to a wedding in Toronto.
We have gone the long way through Lakefield and Peterborough.

We drive past Trent University. It looms like an otherworldly castle rising, dark, out of the land, spanning the river banks. I want Alan to be there. It seems so out of reach. I feel if he were in that dark serene castle he would be happy.

The next spring, Alan is accepted to Trent. He takes an extra year to do a heritage restoration program in Kingston and finish high-school English, and in September 2000 we take him to Champlain College, where the master, Stephen Brown, a former student of George's, welcomes him. Alan takes three courses a year. His grades are uneven. But he stays. And he is happy.

December 2006: My first book, *The Iron Shoes*, is accepted by North Shore Press. I call Alan at Trent and ask if he will take the cover photograph, and he says yes.

January 2007: I am helping Alan with his second-year Latin over the phone. One of the sentences is Cicero's "Horae quidem et dies et anni discedunt, nec praeteritum tempus umquam revertitur, nec quid sequatur potest sciri." We spell it out uncertainly – "Indeed hours and days and years pass by, nor can time that has passed ever return, nor can it be known what may follow."

"Yes," says Alan delightedly, "That's *true*!"

I have a book of poems in press, and he has rediscovered, just for a moment, the joy of reading.

Mother to Vision

SALLY ITO

In summer 1996, when I was pregnant with my first child, I was teaching English to Japanese students at a small college in Cuthbert, Georgia. It was terribly hot and humid outside, and the general lethargy such heat produces often made me sleepy. After the last class was finished, I usually hurried over to the dorm to have a nap. These afternoon naps were of the deep, stuporous kind that produce visions and dreams. It was during one of these naps that a woman's voice came to me. She was an older Nisei woman, and she was telling me the story of her husband, a US Pacific War veteran who had been struck down by a stroke.

I awoke from the dream with the voice ringing in my head. Feverishly, I began writing down the words I heard. Those words became the opening to my novel.[1] What seems strange now in hindsight was that this woman whose voice I heard was old and "barren," to use the Biblical term, and that she had come to me with her story while I was gestating a child deep in the bowels of the southern US.

Later that summer, I had yet another dream. In this dream was an older man, an artist, who told me that I was now entering a new phase in my writing, in which a mature work of art should surely emerge. The dream took place in an attic-like loft with the man emerging into the space from down below as if out of a trunk. The attic symbolized the past; the man's emergence into the space signalled an artistic probing of the haunted past of my characters. The dream was profound. I felt like I had only been in training as a writer up until then for whatever this future work was to be.

When I returned to Canada, I put the dreams at the back of my mind and resumed working on an earlier novel until it was finished. My son, Kenji, was born in February 1997. By this time, I had published one book of poems, and my short-story manuscript was en route to being published as well. It came out as a book in 1998. Luckily, this publisher did not tour their authors. I was loath to leave Kenji in those early years; at one point, I had been invited to attend a festival in Ontario where I was to receive recognition for my earlier published poetry book.[2] I declined in the end because I was still nursing Kenji.

Life with a child changes everything, but it can also make one more determined in one's path in life. To be truthful, I had no real ambition in life to be a good mother. I wanted more than anything to be a good writer. I still wanted to be that even after Kenji was born. So my life after his birth was often about figuring out how to be that good writer with him around.

Kenji, by and large, was not a difficult infant. He was not colicky nor overly active. His only issue was sleep. Sleep deprivation is the worst affliction accorded to some mothers. The constant interruptions of a child at night needing at first to nurse, then to go potty, then to have someone comfort them because of a bad dream, then because of fevers or rashes, can be relentless and wearing. Trying to concentrate on anything, never mind the focused task of writing, after a night of bad sleep is just damn hard.

Sometime after Kenji was born, I met with a writer friend of mine, a man. He, too, had a toddler at home. He'd been working on a novel for several years. When we met for coffee, he had just snagged a lucrative book contract that would allow him to travel to Scotland for a year to write a nonfiction book there. He'd started freelancing and was obviously doing well. I asked him about his novel. He said he'd decided that it was no good and that he'd stopped writing it. He mourned the loss of it for a few days and then decided to get on with the rest of his writing life. I could hardly believe it. Giving up a novel just like that! And yet his act reminded me of something I'd heard Robertson Davies say about writing that first novel to put away in a drawer so that you could write the better work later.

My friend and I chatted briefly about our kids. I confessed to him that I found being with a young child boring. He nodded. It was true. But somehow, being a woman, I felt more guilty about it and about admitting to the fact.

After my talk with my friend, I went home and thought about the novel I'd just finished. Yes, it was done, but slovenly so and needed substantial revision. I thought back to my dream in Georgia about the artist and remembered the snippet of writing I had of the woman's voice I'd heard in my head. I put two and two together. The voice and the notion of that future work – the *better* work. Now had come time to start this novel.

The writer is one who takes a long voyage in a small room, said Richard Wright in his speech for the Giller. But what if on the voyage, there are children, small and tucked under the crooks of your arm like the kind of precious baggage they are?

Kenji grew up in the shadow of my working on this second, better novel. He didn't know and didn't care about this work and is only now beginning to have a dim sense of what I do for a living aside from feeding, clothing, washing him. That's okay. He's a child and is completely entitled to his childishness. I just hoped I wasn't robbing him of what he is entitled to in the only phase of his life neither he nor I will ever see repeated.

A few years later, while still in the early stages of this novel, I moved to Winnipeg. My husband got a job at a small Christian university there. It was a big move away from the family support we had in our home in Edmonton. In September of that year, I became pregnant with our second child.

My husband and I always agreed that we would go wherever he could get a job. I felt that being a writer was pretty much a portable vocation, and that has proved to be true for the most part. But being a writer, a mother, and a wife to a full-time working spouse (and, later, working myself as a part-time teacher) has been a challenge. Setting up house in another city without family support was difficult. I continued to write but became increasingly covetous of my time for the novel. I was still at the stage where I was discovering things about my characters – the stage that Jack Hodgins[3] describes as "ploughing up the field" where things are being "unearthed." Being alone at this time was particularly essential for me to do my work, so I became covetous of my solitude. For it is when writers are alone that they are on their voyages of discovery, when in their little rooms, they stumble on new vistas and terrains of the imagination and experience. How often I wept for characters whose only existence were the words I tapped out onto the computer screen.

Solitude, however, has its drawbacks. So ensconced was I in writing and parenting, I wasn't making friends. I was in need of artistic and spiritual companionship in the journey I had taken on when beginning this novel. I was alone with my characters and was their confessor, but I was only all too human myself and in some ways unable to cope with what I dimly began to perceive as the spiritual crux of the novel. At this time, I began going to a spiritual director. She was a Catholic nun at a retreat centre just outside of the city. I gave up one of my precious writing afternoons per week when Kenji was in kindergarten and drove the half hour drive right through downtown Winnipeg out onto Main Street going north past the Perimeter Highway into a countryside of snow-drifted fields and farmhouses.

One afternoon on arrival at the retreat centre, I overheard the receptionist tell the director that here was the housewife who had come to see her last week. *Housewife!* I thought, shocked and indignant. That was not *me* at all! I was not a housewife. But then what else could a pregnant woman at two in the afternoon visiting a spiritual director be but a housewife? To limited imaginations, that was the only logical conclusion.

And yet, while deeply gestating my second child, I made these weekly visits to the spiritual director where the key epiphany to my novel took place. So significant was this epiphany that I shared it with my spiritual director, vicariously bringing to her my character's spiritual crisis. The protagonist of my story, Satoru, has an encounter with the enemy during the war that marks him forever. As I approached this moment in the novel, the deeper spiritual implications became clear – namely, what is it to be told to love an enemy and fail? Together the director and I worked this dilemma through. If she ever thought of me as a housewife before then, it was likely she didn't afterward! But fundamentally to her, of course, a housewife and a writer are much the same. They are both creatures of God made in His image, fallen and in constant need of grace. There is no ego attachment to one's professional identity. And so was I given a dose of humility as well as a deeper understanding of my own weakness and need for an identity. Still, I had no desire to relinquish the identity nor quit its practice. For better or worse, I *was* a writer.

Seika Magdalen Dyck, my daughter, was born in 2001. Her name had come to me as one my protagonist, Satoru, had wanted to give to the daughter he never had. Seika is a Japanese name, meaning *holy fragrance*. Her birth ushered in a hiatus on the novel. However, feeling pressed, I sent the manuscript in the state it was then to an agent. It came back with a note saying it needed more work. The agent gave me several helpful tips on what to do next, but of course I was not in a position to act.

One of the criticisms of the novel was that I had not explored my protagonist's wartime past enough. Satoru was a Nisei man in his late sixties, a veteran of the Pacific War. I had spent most of my earlier drafts trying to get at him through his wife, whose voice I heard so many years ago. It is significant that I came at this story through her, for as a woman I was coming to the world of war the same way. Although I had done some research, I needed to dig deeper for more details. And so, a year later, I found myself pushing my baby stroller to the public library, where I took out US War department footage of campaigns in the South Pacific. Later at home, while bouncing baby Seika on my lap, I watched colour footage of the grisly aftermath of the battle of Tarawa, Japanese corpses littering the beach head, guns and hardware strewn across the white sand while tall palms quavered in the distance. It was an eerie incongruous feeling, holding a baby, and watching this carnage.

It was also at this time that I began corresponding with some veterans after consulting an online veterans resource website.[4] Some of these men divulged to me stories they never told anyone. Once I even phoned a veteran in California. He was in his eighties and was nursing a sick wife in the hospital. When I heard his voice, it reminded me of an uncle's; there was something warm and familiar in it. The man told me he was tired and couldn't talk much, but if I wanted I could write him a letter with a few questions and he would try and answer them. I wasn't hopeful, but I sent a letter with my questions anyway. A week or so later, a reply came. It was a ten-page handwritten letter on yellow legal size paper; not only did it answer all my questions, but it carefully documented this man's years of service from the time of his enlistment in February 1943 out of a relocation centre in Gila River to his discharge from service in Tokyo in January 1946. The letter arrived on 11 November, the US postmark message across the stamp bearing the words "Veteran's Week."

I felt both privileged and humbled by receiving these testimonies; it became increasingly evident that I must write my novel in a way that honoured these men's experiences. Sandra Birdsell, after finishing *The Russlanders*, visited the graves of her Mennonite forebears to pay homage to those whose experiences she wrote about. I understand that feeling. When you're writing historical fiction of the kind that seeks to illuminate, educate and move readers about a certain community, you feel you owe it to that community to get things right. And if that takes all the time in the world to do, then that is just the way it has to be.

Having two children now restricted my writing time to precious little. Every moment had to be scheduled around their lives. Luckily my son had started school, so I just needed care for Seika. A neighbour agreed to take her in the mornings while my son was at kindergarten. For a year, I ferried my son and daughter back and forth to his school and her babysitter. The walk was a short three blocks, but I remember how, in winter, I bundled up Seika in a blue Inuit parka lent to us by a neighbour and pulled her on a sled. She was so little then, a literal bundle of quilted cloth, her face peering out of the fur-lined ruff of the collar, cheeks rosy as berries.

I had only a few hours a day, a few days a week to work on improving the novel. It was now into its third draft, which meant I was editing *and* creating new scenes. An awkward place to be. Some days, I felt I was in the "bottomless middle" – where you don't know where's it's going or if the parts you've rewritten are all that good or meaningful. This feeling was exacerbated by the fact that I often had to leave the work for days at a time on weekends or because of crises with the children. Sometimes this break was helpful; the perspective you gain from a day or so away can clarify things. Other times, the break was just too long and getting back into the swing of the work was hard. You'd only think you'd just got back into the novel, and then you'd have to leave it again.

A friend told me that having children helped him be a better writer in that he maximized what little time he had to actually get stuff written. I agree, but some of what writing involves is the leisure to think and work things through. Writing is a two-fold process: it involves, in one sense, an engagement with the world of sensory experience and, on the other, the ability to detach and observe the very sensations one is experiencing or engaging in. Time is clearly a factor in this process. Not everything experienced is always understood at once; it often takes time for one to process what has happened. Writing is one of the ways we process experience, including the vicarious experience writers encounter with their characters.

What I began to notice in my life was that if I was not writing, I was not engaging with the immediate world of my family. For some reason, the complete immersion in another world composed entirely of words helped me reap more fully the wonders of my present sensual universe. The act of writing – its interpretation of a world however unrelated to my present existence in time or point-of-view – paradoxically made the immediate world around me more real, at least to me. This made me understand something fundamental about myself. I am a better mother when I'm writing.

Unfortunately, I cannot say I'm a better writer when I'm mothering. My children are only more *real* to me when I have been writing for some part of the day. Likewise can I only be more *real* to them as a mother when I have spent some time away from them in another equally salient reality. For me, life without writing becomes strangely meaningless and banal, and I feel listless, distracted, and purposeless. Without writing, the world does not feel real to me, and I do not feel real to myself.

Only recently have I understood that being a writer means being a parent (if not slave!) to a vision. A vision-led life, I've come to understand, is meaningful. My novel literally arose out of a vision, and I have held and nurtured that vision for years. It is the horse I ride to finish my race.

I love my children, but in the midst of raising them I don't know what's going on all the time. I'm still in the experiential mode with my children and haven't yet reflected much about them. Lately though, I've been writing the odd piece about my son, mostly to figure things out. I'm trying to see through the lens of my words the picture of his being – his particular boyishness, his particular Kenji-ness. *Mom*, he says, *write something about me.* This makes me smile. Now *that* is a role as his mother that I can relish – a scribe to his being, a scribe to his imagination. I see in the distance what *writer* can mean in the context of motherhood. But not yet, not now, while the other vision still has its hold on me, even as the moments of his childhood trickle through my fingers like sand into the sea.

notes

1 Sally Ito.
2 Ito, *Frogs in the Rain Barrel.*
3 Hodgins, *A Passion for Narrative*, 38.
4 Japanese American Veterans Association website www.javadc.org/.

Only a Day to Visit

LINDA SPALDING

One spring three years ago, my mother died and my first grandchild was born. Suddenly everything shifted. My mother dies in February on a cold Kansas day and my grandchild arrives prematurely on an April night in Vancouver, a night when geese are seen roosting on the hospital roof. An old, old woman is lying in cold Kansas ground, and here is a three-pound slip of life.

Which is when I begin to dream of my grandmother. I have only a day in which to visit her. There is a bus to catch, or a plane. There are her closets. Her cupboards. Her house to be reinhabited. There is a lamp under which to read or play a game. She could beat me at checkers without batting an eye. There is her whirring, always-going sewing machine. For awhile, during the first war, this is where she made her meagre living while my grandfather was away. She sewed for a woman of flamboyant fashion. Yes. And they became friends, or so it was said of them.

When my grandfather came back from that first war, he met the flamboyant woman of fashion and fell in love with her.

Later, the flamboyant woman drove up and down the street in front of my grandmother's house. At this time, my mother (the one who is lying in cold Kansas ground) was a small, bobbed hair little girl. The flamboyant woman tooted her horn and shouted in triumph or pain, depending on the disposition of that ill-fated love affair and, from a window in the front room, which is what the main room of the house was called, my mother watched. When my grandmother began to pace and beat at her breast, or pluck at her hair, my mother went into her own room and closed the door.

When I hold my granddaughter, who was that three-pound slip of life, or play with her, or sing to her, or read to her, I feel my grandmother in my hands and arms. I feel her as I never felt my mother while I was mothering my girls. I used to wait for that little invasion, but my mother, who was alive at the time, never seemed to inhabit me. I was busy distinguishing myself from her, setting out the boundaries that separated us geographically and psychologically. I would not do as she had done, although I wanted to make each Christmas perfect (she had done that) and each birthday magical (she had done that) and my house as pretty as hers had been when I was living with her. I wanted my children to read books (most of them were sent by her) and take piano lessons and ballet lessons (as I had done) and to feel comfortable around grownups and go to the theatre and love music and and and ....

But I was a single mother. Actually poor. And, when I couldn't give my daughters what I had been given, I remembered my widowed grandmother. I remembered the long, long summer days that I had spent in her house, when there was nothing to do but go up to the hot attic and look through drawers full of fabric and old, useless beads. Days when there was nothing to do but sit in the bathtub playing with tin pans and soap. Never was I happier. I sat in the bathtub making up stories full of characters and dialogue while she sat at her sewing machine.

At dinner time, my grandmother would call me to the kitchen table and we would eat quietly together, our dishes sitting on her crocheted tablecloth. There was a little ritual after the meal. The washing was done together while the kettle boiled. Then the dishes were put in the old tin tub that had been used to bathe my mother and her brother when they were babies. The boiling water was poured over the clean dishes, and it was my job to dry them and put them away. These were dishes that were plain and inexpensive and often chipped. My grandmother had survived with so much less than my parents had collected for their house. My mother had grown up with so much less than had been vouchsafed to me. It was something to be proud of – the way my grandmother mowed her own grass with a push mower, the way she managed her house. Alone. Without money. Without fear or complaint as far as I could see.

One summer during those years when I spent time in my grandmother's house, it was even hotter than the ordinary 100 plus degrees, and we created a space in her unfinished basement, where we spent all our waking hours. (In the morning, rising from sleep, we might have a hurried breakfast in the kitchen before descending the stairs to escape the heat. We might catch of glimpse, even at that early hour, of birds stalking the grass with thirsty, outstretched wings.)

Down in the basement, without her sewing machine, my grandmother embroidered or crocheted. I was embroidering something, too, but I painted pictures, wrote stories and letters, filled in the pages of my diary, read books, and played solitary pretend-games. It was harder to live in my imagination down there, with my watchful grandmother so close, but she was a woman who had lived alone for so many years that she considered it no affront to sit in silent companionship, and that summer, as long as I didn't move from my wicker chair, I could go anyplace. We sat on wicker chairs, and the concrete floor felt cool against our feet. We ate from the jars she kept stored on her basement shelves: peaches, applesauce, bread and butter pickles, bread and ginger pear jam. We brought the old dishpan down and filled it with water and set a fan behind it to cool us as we worked.

I have tried in various ways to describe the delicious solitude of those lost summer days. They exist as a series of images, much like a dream that, when told, dissolves immediately. I suppose there was the liberation from my parents to take into account, although in all other ways, the brief interlude with my grandmother was more constrained than the rest of my life. So, perhaps that was it, exactly. I should explain that she was deaf, this grandmother, and any effort to communicate with her was severely strained. But we learned, over the years, to move through our days and evenings in silent harmony.

Now, I am left to wonder what kind of grandmother I will be. My grandchildren are too small to amuse themselves in the bathtub all day, or to keep diaries, or to embroider or crochet. I write to an elderly friend for ideas and she sends back an email: Tips on Grandmothering. It includes tea parties, playing school. But I put it away and decide on my own priorities.

1)   A tin tub of water with an electric fan circling in front of it.
2)   Work to do.
3)   Two deep rattan chairs.

4)   Food to eat.

5)   Books to read.

6)   A grandmother's hands, voice, face.

In my list there is no black fur coat (possibly rabbit?) to be leaned against in the dark backseat of a car, although that coat was delicious to me. In my list there is no corset to watch being laced in the morning and unlaced at night, although that ceremony was sacred as was the pinning back of her hair and the rouging of her face. In matters of fashion, the list will change, but during visits one or another of my grandchildren may crawl into bed with me and snuggle down under the sheets. Then, the child will feel the length of leg I inherited from my grandmother, and will feel as I felt, pressed against my grandmother's aging flank. This body I have, that child will say, came to me from a long line of people who suffered and loved and grieved, people who laughed and danced and fried chicken and washed the dishes afterward and put them away.

My grandchildren will inhabit this world long after I am dust, but day by day, minute by minute, I can watch them develop. It is like time-lapse photography, it happens so fast. With my children, this was never the case. I was so caught up in creating them! What I fed them, said to them, put in their rooms and hearts and minds was a slow, slow process that continues to this day. But on my grandchildren I hold a telescope, and sometimes I see my own life through its lens. My heavens. Isn't each one of us the most astonishing result: of the old woman lying in cold Kansas ground, of those who lived before her and beside her and others she never met.

It was my grandmother who got me through those first years as a single mother and fledgling writer. It was an image of her at work. She had taught me to pick up a piece of cloth and plunge a needle in. Make a flower, for example, or a leaf. Choose a colour for the petals. Consider the errant husband if you must but just begin. Begin. So it seemed to me that with enough sitting, pen in hand, I could create something. And once it was created, I could pluck out a seam or adjust a hem. Each word was like a stitch. The thing about creation is: it's mutable. That's its inherent charm. The fabric is there: old stories of war and poverty and heartbreak. The colours are wild characters. Put them together. Take them apart. Start again.

words of advice

Record of a Live Birth, and Other Stories

joanne arnott

"Your life isn't boring!" Theo protests, as I push him on the swing. I am doing this as a personal favour: he is far too big and capable to actually need my assistance with this.

Isidore chimes in, "You're an author!"

Jules wanders too close to the arc of the swing. Shouted warnings, attempts to stop the swing, all to no avail. He is thrust to the dust with the helpless prod of his elder brother's foot. No serious injury.

I am reminded how exciting my life really is.

a writer's life: the fragility of knowing

My first pregnancy ended in miscarriage, and it almost took my life. I was eighteen years old, newly returned to the prairie. I consulted a doctor when my period was long delayed, but by the time of our appointment the bleeding had begun already. As it turned out, the doctor had much more pressing concerns than his job, or my health.

"Soft touch, eh?" he asked, a non-response to the question I'd just spoken. I wanted to know how to tell the difference between miscarriage and hemorrhage. I didn't react, so he posed his question again: "I said, *soft touch, eh?*"

I didn't understand what he was saying, but clearly he needed something from me. I squinted at him, nodded, and waited. He sighed, then, and finally began to answer my questions.

When I left the doctor's office, my defenses failed. I suddenly understood: the doctor had called me a whore, and I had agreed with him. I was mortified and very, very angry.

As this first pregnancy became miscarriage, and miscarriage became puerperal fever, I sweated it out, with only my flower-devil hallucinations for company, and one stupid cat named Pluto whom I'd rescued from a life of abuse. I hadn't named Pluto, but his name always struck me as entirely appropriate. Damaged through malnutrition, neglect, and emotional abuse in his earliest months of life, he was named for the Roman god associated with the underworld, both the physical underworld of wealth hidden within the Earth, and the spiritual underworld and death. As abductor-husband of Persephone, Pluto has become strongly associated with women's sense of power and control in our lives, and – through the story of Demeter's search for her abducted daughter – specifically maternal grief.

Pluto was smart enough to figure out how to use the toilet during my time of incapacitation, generating the mysterious sound that first made me paranoid, then curious enough to crawl out of bed. I did have a number of friends who usually crashed at my apartment, who might have come by to use the toilet, but none of them were staying with me just then. I'd declined their offers of help to the hospital, and, by the time I was so damn sick I was afraid enough to set aside pride and just go, no one was around. Just me and Pluto.

The second pregnancy, in Ontario, ended in a therapeutic abortion. My then-boyfriend, now-husband, walked me from the university to the hospital. As we approached the hospital, we saw a cluster of sign-bearing people near the main entrance. I worried at crossing a picket line, but I reasoned, "This doesn't seem like the kind of thing that can wait."

Upon closer inspection, the apparent workers resolved into an anti-abortion (anti-choice) protest. Wending my way through the small forest of "I know better than you," I went forward with my plans. I said goodbye to my boyfriend at the hospital doors.

When, the next day, I woke from the anaesthetic, I felt two things most powerfully: joy, in that I may well have a say in the course of my life and in the life of my body, and hunger – the nurses were discussing a run for doughnuts, and at the moment that sounded really good!

The third pregnancy, in BC, also ended in a therapeutic abortion. By now I was in a somewhat steadier place: working at a worker-owned moving company and involved in a somewhat-committed relationship with a new boyfriend, a common-law marriage that would eventually last for over a decade.

The list of birth-control methods I used through this period are pretty much a list of what was available at the time: birth control pills, condoms, spermicidal chemicals, diaphragms. In later years, my repertoire of birth-control methods expanded to include an intrauterine device and *long years* of abstinence.

Fertility has led me to mysterious places. I appreciate that.

On the occasion of my second abortion, I wrote "Abortion (like Motherhood) Changes Nothing." This naively titled poem has appeared in anthologies and most recently in an e-journal, *Literary Mama*. Another abortion poem, never published, written on the occasion of the Ontario non-birth, is all about ethics and decision-making: how a very young adult makes a life-and-death decision and moves on.

I called that first abortion poem "The Fragility of Knowing." I presented it at my first public poetry reading, at the Cheshire Cat Café, in Windsor. An older couple stood up and walked out when I read this poem. They cannot have known the nightmares that plagued me throughout those weeks of pregnancy, nor the actual nightmare I'd lived through with my pal, Pluto. Still, they had an opinion, and they voted with their feet, leaving the Cheshire Cat Café for those who could tolerate listening to me.

record of a live birth

On 21 February 1986, and through ten lunar months leading up to that date, magically, I became a mom. My then-partner Brian, my eldest sister Ani, her then-partner Jaki, and our midwives, spent long, long hours together, culminating in a most strange experience, *giving birth*.

> There was snow on the ground on the night you were born. Your father photographed ice on the bushes in our front yard. We will

always remember. We will always remember how you invented us, through the long slow surrender required of us, the reaching, reaching, reaching to understand, how, how do we open, how to receive you. We are, finally, filled with it, the radiant grace with which you arrived, the room and everyone inside of the room, touched with divinity.[1]

What began as a terribly tumultuous experience, where even the names of government forms caused emotional, intellectual, and spiritual gales – *Record of a Live Birth!? Oh My God!* – over time and through experience has become much less terrible, but still awesome and, inescapably, a tumult, creative of joy and of work in equal measures. My notebooks filled to overspilling with detailed accounts of every nuance of my journey. An influential book that I read at this time was Kathryn Allen Rabuzzi's *Motherself: A Mythic Analysis of Motherhood*. Although the author and I have grown from very different roots, the view of a mother's challenges as heroic, and as a journey, proved pivotal for me.

From the first, the experiential process of change – not-a-mother, mother – became a focus for my formal (or public) as well as for my informal, personal writings. Some elements and images have been revisited by me many times in formal writings, through the course of my writing life and mothering life, and others have yet to be tapped. The energetic elements of the experience of birthing and the spiritual reading or interpretation of those energetic changes are fascinations that do make it into my published work on many occasions.

The language of childbirth is unique and antiquated, and lovely for those of us with positive associations to it: "primipara," "multipara," "grande multipara"; "vulva," "conception," "the quickening," "the crowning"; "her laying in." My midwives taught us these words, and so much more. My favoured definition of *primipara* I found in Lewis and Short: "she that has brought forth, foaled, whelped, littered, etc., for the first time." "Pario" is the root word, "to bring forth or bear." Thus, *multipara* has brought forth or whelped on more than one occasion. *Grande multipara* is a woman who has given birth more than five times.

My midwives also asked that I go to my mother and my grandmother and invite them to tell me about their experiences of birth. We had never really spoken of these things before, and the conversations that resulted from asking these questions deepened my understanding of, and my relationships with, both of these women.

My grandmother spent her growing-up years, between the ages of three and thirteen, in a Prairie boarding school, a French girl being raised by French nuns. When she gave birth for the first time, she went to hospital and gave birth to my mother. After the birth, the nurse handed her both baby and bottle and told her to feed the baby: she complied. She continued to bottle-feed at home, despite being perfectly healthy and despite having neither a refrigerator nor an icebox.

My mother gave birth to eight children in Catholic hospitals, each birth lost in a haze of drugs like Demerol. Although she tried breastfeeding, she never felt comfortable with it and soon gave up. The first time my mother saw a human placenta was when I – her fifth-born child – was thirty years old. I am reminded of Maria Campbell's words, "When you look at our history, as women, regardless of our culture, it's terrible what's been taken away from us."[2]

My experiences as a nervous primipara unfurled at a time when anyone connected to homebirths and midwives in this province was more or less afraid. My first choice of midwife, Gloria Lemay, and her partner Mary Sullivan, had been charged in a child's death that occurred during the process of a homebirth they attended. Throughout this time, the private choices around birthing were floodlit, in the public eye, and passionately debated, with insults hurled and accusations rampant. The grieving parents did not press charges. The College of Physicians brought charges against the midwives; whether they were protecting the public good, or simply protecting their own turf, remains an open question.

One of my very earliest impressions upon becoming a mother was a glimpse of my vulva reflected in a silver basin filled with deep red blood and a large placenta. This glimpse of my changed morphology marked my initiation into a blood mystery: vivid in my bodymind, carved into memory, and revisited in my journal, it remained a rich vision that did not find a place in the body of my formal work, until today.

LITErary mIDwIves

In the Downtown Eastside there is a garden, it is called the Four Sisters Housing Co-operative. It was there that you were born, a small enclave of hope in a sea of squalor. The elders, the youth, the mothers and fathers, the single folk in all of their glory, were our neighbours, gathered to make home. Your brother wanted to mount a parade, to sing out to all of our waiting neighbours: a child is born. Congratulations. A community gives birth to itself, and we rest in its arms.[3]

Many long poems, and short, sharp ones, resulted from my early weeks, months, years of becoming a mother. Many poems associated with the second birth were in fact begun with the first, set aside, then taken up again and brought to completion with the new experiences.

In part, this was a result of new encouragements, becoming part of a community when my firstborn son was a nursing child. I learned significant lessons working with my elders, Flo Robertson, Jack Chalmers, Jake Klassen, Peter Chau, and others, met through the multicultural democracy that was my experience of the Four Sisters Co-op. The local rag, *The Carnegie Newsletter*, was a less intimidating showcase for my poetry than any previous venue.

It was also at this time that I met the first of those women I think of as my literary midwives, Beth Brant, Mohawk mother and grandmother. Beth is the editor of the breakthrough anthology *A Gathering of Spirit: A Collection by North American Indian Women* and author of *Mohawk Trail*, *Food & Spirits*, *Writing as Witness: Essays & Talk* and *I'll Sing 'til the Day I Die: Conversations with Tyendinaga Elders*. To become a public writer, to move my stories out of the drawers, boxes, and notebooks in which they were stored, I needed permission, both to live in my skin and to write from that place. This I received from Beth Brant, along with many other nourishing gifts. When I had a manuscript of poems ready, I mailed it away to a publisher in Toronto and sent another copy to Beth. She told Barb Kuhne of Press Gang Publishers about *Wiles of Girlhood*,[4] and Barb called me and asked if she could see it. This is how three of my first four books came to be published by a publisher located in the Downtown Eastside, just a few blocks from my home.

It was at this time, too, that I came across "'You Have to Own Yourself': An Interview with Maria Campbell," by Doris Hillis, published in *Prairie Fire Magazine*. I have returned to this interview again and again over the years and continue to gather nourishment from the wisdom and the plain-speaking Maria choose to share with us there. My first reading of Maria's many books filled this period. I would meet Maria once, in the 1990s, when baby Isidore and I stayed at her home during a book tour. We kept track of each other through a mutual friend, and when I was finally ready to move out of isolation, a full decade later, she welcomed me.

I also met Lee Maracle at this time, when we were both publishing and promoting books through Press Gang. I remember her best during the first year of the Vancouver Writers' Festival, when I had a grant job in the festival office. I arrived at the first festival banquet, and as I looked around I became so anxious, I almost fled home again. Then Lee Maracle arrived with her husband and daughters looking so familiar. I asked if I could sit with them, and they agreed. I have since always remembered Lee as having provided me *a seat at the table,* literally.

Ann Decter, then with Women's Press and now publishing McGilligan Books, was another literary midwife. She assisted my children's book into being, and it was her idea that I should go to the International Feminist Book Fair in Melbourne. Although the fair organizers failed to pay me, along with many other indigenous authors, it was there that I first met Kateri Akiwenzie-Damm. Kateri, too, would later play a major *literary midwife* role.

RIFFING: HAPPILY ever after, a primer for the new mother

Bending to the task of nursing my first son, of maintaining a physical quiet while my mind ran wild, I began to feel strange sensations creeping up my spine, spreading across and over the ribs and muscles and skin of my back. This doesn't seem to be a form of pleasure, nor of ecstasy. I found words and images for it: the awareness of bark forming, as I take up my procreative place on the family tree. An atavistic fear, that the tree's natural and unrelenting growth will completely subsume me.

Whether as a woman giving birth for the first time, as a man on becoming a father, or as a person taking on the care of someone else's young midstream, the reformation of being that is involved in becoming a parent is virtually inescapable. The shocks of giving birth, of finding ecstasy and spiritual replenishment, along with violation and devastation, in an event of the body; of having a stranger coming out of your nether regions and finding familiarity in the face of that newborn stranger/offspring; of offering a private body part for the purposes of nourishment and life maintenance;

of taking responsibility for other lives beyond one's own. The challenges of becoming a parent, undergoing this reformation of being, precipitates interesting, unsettling, even spectacular dreams. These are followed by increasing familiarity, getting into the rhythm of things, becoming more confident and more competent in the unrelenting decision-making, in assisting the young ones' day-to-day survival, as well as their moment to moment happiness.

The lulling times are pocked of course by further sudden happenings: tasting a child's passionate rejection, being bit and hit by one's enraged young; the guilt of saying goodbye for the first time; seeing a child ill, insulted, fevered, or wounded – the helplessness of our best efforts, our inability to stave off the fullness of life.

Feeling rage toward the world or one's circumstances, toward one's partner or family, toward a young loved one – when the accumulated demands from within have been brushed and pushed aside for too long, and the perennial demands from without walk out of some small and unfortunate mouth and, for just a few bad moments, we reveal our bitch aspect, *the wicked princess* as one of my sons put it; the shock of being the bigger one, of being the one who has power, leading to the shame of losing control, whether with sharp words and untruths, or a sharp slap and unhappy hands; the wild and greedy spirit of the creative force in rebellion against the tempering of one's daily habits ... No, I cannot stay up all night pursuing these ideas; no, I cannot sit in cafés for hours of uninterrupted writing, or even of debate; no, I cannot drink or dance or carouse until I am sated, because irrevocably the sleeping child wakes, and hungers, and needs, and I have taken on the gift-task of responding. Finding the way through, for me, meant making friends with structure: locating and exploiting the opportunities that did exist, to practice my craft, and learning to create new ones. My early distressed and stumbling moves have evolved into a skill set, or well-toned muscles, of opportunistic living, balancing the needs and wants and demands of writerself, an artist, a career person, with those of the family woman and old reliable Ma.

For every awesome moment taken on in the interests of childbearing and of childrearing, there are reams of soothing moments that gather, forming the materials that ground us and clothe and feed us, giving succour to our soul-loneliness, forming the complexion of our daily lives. Children need ritual, as do we all, and around these repetitions lives form: sleeping, eating, washing; looking, touching, tasting; storytelling, dancing, singing – these are daily events that nourish young children. The very young are power-ful producers and very good role models. Sharing spacetime with young people who feel free to provoke and invent these celebrations can only be restorative.

Self-mastery is no less important for the person in charge of small chil-dren than for the artist trying to make the leap out of the vast realms of the wannabe and beyond the shallows of the one-book-writer or the one-song-wonder. Many of the same skills are required: flexibility, persistence, a will-ingness and ability to take in the "classics" and examine our "blueprints," to take in the responses and critical opinions of others (large and small), and to set our own goals, values, and agendas. We need to be willing to set out our own content – more like the web pulled from a spider's body than actual blood, guts, or children – in a way that, while hopefully pleasing to editors and marketable to some audience, is fundamentally satisfying to us, the parent/creators. As Maria Campbell has it, "You have to own yourself."[5]

Finding our way between nourishing the artspirit and giving her what she needs, disciplining the artist and setting appropriate boundaries on her behaviour so that productivity is not swamped by a rich but still fantasy life, nor starved by an overliteral sternness, and doing the same for our family members, is an endless improvisation.

THEODORE AND ISIDORE: TWO GIFTS

The point of land on which I gave birth to you, this point of land
has held houses and births from time immemorial. That land on
the day you were born was long grass so golden brown, and it was
wildflowers. The sky was clear and blue. The river melding with the
salt sea ran cold. Your birth was a long, leisurely stroll, it was a warm
summer day, it was a family occasion. You arrived at tea-time. I carried you out, to the land, the grass, the river, the sea, and the sky, the
very next day.

On a deep winter's night, they painted their hands, and they laid
them upon me: painted in that ancient way, painted with spirals, it
was a colourful woman who gave birth to you. Through the evening,
they dipped crystalline ginger in dark chocolate, and they fed me:
handprints woman, spirals woman, chocolate-dipped ginger-eating

woman, it was a colourful woman who gave birth to you. Celebration. We were holding on to what was right, while all the many wrongs made an insubordination of our lives. You were a welcome child. Everything fell apart soon after.[6]

a writer's life: limo service

My plan had been to put the kids to work, helping me to clean the apartment. I would then return the key to the manager and ask him to call a taxi for us. As things turned out, however, the kids weren't a great deal of help, and as they inadvertently knocked a closet door off its moorings, in the bedroom with only three walls, I really didn't feel like engaging with the manager at all. After cleaning the apartment to the best of my ability, I slipped the key through his mail slot and skulked away in not-very-good humour. I carried the vacuum, mop, broom, the bucket of rags and cleaning agents, down to the street. I instructed my two young sons to watch for a taxi, reminding them what a taxi looks like, and asked that they let me know when they saw one.

We watched the stream of traffic pass, pause for the nearby lights, and pass some more – buses, trucks, cars. No taxis. My tension, already high because of an ongoing custody struggle and the usual turmoil of moving house, was mounting: the boys' father, my ex-partner, had agreed to watch the baby while I did the cleaning, and we were running late.

My son Harper noticed a long, white limousine gliding through the traffic. He began energetically waving at the driver.

"Harper!" I snapped. "That is not a taxi!"

The traffic lights changed, and the limo slowed to a stop across the street. The driver looked over at the three of us, standing at curbside, mops and bucket in hand. He unrolled his window and shouted to us.

"Hey, if I pull around there, will you clean my car?"

"No," I responded, tired and embarrassed. "But you can give us a ride home, if you like."

"Where's home?"

We were moving into a subsidized apartment, provided by the Vancouver Native Housing Society. "Not far," I said, and shouted the particulars to him.

"Just a second," he said.

The lights changed, and we watched the limo pull through the intersection. One of my sons asked, "Is he really going to give us a ride?"

No better informed than he was, I said, "I don't know. We'll see."

The driver pulled his long sleek vehicle around, half a block down, and slowly approached us again, on our side of the road this time.

He pulled up, he got out of the car. He proceeded to offer us full limo service: preschoolers, mops, vacuum, stressed-out mom, and all.

LIFE'S WORK: CREATE; MAINTAIN; DESTROY

I survived separation from my children, first as they went off one by one to daycare or to school, and then in a protracted custody battle/negotiation: two years of grieving and insecurity, one month of complete separation. I relived the breakdown of my original family, while struggling to make good decisions as I navigated this one. I found support at the Indian Homemakers Association and other traditional parenting programs for the full two years.

When I lost my children, however briefly, I felt hatred for myself as a writer. I felt that, by taking risks and speaking out, my writerself had betrayed my motherself, left her exposed to a level of loss I could not endure. Yet I did endure; we all did. As a family, we were disrupted; we assumed a new shape, and we found new rhythms over time.

Early in this break-up/breakdown period, I had a book of poetry accepted by a publishing house. Destabilized by the upheaval in my life, I withdrew the manuscript. I agreed to do a number of events, at a festival I'd participated in once before, and then – volatile, vulnerable – I cancelled. These are the aborted works of a woman writer, called to dance with Pluto another round.

I lived for five years as a single parent. My four children lived with me half-time, and so I was immersed in a feast and famine cycle of overwork followed by intense loneliness. One of my sons with *special needs* was struggling – desperately struggling – in the public school system. The economic vulnerability that I lived with, along with the puzzle of my son's heart, took all of my time and energy, although I continued writing poetry and publishing sometimes.

In the fourth year of my single parenting life, I re-fell in love with an old mate, and in the fifth year I married for the first time. This was a time of revisiting the past, dreaming a bright future, and having wishes granted. In my personal romantic and procreative madness, I suggested to Nick that we might have a child, maybe two?

We proceeded to do so:

You were a child dreamed decades before, delayed only by the bends in the lives of your two parents. You are the first-born child of a first-born child, and the fifth-born child of a fifth-born child. Born in a green bath-tub, and born in a green season with the scent of blossoms in the air and the tree-frogs' songs sounding in your ears. You are the only girl-child given to us. Remember: you are a dream come true, and a family's rebirth.[7]

I kept a record of our rekindled romance in poetry, and a year's worth of my efforts became my fifth book.

We celebrated that May Day with no ribbons, with no pole, no meadow, and no guests. We celebrated that May Day with only the clamp used to tie off your umbilical cord, once it stopped pulsing, and the scissors used to separate you from the placenta, once it too was born. A tidal wave of tenderness swept you into our lives. The midwife Esther caught you. Your father Nicholas held me. I was on my way to the garden. You arrived on a fine spring day.[8]

Between the births of these two children, my husband's immigration application was approved, and he moved in.

Kateri Akiwenzie-Damm also returned to my life through this period. She had called me once, shortly after our return from the book fair in Australia, and asked me if I'd done any writing about sex. I realized then that I'd only written about sex in relation to abuse: my life was much improved by the reminder that sex can be fun. The implied challenge – to write beyond abuse and into celebration – is one that I would go on to apply to all the realms of my existence.

Kateri's literary midwifery services have been diverse: first, she sowed the seeds of an indigenous erotica and then, years later, collected the harvest, publishing it as the anthology *Without Reservation*. When I was sitting with my new manuscript of sexy love poetry, wondering how to connect with new publishers, I remembered Kateri's planned anthology, as well as the literary publishing house she started, *Kegedonce Press*, based on Cape Croker Reserve. I submitted work for the anthology and the whole manuscript of poems to the press at the same time. Both were published within two years.

alternate endings

It seems pointless to ask, would I have been more productive as a poet if I hadn't been a mother? Would I have morphed into a novelist, persisted as a playwright, retrained as the sort of writer that actually makes money?

The dance and intermingling of my motherself and artself, the dailiness of my formations as a person in the world and the tracks I leave behind me are inextricably united: one human being. My favourite forms for self-expression – the short nonfiction and the short, long, and medium poem, with the occasional song thrown in – are all a part of my ongoing work. Whether they are favourites because I am able to work them while parenting young children or because it's a natural fit that would not be flavoured by procreative variables, I cannot know.

Although there are similarities between managing a career and managing a family, it is also very different. The consequences – making a book, making a child – are quite different, like an oyster making a pearl, as opposed to an oyster making more oysters. Although we have feelings about our books, and we send them out into the world where they will take on lives of their own, they are much more static – jewels of another sort. To decide to have a child is to decide to bring into being something, someone, more precious than yourself.

a writer's life: family matters

The importance of remaining engaged: it would take thirty-five years for my parents to become friends again after their divorce. This was an inheritance that I tried hard to avoid gifting my own children. The older boys continue to move between the two houses in alternating waves, and, although we run separate households, the boys' dad and Nick and I gather with all the children on a regular basis. We celebrate birthdays and feast days together, raise the children together, and consult with one another, problem-solving. As Jules observed recently, "I have two moms, right? You're my mom at this house, and Brian's my mom at his house."

My life could not have assumed the shape it has, as a writer or as a mother, without the two men with whom I have collaborated most intimately, and through many years. In mundane and daily ways, and in deep-inside spirit ways, this is my team.

My dad and I haven't talked much about his experiences of birth or of becoming a father. He has raised nine children: some have stayed very close, others wandered far. Some, like me, were banished and – eventually – welcomed home again.

I have often reflected back on, and learned from, his years as a single parent, when I was a child in his home. For most of these years, he was the only grownup mainstay in my life, with his guitar in one hand; parenting skills cobbled together from good and bad sources; his sharp mind, exhausted through labour; and the hypoglycaemic roller-coaster of his moods. It was during this time of my life, living in the country with my dad, that I read an article in *The Weekend Magazine* about The Farm in Tennessee and Ina May Gaskin. I decided then, as a young teen, that I would prefer to experience birth naturally, that I would prefer to give birth with midwives, that I would like to breastfeed my children, and that it would be really cool if I could do all of these things with the dad(s).

When my father and I started visiting again, after my first partnership broke down and I was on my own, he was very encouraging. It was through observing his relationship with my stepmother, who suffered with Alzheimer's and was institutionalized for the last five years of her life, that I learned a little more about devotion. Despite strokes that severely restrict his physical freedom and separated him from his guitar, he attended her daily throughout those years; he fed her, and he kept her company.

The passage of twenty-one years in which I have made the walk of child-bearing six times, and six times have given birth at home with midwives – including Mary Sullivan, before her forced retirement, and including Gloria Lemay, before her prison term, this time under the auspices of the new College of Midwives – has resulted in a widening and deepening of my perspective on many elements of the birthing process, internal, physical, and spiritual, as well as in the life of a family and as a community event.

I have never, however, given birth in hospital, nor with a doctor attending. Perhaps it is the echoes of that prairie doctor's voice, *soft touch, eh?* ... but I've never allowed my doctors to come closer than a phone call away when it comes time to give birth. Husbands, sisters, midwives, okay; even other children, even a couple of friends: some births were highly social events, some streamlined and very private, but each and every one of them was mine.

Mother-centered, family-centered birthing care, not always available, is now at least legally entrenched in BC. Deep thanks to Gloria Lemay and to Mary Sullivan, who went all the way to the Supreme Court of Canada with the challenge. Our right to non-institutionalized births has been regained, in part, due to the sacrifices made by these two gentle, knowledgeable women.

muLTIParanormaL

Often multiparas and grande multiparas are associated with ignorance and powerlessness, even (possibly especially) in feminist literature: poor, ignorant, oppressed, our lives are considered – via a simple headcount – to be out of control. I am clarifying my position here as a human researcher, in pursuit of an intentional understanding of a field of knowledge that is quite fundamental to the human race. Being a woman with eight siblings, with whom I like to compare life stories, I might also add that a large family is, in my experience, quite normal.

My personal saint in this shift in perspective, from the one I absorbed through education to the one I evolved through lived experience, is Sylvie. Sylvie is an Armenian-Canadian woman met at the bus stop while making our independent ways to the Richmond Food Bank some years ago. At this beleaguered time in my life, I was feeling the distance between myself and all of the local matrons. This small, dark-eyed lady at the bus stop asked, "Have you children?"

I nodded, and revealed my shameful secret, "I have four."

Sylvie smiled, nodded, threw back her head, thrust out one hip, and announced: "I have six!"

At the age of forty-six, as a mid-career artist, the mother of six children between the ages of three and twenty-one, and as the author of six published books, I no longer carve the expletive FUCK in giant letters on the pages of my journal. It's been a long time. Have I become a less interesting writer, as well as a more temperate mother? I doubt it. Yet, even were it to be proven true, the big picture includes a happier person, both ears still attached to my head, and less and less likely to plath myself with each passing day. Resistance to despair is a form of resilience; it can be learned.

Competence is a form of joy, as is accomplishment and victory. The beginning writer, wherever she begins, can with persistence generate for herself a long history of achievements. Satisfactions large and small await only the acknowledgment of desire and the permission – from self, from at least some others – to try. The emerging mother – like the mid-career mother, and the established mother – is in a unique situation, building muscle and skill, settling questions and raking up new ones for herself. Not every critical view is an accurate one, or helpful, whether it is one's work or one's approach, or one's very being, under review.

On 24 December 2004, I went into day surgery, for a tubal ligation. It was like a day at the spa for me, with plenty of peace and quiet and way less multitasking than I'm used to. Surgery is a job for surgeons. My ob-gyn and I banter sometimes about homebirth and midwives. He agreed to do the initial checkup for my last two pregnancies, then "signed off" on the births. All of his training and experience says, "this is very dangerous." My experiences being quite different from his, I know where my safety lies.

Writing the mother back into the public mind, writing the woman writer, the aboriginal writer, past the narrow gates recreated across so many of our lives, is worthy work. Whether your writing and living are as intimately linked, in terms of subject matter, as my own, or solid boundaries exist between your public and private faces, writer and mother can coexist and feed one another: collaboration is key. Gratitude for what life offers us and kindness aimed at ourselves as well as at others are never amiss. Giving birth unencumbered by the fears and sometime sexism-racism of medical doctors, feeling our full power and possibility in the throes of releasing a new human life from our most intimate domain – no book launch will ever match this, I'm sorry, not even those rare few that end in standing ovations.

notes

1 Arnott, Joanne, "Homebirth." Unpublished prose poem.
2 Campbell, interview with Doris Hillis, *Prairie Fire*, vol. 9, no. 3, 52.
3 Arnott, "Homebirth."
4 Arnott, *Wiles of Girlhood*.
5 Campbell, *Prairie Fire*, 48.
6 Arnott, "Homebirth."
7 Ibid.
8 Ibid.

Stretch Marks

RENEE RODIN

In spring 1979, my father left my bedridden mother in Montreal. He came to Vancouver to join my sister Sandy and me on a holiday. My mother had planned this trip for us, probably feeling guilty that my father had become weary of looking after her.

I was tired, too, never before having worked at a twenty-four-hour-a-day, seven-day-a-week job. I'd been alone with my kids since the oldest was almost four years old, the middle one eighteen months, the youngest four months. My brief marriage to an artist had ended suddenly years earlier. We'd been together since the age of seventeen and had three kids in three and a half years, all very much wanted by both of us. But he hadn't been able to handle the feelings that had come flooding out about his own childhood when he became a parent.

I went for years without a real break until my mother concocted this plan for a trip. My sister and I weren't close to Abe, but saying "no" would have caused a civil war. Sandy was also due for a break from her job, and since our parents were treating us we decided to go for it.

Joey was now eleven years old, Noah nine, Daniel eight, and it was a great time to leave because they were so focused on my daughter's cat, Bushka, who'd just had her first litter, all female. Joey named them Pierre, Elliot, and Trudeau.

Fortunately, Sandy's partner offered to stay with them, otherwise it would have been impossible. Finding a reliable babysitter even for an evening was a dilemma and expensive. I didn't want to impose on my childless friends nor on those who just had one child. It didn't seem right for them to take three of mine, and I didn't want to take theirs three times in order to make it even.

I was determined that the few things I could control would be fair. But I was a piker compared to my watchful kids whose chorus of "no fair" rang out instantly about everything I doled out, physically and emotionally, if it weren't exactly equal in their eyes. Buddhists we weren't.

Underneath my vehement pride that I could do everything on my own was my fear that if I received any real help I'd become a bottomless pit of needs. Better to not scratch the surface, or I'd fall apart. Still, the prospect of a holiday was appealing.

We chose San Francisco because my father, a Montreal taxi driver and tourist guide, had heard the only other place in North America that came even close to Montreal's beauty was San Francisco and he was curious to compare. Also, despite being only a three-hour flight from Vancouver, the city was American and therefore "foreign."

When we arrived downtown, where our cheap hotel was located, the streets were filled with amputees in wheelchairs or on crutches. Many seemed drunk, disaffected. These vets were the embodiment of the war the US had recently lost. Their young lives had barely begun before they'd been so brutally disrupted. Vietnam had never seemed so real to me.

Long before we'd left Vancouver, Sandy and I had made plans to ditch our father as soon as we got to town. Minutes after we dropped our bags off in the room we all shared I muttered to Abe, "We're going to an art show. You won't be interested in it. We'll meet you later, for supper." We couldn't wait to see "The Dinner Party" at the Museum of Modern Art, an exhibition causing a sensation in the art world. As it turned out this would be the only time it would be shown in its entirety.

Headed by Judy Chicago, the collective project took four years and four hundred volunteers to complete. At its centre was a series of thirty-nine ceramic plates using floral imagery to depict three-dimensional vulvas. Each plate was dedicated to a "guest of honour," Sappho, Emily Dickinson, etc., who had contributed significantly to Western civilization. The work was highly controversial. Some thought Chicago was ridiculous to reduce a woman to a body part, others thought she was heroic.

Ecstatic as we were to be able to check out the show for ourselves, it didn't occur to us to ask Abe what he'd do while we were away. Just as we were racing off he told us anyhow. With a sheepish but also defiant expression on his face he said, "Well, while you're doing that, I'll be going to see my first porn movie. I'm going to see *Deep Throat*."

"The Dinner Party" was good and gutsy, though my expectations had been unreasonably high because of the hype. And I was distracted. As we inched alongside the massive tables, peering at the plates and needlework, reading the information on each woman, my mind kept returning to my father, wondering what he was seeing at the movie.

Later Sandy and I talked far less about the show than we did about Abe. Because he was a voracious newspaper reader and "The Dinner Party" was receiving a lot of press, we were sure he knew about it. We were also sure he was equating feminist art with porn, implying that what we were seeing was pornographic, too. This infuriated us.

We also felt guilty, like his accomplices, because we knew he knew we'd never squeal on him. Our parents had enough on their own plates to fight about. If Florence found out he'd been to a porn movie, it would either have set her off laughing or thrown her off her rocker. We could never predict with her and we didn't want to risk finding out.

Had Abe ever been a direct, forthright person, living with our mother had taught him the wisdom of being wily. Going to "Deep Throat" wasn't the worst of his sins. We begrudgingly accepted that a middle-aged man out on the town for the first time without his wife might want to see such a cultural phenomenon. Rather his great crime was telling us, his daughters, that he was going to a porn show. Why hadn't he kept his mouth shut or else lied about it? Sandy and I registered our rage and disgust but only with each other.

The rest of our trip was spent all together during the tourist things: Chinatown, Fisherman's Wharf, the cable cars, and the rhododendron gardens. It was a long four days. Abe conceded that San Francisco had its spectacular sights and was therefore worthy of comparison, but he was eager to return to his beloved Montreal and away from his sour daughters.

A while later Judy Chicago came to give a lecture at a packed hall in Vancouver. I was knocked-kneed with excitement to be able to see this hot feminist art star. After she gave her spiel about the making of "The Dinner Party" she fielded questions.

Someone asked, "Can a woman be an artist and a mother, too?" A hush fell over the audience. You could hear hair growing as we waited for her to answer. "No," Chicago said, "that's simply impossible."

Several people groaned. That was the last thing I heard before my ears went on strike. Then my vision became blurry and it hurt to breathe. An oddly familiar odour permeated the air: it was the smell of defeat. I rushed home to huddle in bed, small and miserable, until my anger brought me back to myself, to my own size.

I burned with betrayal. Here was a woman who had so much support from other women to do her art. Why couldn't she have parlayed that support into helping other women artists? Namely me. She was saying my life as I wanted to lead it was impossible. Since I wasn't going to give up being a mother I should give up being a writer.

For years I bore a grudge against Chicago, whom I doubt I will ever meet. And even if I did get a chance to tell her this story would she remember, recant, deny, or tell me to "get a life?" I shouldn't have placed that much importance on her answer, given her all that power, let her bend me out of shape, reduce me. But I was very vulnerable to opinion then, desperate for support from other women.

It was in the heady days of the Women's Movement, the Second Wave of Feminism, which had followed on the heels of the Civil Rights Movement sparked by the courageous actions of Rosa Parks. Just as women of colour were feeling the Women's Movement was only for "white" women, and working-class women felt the Movement was only for middle- and upper-class women, mothers were feeling the Movement was only for women without children.

Since for centuries most women were forced to have children, the current thinking was that motherhood was too traditional, almost demeaning. Abortions were legal, and the pill was widely available. Instead of opting for "liberation," women who'd wanted to become mothers had made the "wrong choice." We felt alienated, ostracized. We were resented and we resented back. It was complicated and painful.

Even in the best of circumstances, being a mother is daunting. At what other job are you expected to be an expert about things you've never experienced before, take on the world's most enormous responsibility – raising another person – without knowing a thing in advance, all the while knowing that if you don't do it right, even when you don't know what "right" is, you'll forever incur the wrath of your children and/or society?

Along with the original creative energy it takes to make a baby, mothering itself takes a lot of creativity. You have to make order out of chaos, wise decisions in split seconds, fine distinctions between responsibility and control, develop environments that will help your kids grow, build trust between you and your kids, trust your relationship with them. Keep yourself fluid and solid all at once for your rapidly changing children.

Poverty requires creativity, too. You have to practically invent resources, make any and all, including food, clothing, and energy stretch, last as long as possible. Make ends meet.

Mothers, as well as people experiencing poverty, are often maligned. We are as easily pulled off pedestals as we are put on them. In his first term Little Bush declared war on welfare mothers before he declared war on Iraq.

Welfare, Canada Council grants, and subsidies to big corporations all come from the same source, our tax dollars. In the 1970s there was talk about "Wages for Housework" and "Guaranteed Annual Income." But only welfare materialized for single mothers needing to stay at home to look after our kids.

One of my favourite songs is still "Welfare Mothers Make Better Lovers" by Neil Young. He knew. My kids knew that though we didn't have much money we weren't "poor," that we would always have what we needed. They went to a community school where most of the kids came from low-income single-parents families and the few living with two parents were considered freaks.

With advertising targeting ever-younger groups, students were conscious of status symbols even at that school. I tried to keep my kids in the latest jeans and runners so they wouldn't feel stigmatized. Luckily punk came in, and they could wear their clothes until they fell apart and look even cooler.

Whenever I had to see someone at the welfare office, I dressed up in my Sally Ann best and refused to succumb to the stereotypical image of the single welfare mother beaten down by her circumstances. It was important to present a picture of strength and independence no matter how I was feeling.

Because I'd had my first child at twenty-two and two more by twenty-six, I hadn't had much opportunity to establish my identity as a writer, so I was especially insecure. If someone asked me what I did, though mothering was my full-time occupation, I never admitted right away, "I'm a mother," for fear of disapproval. Nor did I admit, "I'm a writer," because when I did and people found out I was also a stay-at-home mother, my writing was relegated to "hobby" and me to "amateur" status.

Like most writers I couldn't and still can't support myself solely by my writing. But no committed writer (or committed anything else) is an "amateur."

All my love relationships were with writers until I realized I didn't need to live vicariously through them, I was a writer myself although I felt like a fraud to even think that way. To the dreaded question "What do you do?" I'd hem and haw or say, "I'm a tennis pro." I'd never played a game in my life, nor wanted to, but it was the most outlandish answer I could give in light of my lifestyle.

One of my few friends who was a mother had a vitriolic argument with another poet after she complained how hard it was to look after a child and write. He looked at her as if she were an idiot and said, "Just go into another room and close the door." Her child was two years old at the time.

A journalist asked me what was the biggest factor that created the "Women's Revolution," as the 1970s was also known. "Daycare," I replied. "Wrong," he snapped, "it's the pill." I repeated this anecdote much later to a friend who has four kids. She howled, "But the pill was for men. We were expected to swallow heavy doses of hormones so they wouldn't have to deal with birth control."

Though contraception remains woefully inadequate for women, reproductive technology has given us more options, including having babies later in life. Same-gender couples are openly raising kids together, and more fathers are involved with their kids in a real way than ever before. But it is still the mother who bears the most responsibility for raising kids.

Relationships come and go. Kids don't. Mothers need good social systems that we can always rely on. "Are you a daycare centre?" strangers would ask when they saw me herding, trundling my close-in-size kids down the street. But real daycare, which used to be decently subsidized, saved my life. It gave me a badly needed breather from my kids and them from me and gave them a chance to be around other adults who were saying the same kind of things I was telling them: "Don't put your hands on the stove" and "Use your words, not your fists" were not just their mother's wacky notions; they could hear them from uninvolved, sane adults.

Though the kids' elementary school was great, the first time I was walking with one of them and saw him run because the bell rang and he didn't want to be late, my heart sank. Here I was sending my kids off to be institutionalized. The first time I had to talk to the principal, I trembled with fear. Having to relate to school as a parent made me conscious of how much I'd been taught to obey authority, the antithesis of creativity. It was also at school that the false distinction between "work" and "play" began to be emphasized. False because anything I apply myself to is "work" and creativity only happens when I let my imagination "play." Make believe.

If one child or another weren't home with the sniffles or for some individual attention, and if I weren't getting groceries, doing laundry, or doing something to make the house more liveable, I'd relish being alone to replenish myself, then steel myself for the scramble of noisy demands that was sure to come after school: the kids' needs for food, actual and emotional.

Rarely did I make art, because what I needed was a blank state of mind, a sense of unlimited time and freedom, and I couldn't decompress in what little amount of free time I had to achieve that blankness.

Like many new mothers I discovered I could barely read a book for a long time after I'd given birth. Most of my body resumed its shape pretty soon, and I began to like, even be proud of, my stretch marks, but my concentration changed radically.

The latest scientific research "proves" that in pregnancy the brain does shrink in its unfamiliar stew of reproductive hormones, but apparently a woman's cognitive abilities start to expand a few weeks after giving birth. The hormonal haze lifts, although new mothers continue to be affected by the lack of sleep, exercise, and relaxation.

We are permanently altered when we become mothers, expanded in a myriad of directions, on totally new psychic territory, in a heightened state of intuition and awareness. And always on call.

Once in a blue moon when the kids were young I did write a poem or a story – something I could work on later – and the satisfaction of that kept my fires stoked. But who knows if my level of creativity would have been any different if I hadn't had kids? It still comes in ways I can't control, the only difference being that with more free time I can make myself available to try to do something with it when it happens.

I recently asked my kids, "Did you ever feel I was frustrated because I didn't have time to write while I was raising you?" Although they're not reticent to speak their minds to me about anything, they each looked at me blankly. None could recall ever thinking of me as wanting to be anything but their mother.

God knows I was frequently laying trips on them. Sometimes I'd say, "Just pretend I'm not here." That inane suggestion never went further than the breath it took to say it. The first word that was imprinted on them was "space." "Give me some space," I'd beg, implore, demand when I felt overwhelmed. In other words, often.

But what do children know about "space"? They just naturally occupy every part of you, body, mind, and soul.

If you haven't had children it's hard to imagine how your entire world changes after they're born, how profoundly your focus shifts. This can be maddening at times but mostly an amazingly wonderful out of ego experience. With infinite rewards. My biggest blessings.

As all-encompassing as it is to be a mother, know that you can also be a writer. Own all parts of your identity. Tell others, in whatever order, that you're a mother and a writer, and tell your kids, too. Tell them you like to make things because they do too and they might before long understand you.

My kids have continued to think with imagination, no matter what they're engaged in, and make things happen in their own way. For years now they've encouraged and expected me to be involved in one creative project or another. They recognize it as my "work" and value it. The very laptop I'm writing this on is a gift from them.

Motherlodes, Muses, Mapmakers

janice kulyk keefer

I thought I'd bonded with my firstborn the moment I finally saw him and held him in my arms; but it was when he spoke his first words that I knew a complete connection and, if possible, an even greater joy. Perhaps this is commonly the case for writers, who are in love, happily or hungrily, with language; perhaps it's mere serendipity, but I was ecstatic at the thought that my son and I could hold speech together, talk to one another, learn from each other. And though there were times, when my children were small, when I seemed to have lost any capacity for coherent thought and the use of polysyllabic words other than snowsuit and potty, there were many more occasions when my children came out with speech that made imagination leap. An observation ventured while I was getting ready for a party: "Don't worry, Mummy, even God has to shave His legs." Or an oath picked up at nursery school, *crotte de bique*, which translates as "droppings of a nanny-goat."

As most parents do, we attempted to raise our sons in our own cultural image. When they were small, we took them to concerts and art galleries: many's the time a child fell fast asleep on a lap despite the best efforts of flutists and percussionists, or rode on a pair of shoulders through this or that National Gallery, always, somehow, catching sight of the paintings we didn't much want him to see, such as Last Judgements boiling over with devils and instruments of torture. We took our children travelling with us, pleading with them to get out of the rental car and away from the Crack-

A-Joke book in order to explore the ruins of Knossos, though their interest never flagged at the prospect of forts or castles, however ancient and fragmentary. We bowed, of course, though not always with good grace, to their need for swings and slides in places boasting far more sophisticated forms of entertainment. And it was thanks to a playground with rubber ponies mounted on giant springs and a modest sandbox that I re-discovered qualities which I thought had disappeared forever once I became a mother, responsible for the very lives, as well as the well-being of my small children.

When our first child was three, we were given the chance to teach for one year at the University of Dijon. During the Easter break we headed south and found ourselves staying in a little town called Mouriès – the seed catalogue capital of France! – not far from Arles, which we set out to visit one morning in our rattletrap of a car. To my husband and me, Arles meant Roman ruins, Van Gogh, secondhand bookstores, cafés; to our son it meant the playground on the outskirts of town. It was April, the sky as fresh as if it had been washed and hung to dry; bits of poplar fleece floated in the air: perfect conditions for strolling among the sarcophagi in the Alyscamps that Van Gogh had painted as an endless earthen avenue bordered by tall but short-lived poplars and small, though, seemingly eternal marble tombs. I was desperate to write. I wanted nothing more, and nothing so badly, than to be on my own, scribbling in a notebook, in the Alyscamps at Arles. Instead, I found myself perched on the concrete lip of a bac à sable, watching our three-year-old play happily with another small boy, while my husband chatted with a couple who turned out to be the boy's parents. It emerged that they were housesitting a villa close to Mouriès and had bused into Arles to shop for groceries. We arranged to drive them home in the afternoon, and it was thus that we found ourselves at an old stone house surrounded by cypresses and umbrella pines and backing on to the Alpilles, which at that time of year were covered in wild iris and flush with the scents of thyme and rosemary.

The parents of our son's new friend were graduate students just as we were; searching for someplace cheerier than an Essex bedsit to spend a winter of thesis-writing, they'd chanced on an ad in a London paper, and had ended up housesitting for poet Stephen Spender and his wife, the pianist Natasha Litvin. Her grand piano graced the living room of the old stone house, along with a drawing by Henry Moore, and thank-you notes from Edith Sitwell and her ilk tacked up on the walls. We were given a tour of the house, including the desk drawer in which, among pens, erasers and paperclips, scrabble scores had been discovered, one of them, astronomically high, belonging to Iris Murdoch.

I did go on to write a short story set in the Alyscamps at Arles, which we'd visited post-playground; this, however, is the first time that I have written about our afternoon at Stephen Spender's villa. And yet without the serendipitous pleasures hatched by that chance encounter at a sandpit, I doubt that the story would ever have been written. For though I'd been itching to write on our way to Arles, my head had been clamped tight by that sense of frustrated urgency common to all those who must fit their work – their "real work" – into the pitifully small spaces they can find for it, spaces created by getting up at four in the morning, or staying up long past midnight to scratch a few words across the silence in which the rest of the house is sunk. You know that clamped state of mind – the one that issues threats more than advice: you only have an hour or two (probably less) to write: what you put on the page has got to be good, worth keeping, a fit exchange for the fog you'll be stumbling through all day as a result of making the time to write.

Spontaneity, serendipity. I owed it to the wine and good food and fine company, and to the ambiance – more encouraging than admonishing – created by that grand piano and those staggering scrabble scores; all that unlocked in my head and freed me to write again, for pleasure. I owed it to the unexpected experiences opened up to me by my small son, that when I did find the time to translate my scribbled notes from the Alyscamps into a short story, the words seemed to write themselves, or at least I seemed to regain that intense, insouciant pleasure in writing without which one might as well be sleeping, deep and dreamlessly.

❧ In taking our son to France and, later, in attempting to expose both our children to a wide range of languages and cultures, I was trying to counter the stamp of my own upbringing, which was focused on a lost, or at least threatened, language and culture – Ukrainian. Because Ukrainians were until extremely recently a colonized people, their language suppressed and sometimes forbidden by imperial *ukaz*, the task of keeping the language alive, of passing it down from mother to child was all-important, especially given the fact that education was carried out in the language of the colonizers: most often Polish or Russian. As primary school children in what was then Poland and is now Ukraine, my aunt and mother took all their lessons in Polish, and witnessed their mother hiding books and newspapers printed in Ukrainian, even distinctively Ukrainian embroidery from soldiers authorized to raid villages and stamp out any signs of Ukrainian national identity in the name of a process called the "Pacification" of minorities.

Among Ukrainians, it is the mothers who have traditionally assumed responsibility for teaching their children the language that defines the very marrow of their culture. Although my mother spoke Ukrainian to her dying day, she never taught us the language herself; that is, I never learned it in the only way that I believe most people become truly fluent, truly at home in another language: by speaking it in childhood, not just at the kitchen table or on special occasions, but constantly, by learning the language which is as much a part of the parent who speaks it as that parent's face or hands. Which means, of course, that I never taught or even spoke Ukrainian to my children; I am only now tackling the language in a concerted way, supplementing the enormous gaps left by long-ago Saturday Ukrainian school. Perhaps it is because of the shame I felt at not knowing what was supposed to be my mother tongue – Ukrainian – that I became a writer in the language that I felt the deepest need to make entirely my own: English. Perhaps because of my background, I took very seriously the role of being cultural motherlode to my children: providing them with as many experiences of the arts as I could, reading to them constantly, choosing both favourites from my own childhood and whatever seemed to appeal to them on the library shelves. My husband did likewise. We also decided not to own a television set until both children were reading for pleasure, with the result that we owned a scavenged black and white set for less than a year, before the kids asked us to get rid of it. They saw all the television they needed to at their friends' houses, they explained; they were happier having their home as a place where they could curl up with the books we'd given them without distractions.

Then came the day when, instead of our children reading books we'd recommended, they gave us for Christmas and birthdays, and sometimes just as loans, the books that fascinated them. I can't pretend that *Ten Days That Shook the World* or *Edible Wild Plants of Ontario* replaced Proust or Woolf in my affections, but recent gifts of Tracey Kidder's biography of US physician and practitioner of "liberation medicine" Paul Farmer by our younger son and of *Upping the Anti*, a journal of political thought co-edited and contributed to by our older son, have kept me from becoming enclosed by the aesthetico-literary cocoon I find all-too consolatory. And so my children's passion for social justice and for understanding systems and structures of inequality serves as a counterpoise to the kind of cultural inheritance I tried to give them: in an important way they have become for me not muses, but mappers, providing new routes for the muse to venture on.

Take, for example, an adventurous experience to which our children introduced us some twenty years later, almost to the day, of our visit with our oldest son to Stephen Spender and Natasha Litvin's villa. I am speaking now of April in Quebec City, and of the plan with which our two sons, now in their twenties, presented us one day: attending the anti-FTAA (Free Trade Area of the Americas) summit, that of the infamous chain-link fence, tear gas, and water-cannon attacks. We duly stocked up on rubberized jackets and the kind of mask you wear when engaged in heavy-duty home renovation; we found a small motel some twenty minutes outside of Quebec City, and we readied our mobile phones, in anticipation of being parted and scattered during the various marches and rallies. As we gathered with thousands of other protestors at the Plains of Abraham Park, we saw a few young couples not only with small children, but with those children's grandparents. The different marches were organized according to potential risk factor, and I hoped that parents pushing strollers would be choosing the safest routes – though I later discovered that one of the "green" or neutral areas set aside as safe havens was tear-gassed by trigger-happy riot police.

We share our children's politics, though in a less radical form; we had attended a few demonstrations with them in times past, but this weekend in Quebec would turn out to be something far more incisive and intense. I speak now as a writer as well as a citizen; what's more, as a poet, for out of the experience of protesting the corporate agenda of the globalizing men in suits locked up behind their multi-million dollar fence came a long poem that developed into a pastiche of T.S. Eliot's *The Waste Land*, which I titled *The Waste Zone*.[1] I think it is a good poem; I know it is the most important poem I have ever written. It emerged from my deeply anxious concern that the world my generation leaves to our children and their children will be a living one, never mind a world worth living in, for all. And this long poem would never have come into being, not only had I not accepted my children's invitation to come to Quebec City with them but, also, had I not explored arguments, exchanged information, and discussed the summit's aftermath with them; had I not been with them there, on the spot and the *qui vive*, and had they not read, commented upon, and helped edit *The Waste Zone* as it finally became.

❧ It's fairly common for writers to use their experiences of having and raising children as material: we have only to think of Alice Munro and Carol Shields to realize how profoundly motherhood and mothering have influenced writers' subject matter and even, we could argue, their methods and angles of approach. In Munro's case, the experience of having had the particular mother she did, of dealing with her long, Parkinsonian decline, has been as strong an influence as raising her own three children and being, for a significant portion of that time, a single mother. We know from her own account that one of Munro's most famous stories, "Miles City, Montana," was written partly from "real life" – her own daughter did nearly drown on a family road trip – and we can guess that many of the stories in, for example, *The Beggar Maid/Who Do You Think You Are?* were drawn from Munro's own, inevitably difficult life as the divorced mother of three daughters.

What do our children make of the way in which we refract, alter, deflect their lives or at least, some of their key experiences, through the lens of our writing? I think of that wonderful Bronwen Wallace poem[2] in which she predicts how significantly her and her son's versions of his childhood, and its key events, will differ. Or of an essay in Bonnie Friedman's *Writing Past Dark*, which argues for the psychological necessity of the adult writer's being able to articulate her own version of familial truth and of the reality of her particular childhood, estranged as it may be from the Official Family Version. Perhaps the best way we could respond to this question would be to ask ourselves how we would feel were our children, one day, to take up their pens and write an account of our lives or of the experience of having grown up with such parents as we proved to be. One of Alice Munro's children has, of course, done just this; one of Irving Layton's as well, and doubtless more of such volumes will appear. The idea of my children writing about me shivers my spine, not that I fear much in the way of skeleton rattling: surely our (nuclear) family was far too dull, too ordinary, to inspire my children to want to write of it or of my specific way of mothering? But the very idea of looking at myself, my actions and omissions through my children's eyes spooks me, and I shut the door on that imagined possibility before there's anything much too see. It's a reflex action, like the way you automatically close your eyes when any object comes too close: inevitably, it seems to me, it would be painful and even perverse, like scraping off my own skin and crawling into theirs. Or at least so my special pleading goes.

My children appear now and then in my writing, or at least what appear are versions not so much of them as their experiences, or experiences through which they have led me to "material." For instance, that year we spent in France, renting the ground floor of an old house whose top storey was occupied by a most reclusive elderly lady whom I would never have met had she not formed the habit of calling down from her windows to my son when she saw him playing in the garden. She had a fascinating history, I was to discover, but the way to that history led through the bonbons she would offer my son when we came to visit and the ancient set of dominos she put out for him to play with. The old lady was childless; the story I wrote about her followed the windings of the triangular relationship that developed between a young, reluctant mother, her small child and a lonely, imperious old lady, not to mention the cat she alternately caressed and bullied. The child in the story was a girl, not a boy, and the mother very different from myself, though I believe that I sketched the contours of *la vieille dame* with some accuracy.

This use we make of our children in our writing – I think of it as being something like the use painters make of models when rendering some historical or religious event requiring a multiplicity of figures. I think, for example, of Vanessa Bell using her daughter Angelica as a stand-in for the Virgin Mary in the wall paintings she did at Berwick Church. Though Bell did paint Angelica in an assortment of domestic interiors, almost by accident, she never produced anything like a penetrating portrait of her daughter, perhaps for fear of what Angelica's face might reveal regarding the painful complexity of their relationship. (Angelica Bell, who says it took her some forty years to free herself of her mother's possessiveness, did write one of those child-of-distinguished-artists-tells-her-side-of-the-story books about her Bloomsbury childhood, a volume with the revealing title, *Deceived by Kindness*.)

This is not to say that writers may not engage in the most profound way with the realities of their relationships with their children or the lives of those children, especially when those lives are harrowing and even tragic. And yet for me there is a kind of taboo that prevents me from approaching my own children's lives or temperaments as the subject of creative writing.

I may have written a poem for, but not "about" each of my sons, but these poems turned out to be the equivalent of casting nets over birds far too alert and strange to ever be caught. Nets whose meshes were made of words very like the birds themselves; meshes that startled and dispersed as soon as they were called on to close in.

I am not proposing that writers who raise or have frequent contact with children are better or more interesting writers than those who don't: think of Emily Brontë or Gwen MacEwan or Mavis Gallant. And I am certainly not trying to make light of those aspects of mothering that turn the Muse into a Frequent Flyer-Away. Although I had the full support of a partner who did his share of parenting our children, taking care of them when I was away for extended periods on research trips or at writing retreats, there were times during that twenty-five years or so when I was responsible for small or teenage children that I hit rock bottom, convinced I could never be either a good writer or a good mother, and certainly not both at once. I can only begin to imagine the courage, stamina, and faith it must require to be both a writer and a single mother, not only when dealing with diapers and measles but also with issues like bullying, drugs, and dropping out of school. I think of Elizabeth Smart, heroic and hapless single mother of four children, one of whom committed suicide; I think of her struggle to feed, clothe, and educate them all, during which time her creative work took the back seat to writing advertising and articles for fashion magazines. As poignantly, I think of her once again putting her writing aside in order to care for a grandchild whose mother was unable to look after her. A superb writer of a few, sometimes uneven works, and one who seems almost unknown. (If Google's search engine is any guide to enduring fame, then the Canadian writer takes a very distant back seat to that Elizabeth Smart who was kidnapped in 2003 and finally returned unharmed to her parents in Salt Lake City.)

And yet, and yet, and yet: if we are writers almost in spite of ourselves and the conditions under which we live; if we need to write the way we need to eat and sleep and open our eyes, we *will* write, however many times we are interrupted or prevented from doing so by this or that demand made by our children and perhaps even grandchildren. This truism may appear a piece of cake for those of us with the means to hire child minders, or lucky enough to have parents to take our children for weekends or sometimes weeks at a time, in order that we may perform that act of extended, internal migration that writing requires. It may appear a crust of stone to those without those means, or whose children's demands are far more serious than those posed by routine childhood illnesses or misbehaviour. But I believe writing to be a vocation that keeps on calling us as insistently as our children do, and far more persistently, as those children grow older and become independent. And when our grown children are able to inform, expand, and contest our settled thoughts and established experiences – to offer us new ways of seeing, thinking, and experiencing the lives we share with them on this small and stricken planet, then we writers are rich indeed in the very things that allow us to write in the only way that matters, at least to this writer, at this time: compassionate intelligence and alert integrity.

notes

1 Kulyk Keefer, "The Waste Zone," *Midnight Stroll.*
2 Wallace, "My Son Is Learning to Invent," *Common Magic,* 17.

Letters to a Young Mother Who Writes

rachel rose

Allow your judgments their own silent, undisturbed development, which, like all progress, must come from deep within and cannot be forced or hastened. *Everything* is gestation and then birthing. To let each impression and each embryo of a feeling come to completion, entirely in itself, in the dark, in the unsayable, the unconscious, beyond the reach of one's own understanding, and with deep humility and patience to wait for the hour when a new clarity is born: this alone is what it means to live as an artist: in understanding as in creating.[1]

– Rainer Maria Rilke

Rainer Maria Rilke wrote his *Letters to a Young Poet* at a time when poets were usually men. He addresses a young man, and writes to the universal young man who is beginning to write. But Rilke is aware, as are some of the great male poets (Blake, Whitman) of the limitations of his time, of what is lost when the sexes are forced to maintain entirely separate spheres rather than celebrate their interdependence. Some women writers who were also my teachers have positioned mothering and writing as incompatible.

I came of age after a renaissance of women writers, some of whom were also mothers, wrote the truths of their lives. I write and mother in an age where much has become possible for some women writers, but an age also where much has also stayed stubbornly fixed, and some things have gotten harder. When I think of the young writer who has just become a mother, my heart aches for her, and yet I consider her fortunate among writers. I do not believe that caring for those one loves hinders a writer's creative development. During these years of relatively marginal production, I feel my soul to be tempered and my interconnectedness with all that is creative and life-affirming to be deepened. I write with great expectation.

Let me share two truths I have gleaned after years of mothering and writing: being a full-time writer is dreadful preparation for motherhood, but being a mother offers excellent opportunities to writers, if we are only supported enough in the world to be able to grasp them.

Writing is a selfish act. Don't try to tell me otherwise. Sure, it can be incredibly hard work. But most of the time writing is pure pleasure, that honest, hard-won pleasure that comes from making something out of nothing, something entirely new. Pregnancy is like that, a little, or maybe conception is. But once the babe is birthed, the skills a writer demands don't help in any way. Selfish devotion to the desk, the keyboard, the espresso machine, and the whims of the muse all yield to being available to a small, gassy, ravenous being.

Many have written that the ideal life for an artist is to be alone, independently wealthy, devoted to no one and nothing but art. Rilke often spoke of himself as a solitary soul, and proposed that the test of a true writer was whether one would die if unable to write. He stopped living with his wife and child when his daughter was only a year old, and never returned. Rilke has been one of my wisest guides, and still I marvel that he could have such insight, such exquisite sensitivity, and remain so frustratingly limited. I continue to argue the point with him. Once you have other lives connected to your own, preserving health and wellness take on a whole new significance, and being alone for a whole night becomes a rare gift. I would die for my children, but not for lack of a pen and paper. I am made of tougher stuff than that. I would pine and mope and become less and less the mother I wish to be, but these days my focus is on staying alive. These days such romantic notions seem, let me say it, *silly*. That's what I want to say to Rilke, the same way I'd say to my son: *Don't be silly. Enough of this talk of dying. Let's talk about birth.*

But behind that refusal of mine to become preoccupied with pining to death for want of a pen lies a deeper fear: I focus on life because I know there are no guarantees I can keep my children alive, no guarantees that they will outlive me. In this way, too, the examined life of a mother who writes has been a gift. When my son was small, I whispered to myself that, if I lost him, I would die, too. It was a pure, uncalculated emotion: he was my life, my heart, my vitality. Then I watched mothers I know lose their children and struggle through the darkness. Two events taught me to bite my tongue and face my deepest fear: my daughter's blood disorder and long week in the NICU after birth, and a brief incident with my boy and a speeding car. After we had cried together at almost losing our son, Isabelle said to me, fiercely, "You can't just check out if you lose him. You can't do that." Now I'm a bit ashamed of having said that I'd die if I lost either of my children, because I want to live with gratitude most of all for this unexpected, uncontrollable gift that is my life, our lives entwined. If I died for love of them, where would my love for them go? I believe now I could go on, broken, loving with whatever I had left. The end of the story will not be mine to write. Mothers face these fears in flashpoints of focusing terror, and mostly we find ourselves stronger than we thought imaginable. We love, as Rilke taught us. But we cannot hold.

❧ For a long time you won't be alone, and, even when you are, your mind will be as cluttered as your house. That, for me, was the biggest shock to my system. I went from loving long stretches of solitude, *needing* my time alone, to having an infant at my breast, all the time. I thought the intensity of the bond would drive me mad; at the same time, I didn't feel comfortable unless he was in my arms. To be with someone and still be lonely was a novel and uncomfortable sensation.

Mothers have often been so busy with the heavy duty of human attachments that artistry has been marginalized, but mothers have never, as a group, been silenced. Women have written diaries and penned letters as they crossed the prairies in pioneer wagons. They have created poems and lullabies, resonant rhymes and quilts that told stories. They have written novels while their children slept – and those who never learned to read have still passed down songs and poems. But we have not created the canon. We have not defined the perimeters of what qualifies as literature. We are, however, beginning.

When Tillie Olson wrote *Silences*, her important essay on mothering and writing, there were few examples of women who managed to mother and to have successful writing careers; more women were silenced or driven to suicide by the demands of both spheres. But I have Alice Munro, Alice Walker, Carol Shields, Margaret Atwood, and Audre Lorde. And I can go back further and find the women that Tillie Olson did not speak of, because, as Alice Walker writes, their histories were buried (and what a bittersweet pleasure to find their treasures!), though they were always there. Murasaki Shikibu wrote her masterpiece, *The Tale of Genji*, in the eleventh century, likely with the help of her daughter, Daini no Sanmi. Before them there was Sappho: mother, poet, lesbian, mystery. We are not the first to discover the Earth is round.

A childless-by-choice friend of mine recently expressed her irritation with all her girlfriends becoming mothers. "They go on *for hours* about how unselfish they are, how much they've given up. You can't get a word in edgewise. That's all they can hear. That's all they want to talk about."

Though the words stung, they stung because they had the smart of truth to them. We *do* want to talk about how much we've given up, how little we're sleeping, how hard we're working, how incredible our new creations are. We *do* become monotonous. Everything I said to try to explain only proved her point. Never has there been a greater rupture in my life than that which came with becoming a mother. I thought I would never write again. I thought I would never look the same again, or be alone. My body had been turned inside out, my uterus sitting on my hips like a Christmas ham. I thought, and to some extent it's true, that I'd never feel free of worry again. I wanted the whole damn world to mourn and celebrate with me. I wanted everyone to be where I was, on this new planet. I was so lonely, and I couldn't even write about it.

Instead, I walked. I put the baby in his stroller for his twice-daily naps, and I walked: up one side of Mont Royal, down the other. I wandered through the cemetery, past the small crosses where dozens of babies lay buried, snatched from their mothers' arms at birth, at seven months, at two years, and I wept for them, wept for myself, for all humanity. I was porous those first few months, terribly open. I sat in the hot, dry grass, nursed my baby and trembled with a wild delight at this new gift I'd been given. But I could not write. I was wholly preoccupied with making sure he was still breathing, with attending to my bleeding nipples, my new scars, his hungers and needs. Even when my partner was holding him, even when I had those blocks of time for myself, I had nothing to say. I couldn't write; I couldn't even read deeply. Was I suffering post-partum depression, or was my experience normal? I don't know. I was in a soupy quicksand, trying to keep my head up; I despaired. I was also falling deeper and deeper into the truest love I had ever found. My muse had deserted me entirely.

At first, I was determined not to change too much. I wanted my autonomy, which is so precious for writers: I wanted that lonely wildness, the ability to go deep, wherever my imagination took me. I was afraid of going deep with him and losing myself entirely. I took him to the best daycare I could find, and I kissed him and left him in his little swing. At home I pumped my breasts and lined the milk with its hardening cream in bottles in the fridge. I wandered around the empty apartment, searching for myself like a book I'd mislaid.

After a week or two, I took him out of the daycare. I surrendered myself. I had that choice, that luxury – though it felt like being swallowed whole. I wasn't myself anymore, and I couldn't be happy with him or away from him. But maybe it wasn't about being happy, that first year.

There are a few things I wish I'd known, or been able to hear: that time when they are small and wholly yours is finite and precious. If you are able to give yourself to the process, don't be afraid to – you will experience wonders amidst the quicksand of your daily routine. And you will come back to yourself, or to a close enough approximation of yourself that you'll be fine. One day, you'll be able to go deep into the writing again, you'll be able to be a lonely wanderer and poet, you'll be a lover again, and an adventurer, if only part-time. Perhaps, after giving yourself to your baby with compassion and love for a generous period, you'll like yourself better than you did before.

My muse came back after a few years. I became an approximation of my old self; I healed. I began a second book. I allowed myself to be apart from my beloved baby. So that is something I must tell you: your muse may flee, but it is very unlikely to be a permanent departure. Wait for her. It's okay to find motherhood all-consuming for a little while.

My wise friend, the writer Wendy Lustbader, wrote an essay about growing old and becoming dependent. She asks: "Once we begin living in terms of the question, *Who would take care of me if I got sick?* the whole of life transforms. The question mandates a shift in the order of things, making a life rich with generosity and kindness more desirable than any other kind of fortune."[2]

If we mother with those questions in mind, we gentle our hands, we accept the new rhythms. No matter the difficulty of our circumstances, we have a choice to be kind and honest. We can apologize when we are not and learn from our mistakes. We can strive to have compassion not only toward our own children but to the children in their classes who are struggling with aggressive behaviour, to all the children who will outlive us. We can let them see that we are women who love them passionately and had lives before they came, are in love with books and creating literature, with *creating*, with all creation, and preservation.

✿ Many women suffer ambivalence about whether or not to mother. I was not one of them. It was not the mothering that frightened me, but the rest that goes along with it: how to be with a partner in a true partnership when you are made dependent by a child, how to earn money and also write poetry, how to be an involved mother and an independent woman in a sexist world that values material wealth and power over interconnectedness. I cobbled together something that works well for me, and I have seen other mothers who write do the same in their own relationships. It's possible, but it's by no means easy.

Oppressive elements attach themselves to motherhood; they are not intrinsic to motherhood. More important by far are the circumstances under which a young writer enters into motherhood. Like marriage, motherhood has an oppressive history to answer for, but marriage between two equals can also be a source of strength and joy. We speak of how becoming a mother damages and diminishes a writer, with its broken attention span and many obvious burdens. But what if motherhood brings with it the greatest gift to a writer: empathy, interconnectedness, a consciousness that is bigger than the individual woman who writes? What if mothering offers a shortcut that other writers who don't have this opportunity must work for years to imagine in their own work?

I do not have the struggle that many heterosexual women face, of forging insistence that their role of nurturer is valued in a sexist world or by a particular beloved man. I mother with another mother, and in some ways we are the most harmonious of families, the most intimate. How could we not respect the mother we see in one another, nursing our children as we have together? Our struggles are different: they are external to our relationship. We fear the way our children will be treated because of us. We fear the pitfalls they will have to negotiate growing up without a father.

There are still no easy paths, but women are creating true marriages, giving birth, mothering and writing and working hard. They are insisting on both the books and the baby in the same lifetime. Some of us are living in a time of possibility, of hope.

For most mothers, of course, that's not the case at all. Globally, most mothers are still silenced, fettered, hemmed in, controlled by brutal poverty, racism, and sexism. I don't pretend that reality is not bleak. I am writing to the young mother who has enough food and isn't being beaten at night and already knows how to read and expects her newborn baby to survive past its fifth birthday, because, without this, what else matters? I am writing from a place of such incredible privilege that sometimes I feel the heat rise in my face: I am speaking to so few mothers when I write of choosing to listen to the muse, to the child. What of the long hours of monotonous work most mothers must do, often far away from their babies, just to survive? What about when there is no paper, no pen, no words?

Yet I am thinking of all mothers, all mothers who endure, all the poems not written down, half-formed and forgotten, all the grief-chants. It is dark indeed, and I cannot say that I see much hope globally. But here and there are sparks of light, like fireflies in fog. Here and there – a song, remembered.

❧ As a child on Hornby Island, British Columbia, I wandered in the woods and fields. I found a nest of voles ripped open by a combine and brought them home, fed them every few hours round the clock with an eyedropper, and, when they died, I cried until I couldn't breathe. I helped my father nurse an injured red-tailed hawk, staring straight into its wild, dilated eyes, and I was there to release it when its wing mended and it left me. I bottle-fed the lambs and let the dog sleep on my bed. I learned from my mother how to brush and comb the bodies of our horses and how to clean the dirt from their heavy hooves. Their hot breath on my shoulders was my reward, the galloping where I become part horse: that fusion of self into other.

Holding a bullfrog is not so different from holding a newborn. How I stared into those otherworldly gold-flecked eyes and shuddered as it peed all over me. How strange, to be so connected with another living thing that I forget my own self in the moment of wonder, even as my hands fill up with frog pee.

All this was work, but it was a privilege, because it gave me an intimate connection with something outside myself, and who I was changed as a result. There are other ways to lose the self, to become egoless. One can study the bullfrog, follow the red-tailed hawk, meditate for years in a Tibetan temple. But the miracle of giving birth is that one becomes two-in-one, two become a trinity. If you find yourself in the situation of recently having created life, it won't hurt to recognize the spiritual doors that have opened to you. Should such an opening be free of pain? Even following the barn owl for a day makes the back ache and the knees stammer. The pain of such knowledge is indistinguishable, in the end, from joy.

And so I say this: remember to play wildly. You can learn the names of all the shorebirds together; it's not too late. If your son and daughter see you peeling a persimmon, they will almost certainly be curious enough to want a taste.

❧ With the second pregnancy, things were a little less intense. I knew what to expect. I worked to complete the second manuscript in time, knowing that I would once again be overwhelmed. A week before my due date, just after midnight, I woke my partner to whisper that maybe I'd wet the bed; was I suffering from pregnancy-induced urinary incontinence? Every giggle brought a little rush of fluid. Then I stood up and the waters spilled out of me, and I realized what was happening. Isabelle pulled me back into bed. We lay together holding hands, our son sleeping between us, and we talked about the baby that was coming. She went to sleep, and I went upstairs to write for a few more quiet hours. I wanted them badly, those last hours alone with my poems. I did not think much about the baby that was going to come. Just before dawn, the contractions got so heavy I had to stop. Poetry didn't matter anymore. I was holding on to a rope of sheets, dipped in a well of pain and then drawn up again, a dripping bucket. This time, I was not so afraid to be emptied, to be returned entirely to my body. It is not a bad thing, once in a while, for a writer to be poured out, emptied of ego.

❧ Rilke hated critics. He wrote, "Works of art are of an infinite solitude, and no means of approach is so useless as criticism. Only love can touch and hold them and be fair to them."[3]

As soon as you become a mother, you will be vulnerable to the critics. They will ask you if your baby sleeps through the night and judge your answer. If your baby is adopted, or doesn't look like you, they will want explanations. If your baby cries a lot, they will tell you what you are doing wrong. They will tell you to ignore your baby's cries so you don't spoil him, to ignore your own heart and listen to them.

But an experienced writer knows that at the beginning there is no sense in showing your fledgling work to the public. You must be alone with it. You must love it and help it grow without shame, with only the purest intimacy. Wear cotton in your ears when you walk with your baby. Smile vaguely, and let yourself be guided by love. Listen to those you trust, but always make your own way. Ask yourself: would you like to be the child of the mother that you are now? Let this alone guide you.

You will hurt your child. You will get divorced, or sick, or she will get sick, or you will be too fat or too busy or not the biological mother or you won't notice she's being molested or you will not change him to a better school soon enough or the one time you aren't paying attention will be the time he falls out of the tree. You can't keep them safe, but that does not absolve you from trying.

I walked in the cemetery with my sleeping baby and wrestled with this truth. I love my son, my daughter, with my whole being, and I can't protect them. And I am a lesbian, raising children in a family with two mothers. They have to deal with social prejudice, with being different. I chose that fate for them with great deliberation when Isabelle and I set their lives into motion. At times the responsibility I have taken on terrifies.

I lie awake at night sometimes, preparing to fight for them, to defend them against those who will try to hurt them because of who I am. I'm a writer who writes about family, who writes about her children. The idea that they may suffer because of who I am is acutely painful. Isabelle wisely points out that if they do suffer, it will not be because of us, but because of others' prejudices against us. This is a distinction I must bear in mind and make sure they understand, too. But I can't kid myself. I could put down my pen. I could write about something else, but I choose not to. I am a writer; this is the family they ended up with. So far, I have censored little. I give them my flawed perceptions, my body, my hope, my presence.

❦ Writing, for me, is a process of controlled creativity. I create a world in miniature in a poem or story. Even in a memoir, I pick and choose what I will write about, what I will keep silent. Mothering is a process of letting go of control, while simultaneously loving intensely. The process happens to you: your choices are only partially in your hands as to when or whether you'll get pregnant, if your birth will be free of interventions or invasively high-tech, if your child will love to read with you as you've always imagined, or will have a learning disability and never read with ease. Writing is ego; mothering makes you realize that *hey, shit!* it's not all about you. It's a dance, and you are the lead partner; your steps are important, you should never step on your partner's toes without apology. But you don't choose the music or the partner.

There are many options available if a writer is struggling with a manuscript. You can kill off the difficult characters, or make them have a life-changing revelation. You can render them mute from an accident. You can shut the manuscript in a drawer until you want to deal with it again, or burn it altogether and start fresh. You can send it to someone else and pay them to try to fix it.

If you are struggling with a child, here is the singular option available: keep struggling. Call up reserves of strength and patience you never knew you had to deal with the incessant screaming of colic, the anorexia your daughter is flirting with, the terror that strikes as your son runs in front of an oncoming car, the last meal in the house. Here's what I've learned: we mothers are tougher than we knew, tougher than we've ever acknowledged. We stay and face the unknown, the unexpected, the unsolvable. We can survive on air instead of sleep, hope instead of present happiness.

There are times where I would have given my right arm for a whole week alone. But I learned nobody wants my right arm. No offers. I'd give my life for my children's lives in an instant, but most of the time it doesn't work like that. We mothers learn to endure. With a little luck, we learn grace under pressure.

I have learned, as a mother, to memorize the one true line of a poem before I fall asleep at night, to carry the germ of a short story in me as I push a stroller along the beach, working it like the waves work a pebble. What a gift, to know I can keep the seed of a poem within until I can sit with it! But I have learned, also, to make time for the sitting and the planting before the seeds rot and are gone.

Certainly mothering has made me a better writer. Writer's block? Who has time for it? Give me a free afternoon, and I'll give you a full afternoon's work.

Writing is a luxury. It's much easier to be upstairs writing in my quiet study than it is to be downstairs sudsing the children as they flail in their baths. It's often more peaceful to write about motherhood than to descend into it. But mothering, as I have mentioned, has made me reconsider what we call *work* and *happiness* and *easy*. I asked myself what I want to do with the years I have been allotted, and the answer is this: love Isabelle. Raise children. Write books and read books. Learn the stories of everyone whose path crosses my own, and try to ease suffering when the opportunity presents itself. Walk on the beach barefoot whenever I can. Share my sensory delight in the world with my son and daughter.

Poets write poetry for its own sake. We don't write and publish poetry planning to get rich or famous. The rewards are intrinsic to the work. Mothering, I think, is much the same. As I've written this essay, I've been sleeping sitting up with my daughter the past four nights as she struggles to breathe through the first cold of the season. I look at myself in the mirror and see new lines under my eyes. The china has cracked. I barely recognize myself. I can't remember what I was told or said five minutes ago. My hair has thinned from nearly four years of nursing.

But the compensation is in the creation of a family on my own terms. The compensation is having my two-year-old yell at her friend when I pick him up, "You don't love *my* mama. There's your mama over there. This mama is *my* sweetheart!"

notes

A few of the ideas in this essay began to take shape in an earlier essay, "Creating Benjamin," which won third place in *Prairie Fire*'s 2001 Personal Journalism contest and was published in *Prairie Fire*, vol. 22, no. 4.

1 Rilke, *Letters to a Young Poet*, letter 3, 23–4.
2 Lustbader, "At the Mercy of Strangers," *Generations*.
3 Rilke, *Letters to a Young Poet*, letter 3, 23.

about the authors

luanne armstrong

Luanne Armstrong has published over ten books: novels, poetry, and children's books. Her most recent children's book, *Jeanie and the Gentle Giants*, was nominated for the Sheila Egoff BC Book Prize, the Canadian Library Association Book of the Year, the Ontario Library Association Silver Birch Award, and the Red Cedar Award in BC and was named by McNally Robinson Booksellers in Winnipeg as one of their top ten all-time best children's books. Her novel *The Bone House* was shortlisted for the Canadian Sunburst Award for Science Fiction and the Relit Prize for Fiction. Her memoir, *Blue Valley*, was published by Maa Press, and her new children's book *Pete's Gold* will be published by Ronsdale Press. She has four children and two grandchildren, an MFA in creative writing, and a Ph.D. in education from UBC.

joanne arnott

Joanne Arnott is a Métis/mixed-blood writer, originally from Manitoba. She was raised in both urban and rural communities, studied English at the University of Windsor, Ontario, and has lived on the West Coast of BC since 1982. Her poetry books include *Wiles of Girlhood* (Press Gang, 1991), which won the Gerald Lampert prize for poetry; *My Grass Cradle* (Press Gang, 1992); *Steepy Mountain: Love Poetry* (Kegedonce Press, 2004); and *Mother Time* (Ronsdale Press, 2006). She has also published a children's book, *Ma MacDonald* (Women's Press, 1993) with Mary Anne Barkhouse, and a nonfiction collection, *Breasting the Waves: On Writing & Healing* (Press Gang, 1995). She is currently working on a new nonfiction collection. She has five sons and one daughter.

STEPHANIE BOLSTER

Stephanie Bolster's first book, *White Stone: The Alice Poems* (Signal/Véhicule), won the Governor General's Award and the Gerald Lampert Award in 1998 and appeared in French with Les Éditions du Noroît in autumn 2007, translated by Daniel Canty. She has also published *Two Bowls of Milk* (McClelland & Stewart), which won the Archibald Lampman Award and was shortlisted for the Trillium Award, and *Pavilion* (McClelland & Stewart). Her several chapbooks include, most recently, *Biodôme* (above/ground) and *Past the Roman Arena and the Cedar of Lebanon* (Delirium). She is the editor of *The Ishtar Gate: Last and Selected Poems* (McGill-Queen's) by the late Ottawa poet Diana Brebner and of *Best English Canadian Poetry 2007* (Tightrope) and is currently editing an anthology of poetry and prose excerpts pertaining to zoos. She teaches writing at Concordia University in Montreal.

DI BRANDT

Di Brandt's poetry titles include *questions i asked my mother* (1987), *Jerusalem, beloved* (1995), *Now You Care* (2003), and *Speaking of Power: The Poetry of Di Brandt* (2006). Her nonfiction books include *Wild Mother Dancing: Maternal Narrative in Canadian Literature* (1993), *Dancing Naked: Narrative Strategies for Writing Across Centuries* (1996), *This Land That I Love, This Wide Wide Prairie* (NeWest, 2006), and *So this is the world & here I am in it* (2007). She has received numerous awards for her poetry, including the CAA National Poetry Prize, the McNally Robinson Book of the Year Award, and the Gerald Lampert Award. Di Brandt holds a Canada Research Chair in Creative Writing at Brandon University.

sHannon cowan

Shannon Cowan is the author of two novels: *Leaving Winter* (Oolichan, 2000) and *Tin Angel* (Lobster Press, 2007). She was shortlisted for the CBC Literary Competition in 2003 and received the Norma Epstein Award for Creative Writing the same year. For the past four years she has written sporadically on books and ideas for the *Times Colonist*, the *Vancouver Sun, Books in Canada, Quill and Quire*, and the *Globe and Mail*. She holds an MFA from UBC, where she was once the associate fiction editor of Prism International, and lives on Vancouver Island, where she is mothering her two children.

eLIzaBeTH Greene

Elizabeth Greene taught English from 1969 to 1998 at Queen's University, where she was instrumental in establishing the program in Women's Studies and courses in Creative Writing. She edited and contributed to *We Who Can Fly: Poems, Essays and Memories in Honour of Adele Wiseman* (Cormorant, 1997), which won the Betty and Morris Aaron Prize for best Scholarship on a Canadian Subject at the Jewish Book Awards in 1998, and edited and contributed to *Kingston Poets' Gallery* (Artful Codger Press, 2006). She has also co-edited *The Window of Dreams* (Methuen, 1986), with Mary Alice Downie and M.-A. Thompson, and *On the Threshold: Writing toward the Year 2000* with Foxglove Collective (Beach Holme, 1999). Her essay, "Dark Night and Fireflies," part of a memoir about her son Alan, is posted on the *Dropped Threads 3* website. Her book of poems, *The Iron Shoes,* is forthcoming from North Shore Press. Elizabeth lives in Kingston with her son Alan.

corI HowarD

Cori Howard is a writer and radio and television producer in Vancouver. She has written for *Maclean's*, the *National Post,* the *Globe and Mail, The San Francisco Chronicle*, and magazines including *Elle, Condé Nast Traveller*, and *Saturday Night*. She is currently a producer with CBC Radio and lives near the beach with her husband, little boy, and baby girl. Her anthology on motherhood, *Between Interruptions: Mothers Write about Guilt, Ambition, Anxiety, Love and More*, was published by Key Porter in autumn 2007.

sally ito

Sally Ito's first book of poetry, *Frogs in the Rain Barrel* (Nightwood, 1995), was chosen first runner-up for the Milton Acorn People's Memorial Award in 1997. She has also published a second, *Season of Mercy* (Nightwood, 1999). Her book of short fiction, *Floating Shore* (1998), won the 1999 Howard O'Hagan Award and was also shortlisted for the Danuta Gleed Award for short fiction and for the City of Edmonton Book Prize. While parenting two children in Winnipeg, Manitoba, Ito is currently at work on a novel about a Japanese-American veteran who fought against the Japanese in World War Two. She has also been a judge for the Kiriyama Pacific Rim Book Prize.

marni jackson

Marni Jackson is a senior editor at *Walrus* magazine and has recently been appointed Rogers Communications Chair at the Banff Centre, heading up the Literary Journalism Program there. She has won numerous National Magazine Awards for her features, columns, and humour writing and is the author of *Pain: The Science and Culture of Why We Hurt.* She was one of the first authors to tackle the myths of contemporary motherhood in her Canadian bestseller, *The Mother Zone*, which has been reissued by Vintage Editions.

janice kulyk keefer

Janice Kulyk Keefer was born in Toronto and teaches at the University of Guelph. She has two sons. Her books include *The Green Library* (Harper-Collins Canada, 1996), *Rest Harrow* (HarperCollins Canada, 1992), *Travelling Ladies* (HarperCollins Canada, 1992), *Reading Mavis Gallant* (Oxford University Press, 1989), *Constellations* (Random House Value Publishing, 1987), *Under Eastern Eyes: A Critical Reading of Maritime Fiction* (University of Toronto, 1988), *The Paris-Napoli Express* (Oberon, 1986), and *White of the Lesser Angels* (Ragweed, 1986). She has won the CBC Radio Literary Contest for fiction twice: for "Mrs. Putnam at the Planetarium" and for "The Wind." She has also won a National Magazine Award for poetry for "Fields," and the *Malahat* Long Poem Prize for "Isle of Demons." *Under Eastern Eyes* was shortlisted for the Governor General's Award for nonfiction and *The Green Library* for the Governor General's Award for fiction.

CATHERINE KIRKNESS

Catherine Kirkness was born in New Zealand in 1967 and grew up in Scarborough, Ontario. In 1989 she graduated from Trinity College, University of Toronto, with an English Specialist BA and was awarded the Philip Child essay prize for her work on Janet Frame. She has a Master's degree in English literature from UBC. She lives in Vancouver with her husband, mother, and two children. This essay is part of a larger work in progress.

FIONA TINWEI LAM

Fiona Tinwei Lam is a Scottish-born Chinese Canadian writer and former lawyer. Her poetry has appeared in major Canadian literary magazines including *Grain, The Malahat Review* and *The Fiddlehead,* and in anthologies such as *Swallowing Clouds: An Anthology of Chinese Canadian Poetry* (Arsenal Pulp Press, 1999), *Fine Form* (Polestar, 2005), and *White Ink* (Demeter Press, 2007). Her book *Intimate Distances* (Nightwood, 2002) was a finalist for the City of Vancouver Book Prize. She has twice been shortlisted for *Event Magazine's* Non-Fiction Contest. She is the single mother of a five-year-old son.

DEIRDRE MAULTSAID

Deirdre Maultsaid was born in Saskatchewan and now lives in Burnaby, British Columbia, as the single mother of two teenage sons. She won Third Place in *Prairie Fire's* 2003 Creative Non-Fiction Contest and Honourable Mentions from *This Magazine* and *Rippleffect Press*. She has been published in *Canadian Women's Studies, The Danforth Review, Other Voices, Zygote,* and anthologies by Rippleffect Press and Rowan Books. She has also been published online at *Ariadna* (Spain), *Amnesia* (Spain), *The Barcelona Review,*

Conspire (US), *Moxie* (US), the *Southern Cross Review* (Argentina), and the *Vestal Review* (US). She has recently published a book of lyrical essays: *These Blessings, This Crisis: Essays* (Trafford, 2006).

susan musgrave

Susan Musgrave's most recent novel, *Cargo of Orchids* (Knopf), is the story of three women on death row for the murders of their children. Her latest collection of poetry is *What the Small Day Cannot Hold: Collected Poems 1970–1985* (Beach Holme). *You're in Canada Now ... A Memoir of Sorts* was published in autumn 2005 by Thistledown. She has been nominated, and has received awards, in five different categories of writing: poetry, fiction, nonfiction, personal essay, and children's writing, as well as for her work as an editor. A mother of two grown daughters (Charlotte, twenty-four, and Sophie, eighteen) she lives on Vancouver Island and on the Queen Charlotte Islands / Haida Gwaii.

susan olding

Susan Olding's prose and poetry has appeared in literary journals throughout Canada and the US including *CV2*, *Queen's Quarterly*, *River Teeth*, and *Water-Stone*. A two-time winner of the *Event* Creative Non-fiction contest, she has also received first prize, third prize, and honourable mentions in *Prairie Fire's* annual contest. She has been a finalist for the CBC Literary Awards, the Western Magazine Awards, and The National Magazine Awards. She is stepmother to three now-adult children and the mother of a daughter adopted from China. Her book of essays, *Pathologies*, is due out from Freehand Books in autumn 2008. Her essay "Mama's Voices" won the 2007 Edna Staebler Award.

catherine owen

Catherine Owen's work has appeared in journals across Canada, New Zealand, Australia, and Germany. Titles include *Somatic: The Life and Work of Egon Schiele* (Exile Editions, 1998), nominated for the Gerald Lampert Award; *The Wrecks of Eden* (Wolsak and Wynn, 2002), shortlisted for a BC Book Prize; and her new collections, *Shall: ghazals* (Wolsak and Wynn, 2006) and *Cusp/Detritus* (Anvil Press, 2006). Her poems have been shortlisted for the CBC Literary Awards. She holds a Master's degree in English from Simon Fraser University. She has two children.

SHarron ProuLX-Turner

Sharron Proulx-Turner is a member of the Métis Nation of Alberta, the mother of three children, and the grandmother of two. Her ancestry is Mohawk, Algonquin, Huron, Anishnabe, Mikmaw, French, and Irish. Her previously published memoir, *Where the Rivers Join*, was shortlisted for the Edna Staebler Award for Creative Non-Fiction and her second book, *what the auntys say*, was shortlisted for the League of Canadian Poets' Gerald Lampert Prize for best first book of poetry. Sharron's work appears in seven anthologies, including *An Anthology of Canadian Native Literature in English, Third Edition, Crisp Blue Edges: Indigenous Creative Non-fiction, My Home as I Remember*, and in several literary journals, including *Gatherings: The En'owkin Journal of First North American Peoples, Prairie Fire, tessera*, and *absinthe*.

renee roDIn

Renee Rodin moved from Montreal in the 1960s to Vancouver, where she raised her three children. She ran R2B2 Books along with its weekly reading series, 1986–94. Her essays, poetry and fiction have appeared in many literary periodicals. Her published work includes *Bread and Salt* (Talonbooks, 1996) and *Ready for Freddy* (Nomados, 2005).

DenIse roIG

Denise Roig is the author of two short-story collections: *Any Day Now* (2004) and *A Quiet Night and a Perfect End* (1995), both published by Signature Editions. The latter was translated into French as *Le vrai secret de bonheur* (Éditions Pleine Lune) in 2000, and five stories from this collection were broadcast on CBC Radio One's *Between the Covers* in autumn 2003 and again in autumn 2006. *Any Day Now* was shortlisted in 2005 for the Quebec Writers Federation's Hugh MacLennan Prize for Fiction. She has co-edited two collections of new fiction in English by Quebec writers and has taught writing in Concordia University's journalism department and through Quebec's Writers-in-the-Schools program. She is working on a book of nonfiction, *Butter Cream: A Year in a Montreal Pastry School*, and another collection of stories.

rachel rose

Rachel Rose is a dual Canadian/American citizen whose work has been published in various journals in both countries, including *Poetry, Verse, The Journal of the American Medical Association, The Malahat Review*, and *The Best American Poetry*. Her work appears in several anthologies, including *Uncharted Lines: Poems from the Journal of the American Medical Association* and *In Fine Form: The Canadian Book of Form Poetry*. Her first book, *Giving My Body to Science* (McGill-Queen's University Press), was a finalist for The Gerald Lampert Award, The Pat Lowther Award, and the Grand Prix du Livre de Montréal and won the Quebec Writers' Federation A.M. Klein Award for the best book of poetry for 2000. Her second book, *Notes on Arrival and Departure,* was published by McClelland *&* Stewart in 2005. She has two children.

robyn sarah

Robyn Sarah is the author of seven poetry collections, two collections of short stories, and most recently a book of essays, *Little Eurekas: A Decade's Thoughts on Poetry* (2007). Her writing has appeared widely in Canada and the United States. Her poetry collections include *The Touchstone: Poems New and Selected* (1992), *Questions about the Stars* (1998) and *A Day's Grace* (2003). One of seventeen poets newly included in the *Norton Anthology of Poetry,* she has participated in the Festival franco-anglais de poésie in Paris and the Oxfam Poetry Series in London. Les Éditions du Noroît recently published *Le tamis des jours*, a selection of her poems in French translation with parallel English text. Her son, daughter, and stepson are now all past twenty-five.

noreen shanahan

Noreen Shanahan is a lesbian mother co-raising her fourteen-year-old son with two gay men in Toronto. Her prose has appeared in *Toronto Life, New*

Internationalist, Geist, Reader's Digest (Canada & Worldwide), Pacific Tri-bune, The Globe and Mail, Kinesis, Herizons, Our Times, and other publications. Her poetry has been published in various Canadian literary jour-nals and poetry anthologies, including *CV2, Jewel in the Lotus of the Instant Anthology* (Small Press Fair, Toronto) and *She's Gonna Be* (McGilligan Press). Her poems have also appeared in the *Lesbian Mother Journal*, York University. She is currently completing a poetry manuscript, *You Catch My Breath,* and a memoir about working as a housecleaner, *Dirt: A Writer's Survival Guide.*

THeresa sHea

After completing her Ph.D. in English Literature, Theresa Shea put most of her energy into family life. The mother of three children under the age of ten, she is now devoting more of those energies to the writing of poetry, fiction, and nonfiction. Her work has appeared in *Grain, Antigonish Review, Matrix, Queen's Quarterly, CV2*, and *AlbertaViews* and has been broadcast on CBC Radio. She currently lives, writes, studies violin, and homeschools her children in Edmonton, Alberta, with her husband, Tim Bowling.

jane SILcoTT

Jane Silcott was born in Toronto and now lives in Vancouver. Her stories have been published in *Room of One's Own, Prairie Fire*, and *The Malahat Review*. Her nonfiction has been published in *Fugue, Geist*, and *enRoute*. Her essay for *Double Lives* won second place in the creative nonfiction cat-egory of the 2005 CBC Literary Awards; while at UBC, she won the Elsie and Carl Halterman Scholarship for nonfiction. She has also won an Alcuin Society Design Citation for her art direction of the third edition of *Empire and Communications*, by Harold A. Innis. She is a former editor of *The Cap-ilano Review*. She has two children.

anne SImpson

Anne Simpson lives and works in northeastern Nova Scotia. Her most recent book of poetry is *Quick* (McClelland & Stewart, 2007). Her second poetry collection, *Loop* (McClelland & Stewart, 2003), won the Griffin Poetry Prize. She has also written a novel, *Canterbury Beach* (2001), and her second novel, *Falling*, is forthcoming in 2008.

LINDA SPALDING

Linda Spalding was born in Kansas, has lived in Mexico and Hawaii, and moved to Toronto in 1982. She is the editor of *Brick: A Literary Journal*. She edited *The Brick Reader* (Coach House Books, 1999) and *Riska* (Knopf Canada, 1999). Her other books include *The Paper Wife* (Knopf Canada, 1994), *Daughters of Captain Cook* (Key Porter, 1987), and (with her daughter Esta) *Mere* (HarperFlamingo, 1991), as well as a nonfiction work, *The Follow* (Key Porter, 1998), which was shortlisted for the Trillium Award and the Writers' Trust Non-Fiction Prize. Her new book, *Who Named the Knife* (McClelland & Stewart, 2007), is based on her experience as a juror in a murder trial in Hawaii more than twenty years ago.

CATHY STONEHOUSE

Cathy Stonehouse was born and raised in the UK and moved to Vancouver in 1988. Educated at Oxford University and UBC, she was the editor of *Event* magazine between 2001 and 2004 and is the author of the poetry collection *The Words I Know* (Press Gang, 1994) and a chapbook of juvenilia, *Keys to the City* (2000). Her poetry, fiction, and nonfiction have been published in a wide variety of magazines and anthologies, including *Grain, Descant, The Malahat Review, The Literary Review of Canada, eye wuz here* (Douglas & McIntyre, 1995), and *Beyond the Small Circle: Dropped Threads 3* (Random House, 2006). A chapbook of her poems was recently published online by *The Drunken Boat*, www.thedrunkenboat.com. Poems were also included in *White Ink* (Demeter Press, 2007). She lives in Vancouver, where she teaches Creative Writing and is the mother of a three-year-old daughter.

acknowledgments

Deirdre Maultsaid's "The Sun Knows What It Does" was recently published in her essay collection *These Blessings, This Crisis* (Trafford, 2006).

Susan Musgrave's "Mothering and Other Possibilities" is adapted in part from three previous essays: "The Price of Words" and "One Blank Page at a Time," from *Great Musgrave*, (Prentice-Hall Canada, 1989), and "Other Possibilities," from *Musgrave Landing: Musings on the Writing Life* (Stoddart, 1994).

Susan Olding's "Mama's Voices" first appeared in *The New Quarterly* 103.

Rachel Rose's "Letters to a Young Mother Who Writes" was developed in part from an earlier essay, "Creating Benjamin," which won third place in *Prairie Fire*'s 2001 Personal Journalism Contest and was published in *Prairie Fire*, volume 22, no. 4.

Jane Silcott's "Drafts 1–12 (Not Including 11)" won second prize in the 2006 CBC Literary Contest, Nonfiction Category, and was subsequently published in *EnRoute* magazine.

BIBLIOGraPHY

Arnott, Joanne. *Wiles of Girlhood*. Vancouver: Press Gang Publishers, 1992.

— *Steepy Mountain: Love Poems*. Ontario: Kegedonce Press, 2001.

Akiwenzie-Damm, Kateri, ed. *Without Reservation*. Ontario: Kegedonce Press, 2003.

Atwood, Margaret. "Five Visits to the Word Hoard." Bill Duthie Memorial Lecture, Vancouver Writers and Readers Festival, October 2005.

Bolster, Stephanie. *Two Bowls of Milk*. Toronto: McClelland & Stewart, 1999.

— *Pavilion*. Toronto: McClelland & Stewart, 2002.

— *Biodôme*. Ottawa: above/ground, 2006.

Bowden, Darsie. "The Rise of a Metaphor: 'Voice' in Composition Pedagogy." *Rhetoric Review* 14, no. 1, Autumn 1999.

Brandt, Di. *questions I asked my mother*. Winnipeg: Turnstone Press, 1987.

— *mother, not mother*. Toronto: Mercury Press, 1992.

— *Wild Mother Dancing: Maternal Narrative in Canadian Literature*. Winnipeg: University of Manitoba Press, 1993.

Brant, Beth. *Mohawk Trail*. Boston: Firebrand Books, 1985.

— *A Gathering of Spirit: A Collection by North American Indian Women*. Boston: Firebrand Books, 1989.

— *Food & Spirits*. Vancouver: Press Gang Publishers, 1991.

— *Writing as Witness: essays & talk*. London: Women's Press, 1994.

— *I'll Sing 'til the Day I Die: Conversations with Tyendinaga Elders*. Toronto: McGilligan Books, 1995.

Campbell, Maria. Interview with Doris Hillis. *Prairie Fire*, vol. 9, no.3.

— Interview with H. Lutz in *Contemporary Challenges: Conversations with Canadian Native Authors*. Fifth House, 1991.

Cosman, Carol, et al., eds. *The Penguin Book of Women Poets*. Penguin, 1978.

Didion, Joan. *Slouching towards Bethlehem*. New York: Farrar, Straus, Giroux, 1968.

Dillard, Annie. *Pilgrim at Tinker Creek*. New York: Bantam Books, 1974.

— *Holy the Firm*. New York: Harper and Row, 1977.

— *The Annie Dillard Reader*. New York: HarperCollins, 1994.

— "To Fashion a Text." *The Fourth Genre: Contemporary Writers of/on Creative Nonfiction*, Robert L. Root and Michael Steinberg, eds. Boston, London, Toronto, Sydney, Singapore: Allyn and Bacon, 1999, 276.

Friedman, Bonnie. *Writing Past Dark*. Toronto: HarperCollins, 1993.

Garnett, Angelica. *Deceived with Kindness*. Oxford: Oxford University Press, 1985.

Gorey, Edward. Interview in *Vanity Fair*, from McDermott, *The Elephant House*. California: Pomegranate Communications, 2003.

Graves, Robert. *The White Goddess*. London: Faber & Faber, 1948.

Greene, Elizabeth. *The Iron Shoes*. Trenton, Ontario: North Shore Press, 2007.

Gunn Allen, Paula. *The Sacred Hoop: Recovering the Feminine in American Indian Traditions*. Boston: Beacon Press, 1982.

Hall, Nor. "Channel a Muse." *Spring Journal: A Journal of Archetype and Culture*, Spring 2004.

Heaney, Seamus. "Feelings into Words." *Preoccupations: Selected Prose, 1968–1978*. Vancouver: Douglas & McIntyre, 1981.

Heilbrun, Carolyn. *Reinventing Womanhood*. New York: Norton, 1981.

Hillis, Doris. *Plainspeaking: Interviews with Saskatchewan Writers*. Saskatoon: Coteau Books, 1988.

Ito, Sally. *Frogs in the Rain Barrel*. Sechelt: Nightwood Editions, 1995.

Jackson, Marni. *The Mother Zone*. Toronto: Random House of Canada, 2002.

Japanese American Veterans Association website: www.javadc.org/.

Jeffers, Robinson. *The Collected Poems of Robinson Jeffers*, ed. Tim Hunt. New York: Random House, 2000.

King, James. *The Life of Margaret Laurence*. Toronto: Alfred A.Knopf, 1997.

Kulyk Keefer, Janice. *Midnight Stroll*. Toronto: Exile Editions, 2006.

Lang, Andrew. *The Orange Fairy Book*. Dover, 1968.

Lazarre, Jane. *The Mother Knot*. New York: McGraw, 1976.

Lam, Fiona Tinwei. *Intimate Distances*. Sechelt: Nightwood Editions, 2001.

Laurence, Margaret. *Dance on the Earth: A Memoir*. Toronto: McClelland & Stewart, 1989.

Lessing, Doris. *Under My Skin: Volume One of My Autobiography, to 1949*, quoted in *Mother Reader: Essential Literature on Motherhood*, Moyra Davey, ed. New York: Seven Stories Press, 2001.

Literary Mama, www.literarymama.com.

Lustbader, Wendy. "At the Mercy of Strangers." *Generations*, Winter 1999–2000 (copyright American Society on Aging, www.asaging.org).

Malin, Jo. "Babies and Books: Motherhood and Writing." *Literary Mama*. www.literarymama.com/litcrit/archives/000105.html.

Middleton, Diane. *Her Husband: Hughes and Plath – A Marriage*. New York: Viking, 2003.

Moure, Erín. *Sheep's Vigil by a Fervent Person*. Translation of Alberto Caeiro / Fernando Pessoa's *O Guardador de Rebanhos*. Toronto: House of Anansi, 2001. Portuguese text copyright Assirio and Alvim, Lisbon.

Munro, Sheila. *Lives of Mothers and Daughters: Growing Up with Alice Munro*. Toronto: McClelland & Stewart, 2001.

Olsen, Tillie. *Silences*. New York: Feminist Press at CUNY, 2003.

Owen, Catherine. *And the Silence, Stones*. Vancouver: Wet Sickle Press, 1992.

– *Her*. Vancouver: Wet Sickle Press, 1995.

Prose, Francine. *The Lives of the Muses: Nine Women and the Artists They Inspired*. Toronto: HarperCollins, 2003.

Rabuzzi, Kathryn Allen. *Motherself: A Mythic Analysis of Motherhood*. Indianapolis: Indiana University Press, 1988.

Rich, Adrienne. *Of Woman Born: Motherhood as Experience and Institution*. New York: Norton, 1995.

Rilke, Rainer Maria, *Letters to a Young Poet*, Translated by Stephen Mitchell. New York: Random House, 1986.

Roig, Denise. *A Quiet Night and a Perfect End*. Montreal: Nuage Editions, 1995.

Sarah, Robyn. *The Space Between Sleep and Waking*. Montreal: Villeneuve Publications, 1981.

Schwartz, Steven. "Finding a Voice in America." *Bringing the Devil to His Knees: The Craft of Fiction and the Writing Life*, Charles Baxter and Peter Turchi, eds. Ann Arbor: University of Michigan Press, 2004.

Sheldrick Ross, Catherine. *Alice Munro: A Double Life*. Toronto: ECW Press, 1992.

Simpson, Anne. *Falling*. Toronto: McClelland & Stewart, 2008.

– *Light Falls through You*. Toronto: McClelland & Stewart, 2000.

Sullivan, Rosemary. *The Red Shoes: Margaret Atwood Starting Out*. Toronto: HarperFlamingo Canada, 1998.

Trillin, Calvin. *About Alice*. New York: Random House, 2006.

Wallace, Bronwen. "My Son Is Learning to Invent." *Common Magic*. Ottawa: Oberon, 1985.

Wideman, John Edgar. "Looking at Emmett Till." *In Fact: The Best of Creative Non-Fiction*, Gutkind, ed., 24–8. New York: W.W. Norton & Co., 2004.

Wilkinson, Anne. *The Collected Poems of Anne Wilkinson*. A.J.M. Smith, ed. New York: St. Martin's Press, 1968.

Winnicott, D.W. "Transitional Objects and Transitional Phenomena." *International Journal of Psychoanalysis* 34, 1953.

Wiseman, Adele, and Margaret Laurence. *Crackpot*. Toronto: New Canadian Library, 1989.

Woolf, Virginia. *A Room of One's Own*. New York: Harvest Books Reprint Edition, 2005.

Yalom, Marilyn. *Maternity, Morality and the Literature of Madness*. Pennsylvania State University Press, 1985.